The dialogics of critique

The work of Mikhail Bakhtin and the Bakhtin Circle has generated a tremendous amount of interest with respect to our under-standing of textuality, aesthetic creativity and the philosophy of language. Yet existing critical studies have concentrated more or less exclusively on his influence as a literary theorist. Michael Gardiner challenges this literary appropriation of Bakhtin's ideas, depicting him instead as a social thinker with a significant contri-bution to make to contemporary debates in social and political theory.

Gardiner introduces Bakhtin's core concepts – dialogism, poly-phony, carnival – through an examination of the Bakhtin Circle's major writings. He scrutinises Bakhtin's insights into the nature of the text, showing how they engage with Marxist theories of ideology, the hermeneutic tradition as represented by Gadamer, Habermas and Ricoeur, and the poststructuralism of Barthes and Foucault. The book concludes with critical assessment of Bakhtin's contribution to ideological and cultural criticism and an appraisal of his legacy for the purposes of *Ideologiekritik*.

Written with clarity and precision, *The Dialogics of Critique* provides an excellent, reliable guide to the important ideas of Bakhtin. The book will have a wide appeal, and will be of special interest to students of social theory, sociology, cultural studies, literary theory and philosophy.

Michael Gardiner lectures in sociology at the University of York.

The dialogics of critique

M. M. Bakhtin and the theory of ideology

Michael Gardiner

London and New York

First published in 1992
by Routledge
11 New Fetter Lane, London EC4P 4EE

Simultaneously published in the USA and Canada
by Routledge
a division of Routledge, Chapman and Hall Inc.
29 West 35th Street, New York, NY 10001

© 1992 Michael Gardiner

Typeset in Baskerville by Laserscript Limited, Mitcham, Surrey
Printed and bound in Great Britain by
Mackays of Chatham PLC, Chatham, Kent

British Library Cataloguing in Publication Data
A catalogue record for this book is available from the British Library.

Library of Congress Cataloging in Publication Data

Gardiner, Michael, 1961–
   The dialogics of critique : M.M. Bakhtin and the theory of ideology /
by Michael Gardiner.
   p. cm.
   Includes bibliographical references and index.
   1. Bakhtin, M.M. (Mikhail Mikhaïlovich), 1895–1975.
2 Criticism – History – 20th century. 3. Ideology. 4 Hermeneutics.
I. Title.
PG2947.B3G37 1992
801'.95'092 – dc20   91-37484
                                                                          CIP

ISBN 0-415-06064-8
      0-415-07975-6 (pbk)

Contents

For my mother and father

Acknowledgements

The present study is based on D.Phil. research undertaken at the Department of Sociology at the University of York (UK) between October 1987 and February 1991. I gratefully acknowledge the Social Sciences and Humanities Research Council of Canada for providing me with a doctoral fellowship during this period. I would also like to extend my gratitude to Dr Barry Sandywell for his invaluable input and advice, and also Mr Phil Stanworth and Mr Arthur Brittan. I would also like to thank my parents George and Mary and the rest of my family in Canada for their emotional and material support. Finally, I would like to give my special thanks to my friend and partner Rita Caine whose encouragement and practical help made the difficult task of producing this work a very much happier one.

Michael Gardiner
York, December 1991

Introduction

What can oppose the decline of the West is not a resurrected culture but the utopia silently contained in the image of its decline.

T. W. Adorno

M. M. Bakhtin was an enigmatic, even mysterious figure who lived and worked under extremely difficult circumstances. He was always a marginal individual within the Soviet intellectual establishment, mainly because his rather unorthodox views contradicted the official Party line on aesthetic and literary matters. Many of his writings have failed to survive; much of what remains is only now being translated, and many of the existing manuscripts exist in the form of rough notes and fragments which were not intended for publication. And, as has been frequently commented upon, his texts do not resemble straightforward academic treatises: they are frustratingly vague in their terminology, often deliberately repetitious, and encumbered with multiple and ambiguous levels of meaning. Bakhtin's cryptic, dense style, his use of distinctive metaphors, allusions and neologisms, and the diversity of philosophical and scholarly influences he draws upon have presented formidable interpretive problems. None the less, since the late 1970s, the work of Mikhail Bakhtin and the 'Bakhtin Circle' has generated an enormous amount of interest in the scholarly world. Literally hundreds of articles, reviews and essays covering virtually every aspect of Bakhtin's thought have appeared, and his central concepts have been applied to an astonishing range of cultural and literary texts ranging from Homer's *Iliad* to Soviet puppet theatre to 'rap' music.[1] This situation has prompted the American literary critic Edward Said to refer to the 'cult of Bakhtin' in fairly disparaging terms.[2] It has also encouraged the appropriation of his work by a number of competing schools of thought, each claiming Bakhtin as 'their' own. He has been portrayed as a poststructuralist long before Derrida and Foucault decentred the subject, a Russian Formalist (albeit a rather unorthodox one), a nascent modernist or postmodernist, and even a religious thinker. However, despite the inordinate amount of attention lavished upon Bakhtin, his work does contain a number of rich and suggestive elements which have much to offer to a radical cultural theory and politics.

The lack of accessibility of his work to Western critics has (at least until recently) been compounded by the fact that many now attribute several important writings of the Bakhtin Circle to Bakhtin himself, in what has become known as the 'authorship debate'.[3] In this study, I take up a position of agnosticism with respect to this controversy, if only because it has little overt relevance to the central concerns of this study. Yet even if we choose to set aside the question of authorship, it is none the less apparent that Bakhtin wrote on a prodigious range of subjects. A brief index might contain the following topics: the theory of the novel, sociolinguistics and the philosophy of language, aspects of Renaissance and medieval folk culture, cultural and literary history, the psychology of perception, and numerous epistemological and interpretive issues in the human sciences. His influences were equally diverse: besides Marxism, these include neo-Kantianism, Formalism and other early Soviet *avant-garde* movements, evolutionary biology and Einsteinian physics, and classical thought. Yet in spite of the manifestly wide-ranging nature of his work, it can be argued that Bakhtin's interests were guided by a remarkably coherent series of meditations on the nature of the self and the centrality of language within social life. Indeed, it could be said that his life-long ambition was the development of an interdisciplinary approach to the study of socio-cultural life as it is constituted in and through forms of symbolic interaction – what has been generally referred to as 'metalinguistics' or 'translinguistics'. It is also evident that Bakhtin was motivated by a discernible (if largely implicit) political and moral stance. Bakhtin's politics of culture can be characterized as the desire to understand and indeed encourage what I will call the 'popular deconstruction' of official discourses and ideologies. This standpoint has a distinct ethical corollary: his staunch belief that the establishment of linguistic and cultural freedom is a necessary prerequisite to the emergence of a truly egalitarian and radically democratic community – a position which, in many respects, resembles Jürgen Habermas's notion of the 'ideal speech situation'. The construction of such a community was in Bakhtin's opinion not only inherently desirable; it was something akin to a categorical imperative. He felt that we required a dialogical interaction with others before we could develop a coherent image of self and engage in morally and aesthetically productive tasks. Such a co-endeavour is ideally conducted in a spirit of mutual recognition and trust, even love. By encouraging rather than suppressing social difference and by tracing out how this diversity was sustained in the utterances and cultural practices of everyday life, Bakhtin believed that the authoritarian structures of modern bureaucratic societies could be challenged and subverted. However naive this might seem today, Bakhtin unarguably maintained a pronounced faith in the liberating potential of popular cultural forms, even during the darkest moments of Stalinist repression.

In studying Bakhtin and the various debates his work has generated in the human sciences, one is reminded of a recurring metaphor that Bakhtin himself often refers to: that we can never find the word in a 'virginal state', as if we were a primordial Adam or Eve, because any word is 'always-already' imbued with the evaluations and perceptions of others. The same insight can, of course, be applied to Bakhtin himself: his legacy is inescapably coloured by a posteriori interpretations, to the extent that any kind of purism or 'theoretical innocence' is simply out of the question. The intellectual and political appropriation of Bakhtin's legacy to a myriad of competing theoretical discourses has been documented at length elsewhere.[4] Rather than enter into this debate directly, except to say that I consciously identify with so-called 'left readings' of Bakhtin, I wish to turn to another issue: the overwhelmingly literary affiliation of most of the existing work on Bakhtin.[5] With some important exceptions, Bakhtin has been treated more or less exclusively as a literary theorist and critic or, perhaps more reluctantly, as a philosopher of language with an acute interest in literary matters. Accordingly, the utilization of his main concepts has generally been restricted to the description and analysis of literary texts, a situation which has precluded a more systematic assessment of the relevance of Bakhtin's ideas with respect to broader social and cultural phenomena. This is certainly not to devalue this use of Bakhtin, which has yielded many worthwhile results, but to suggest that this is only one area where his insights can be fruitfully applied. Accordingly, while I make frequent reference to recent developments in literary theory throughout this study, I will engage with Bakhtin's writings on a different conceptual terrain: that of critical social and cultural theory.

Of course, now that something approaching the full corpus of Bakhtin's writings has appeared in translation, and given that the secondary literature is almost literally boundless, it would prove exceedingly difficult to write a general study of Bakhtin's *oeuvre* that would adequately address all or even most of the issues raised by his work. Accordingly, I have chosen to focus on one major area: the theory and critique of ideology. With reference to Bakhtin, this injunction may at first glance seem rather odd. For anyone with even a cursory knowledge of his texts will undoubtedly know that they are replete with references to the phenomenon in question. However, it is also evident that Bakhtin's writings do not contain anything like a fully worked-out theory of ideology. To glean such a theory from his texts requires a close or 'symptomatic' reading and an extended process of conceptual reconstruction. Yet such a project is not impossible: on a broader level, it is clear that Bakhtin was concerned with the critique of certain theoretical discourses (Formalism, structuralism, and so on) which he felt constituted serious threats to the 'dialogical integrity' of the social world. In other words, although Bakhtin's texts do not appear at first glance to offer much of a directly programmatic or methodological nature vis-à-vis a theory of ideology, at a deeper level it can be argued that an ethically-informed analysis of ideological discourses is implicit in his critical project. Thus, I would agree with Susan Stewart (in one of the few essays that touch on this issue) that it is 'more appropriate to place Bakhtin among theorists of ideology rather than among theorists of linguistics and semiotics' (1986: 49).

This leads me to a second important point: that although Bakhtin has been coveted by Marxists (and some 'post-Marxists') as a figure who offers a middle path between the twin pitfalls of economic reductionism and the 'hermeneutical nihilism'[6] of post-structuralism, little attempt has been made to situate Bakhtin in relation to the Marxist tradition and its various offshoots and derivatives.[7] Given that Bakhtin and his followers took Marxism and the project of constructing socialism seriously (at least during the initial post-revolutionary period of Soviet Russia), such a theoretical 'dialogue' would seem to be of considerable importance. Of course, one cannot reconcile Bakhtin and Marxism simply by glossing over the many differences between them. The relationship between them is complex and equivocal: instead of adapting existing Marxist theory to the study of language and culture, Bakhtin attempted to formulate a completely new analytical framework by drawing on an eclectic mix of philosophical and theoretical sources. None the less, I construe Bakhtin as a theoretician whose central interests and preoccupations are largely congruent with those of the Western Marxist tradition.[8] For instance, like the major Western Marxists (Bloch, Gramsci, Adorno, etc.) Bakhtin's thought matured during the political and cultural tumult of the inter-war years, which produced a libertarian-humanist vision of socialism that was inimicably opposed to the authoritarian tendencies of Leninism and Stalin's 'barrack communism' as well as the vacuity of official social democracy. On a more theoretical plane, Bakhtin no less than the Western Marxists was relatively unconcerned with the causal efficacy of political and economic structures, and instead focused on so-called 'superstructural' phenomena. In this, Bakhtin fully participates in the general realignment towards aesthetic and cultural themes which characterized left European thought after the early 1920s. Moreover, both were deeply concerned with the destruction of human values and with the progressive incursion of the commodity form into every sphere of cultural and civil life in modern society. They equally decry the treatment of the human subject as a means to an end (whether for the maximization of surplus-value and the accumulation of capital, as with the Western Marxists, or in more Kantian terms, as with Bakhtin). This in turn engendered a preoccupation with problems of human alienation and the reification of social relations under capitalism (and bureaucratic socialism), in which the analysis and critique of regressive ideologies occupied centre stage. And finally, both considered their studies to be 'critical' and not scientific in the orthodox (and especially Soviet) Marxist sense. Bakhtin would certainly have subscribed to Karl Korsch's sentiment that the critique of everyday life necessitated a philosophical confrontation with the 'intellectual (ideological) structure of society'.[9] Such a critical orientation refuses to fetishize science – that is, to appeal dogmatically to objectivistic standards of verification – and is ultimately grounded in a 'humanist' rather than a positivist epistemology, one that is not wholly dismissive of the value of utopian thought. Critique in this Western Marxist (and Bakhtinian) sense aims at a reflexive understanding of (and autonomy from) those repressive social structures and impoverished modes of thought which characterize contemporary social relations.[10]

The first section of this study will be concerned with a synoptic or exegetical discussion of Bakhtin and the Circle's major texts in relatively general terms. Chapter one will concentrate on those writings originally produced during the 1920s, including V. N. Voloshinov's *Marxism and the Philosophy of Language* (1973), P. N. Medvedev's *The Formal Method in Literary Scholarship* (1985), and M. M. Bakhtin's *Problems of Dostoevsky's Poetics* (1984). In the second chapter, I will examine Bakhtin's writings from the 1930s and early 1940s, encompassing the famous essays on the theory of the novel (now collected in the volume *The Dialogic Imagination*, 1981) and what constitutes his most challenging and stimulating work, *Rabelais and His World* (1968).[11] The central aim of these first two chapters will be to introduce Bakhtin's main concepts ('dialogism', 'heteroglossia', and 'carnival') within the corpus of his (and the Circle's) work as a whole, notions that will be continually referred to in the following chapters. The decision to discuss these texts in a roughly chronological fashion is not a whimsical one: as his intellectual career develops, Bakhtin progressively moves away from the phenomenological and literary orientation of his earlier works to embrace a more sociologically and historically-attuned approach which is concerned with the elucidation of a wide spectrum of cultural texts and practices. Moreover, Bakhtin's later writings become more overtly political, probably because of the changing historical context (the consolidation of Stalinism and the degeneration of Soviet Communism into a second Thermidor), and are thus closer to the aims and methods of a Marxian *Ideologiekritik*.

The second part of this study will narrow the thematic focus considerably. In chapter three, I utilize Bakhtin's insights into the nature of the text, ideology and power in order to criticize the orthodox Marxist theory of ideology. My position will be that because Bakhtin unequivocally rejects the abstract base–superstructure nexus propounded by economistic forms of Marxism, he dodges the epistemological conundrums of this classical problematic and the debilitating dualisms it contains (false vs. real, science vs. ideology, etc.). Rather than interpreting ideology in the usual ways (as a form of 'false consciousness', or as a coherent 'belief system'), Bakhtin views ideology as the essential symbolic medium through which all social relations are necessarily constituted. Thus, like Althusser and Gramsci, Bakhtin conceives of ideology not as epiphenomena, or as a distorted representation of the 'real', but as a material force in its own right. But he also attempts to conceptualize ideology along linguistic and semiotic lines, as a signifying practice which is produced within particular social contexts. Yet Bakhtin does not disavow the Marxian stress on the centrality of class conflict, because for him ideology understood as a social practice is intimately connected with wider antagonisms in the social world. When colonized (or 'monologized') by dominant cultural forms and institutional arrangements, particular ideological discourses can play a crucial role in the maintenance of asymmetrical power relations. Yet language, being inherently 'dialogic', is always the site of ideological contestation, which explains Bakhtin's stress on the 'struggle over the sign'. As such, Bakhtin's conception of ideology does not lose its critical or radical edge.

In chapter four, I turn to the problem of 'critique' in more detail. Here, I will pursue two major aims: firstly, to attempt to situate Bakhtin's critical-interpretive *Hermeneutik* with respect to three central figures of the hermeneutic tradition (Hans-Georg Gadamer, Jürgen Habermas and Paul Ricoeur), in order to assess the methodological and philosophical substance of Bakhtin's texts in relation to these thinkers and to evaluate the possible contributions his theories might make to the critique of ideology. Secondly, I will elucidate the difficult problem of the justification of ideological critique by considering some of the possible standpoints whence the exercise of critical reason and reflection might be conducted. Insofar as Bakhtin declines to portray ideology as a 'negative' or distorted form of knowledge, he does not strive to justify his critical interpretations of particular texts by recourse to a positivist epistemology. This anti-foundationalist stance (as is often supposed) does not entail relativism or nihilism, but it does necessitate an appeal to particular grounds or standards with respect to rival interpretations. In Bakhtin's case, such an appeal is made to normative precepts which are ultimately based on his idiosyncratic philosophical anthropology and a utopian conception of the dialogic community. This explains his Kantian

Sprachethik, his unwavering position that 'A philosophy of life can only be a moral philosophy'.[12] Accordingly, an understanding of Bakhtin's critical hermeneutics will constitute the second major focus of this thesis, and it addresses a significant gap in the current literature which has predominantly considered Bakhtin in relation to the semiological or the Formalist traditions.

That 'ideology' cannot be satisfactorily theorized without conjoining it to a philosophy of language is a position that has been voiced with increasing regularity by thinkers as diverse as Pierre Bourdieu and A. J. Greimas.[13] Bakhtin has close affinities with this development, but what is most remarkable is that he (in tandem with Medvedev and Voloshinov) formulated this stance some forty years before it (re-)emerged elsewhere. Nor did Bakhtin seek inspiration from the structuralist problematic; indeed, he fashioned his theories as a conscious repudiation of Saussure's structural linguistics. In chapter five, I consider Bakhtin's conception of ideology in relation to two contemporary approaches which would appear to occupy much of the same theoretical terrain: Roland Barthes's construal of 'ideology as myth', and Michel Foucault's innovative effort to displace the category of ideology with the Nietzschean-inspired notion of 'power/knowledge'. By developing a Bakhtinian-inspired critique of Barthes and Foucault, I want to demonstrate the superiority of a 'dialogic' theory of ideology in certain key areas. In the final chapter, I turn to a more critical assessment of Bakhtin's contribution, addressing such lacunae as his tendency to undertheorize the complexity of the social and to overestimate the liberatory potential of popular culture, and the negative aspects of his unfettered utopianism. This study will conclude with some brief reflections on how his insights into the dynamics of ideology, power and discourse might be productively appropriated by a radical cultural and social theory.

Chapter 1

The 1920s writings

INTRODUCTION

In this chapter I will discuss three seminal texts produced by the
Bakhtin Circle during the 1920s. I begin with Valentin N.
Voloshinov's *Marxism and the Philosophy of Language*, which I argue
is of acute importance with respect to the project of conjoining the
theory of ideology with a sophisticated philosophy of language. I
then move on to Pavel N. Medvedev's *The Formal Method in Literary
Scholarship*, which contains an extended critique of the school of
Russian Formalism that was briefly influential in Soviet intellectual
circles in the 1920s. I conclude with an examination of M. M.
Bakhtin's portrayal of the 19th-century Russian writer Fyodor
Dostoevsky as the first 'polyphonic' novelist in his seminal trans-
itional text *Problems of Dostoevsky's Poetics*.

V. N. VOLOSHINOV: TOWARDS A TRANSLINGUISTIC MARXISM

Voloshinov's *Marxism and the Philosophy of Language* (1973) is a
work which elucidates the Bakhtin Circle's general approach to
the nature of language, signification and ideology in a particularly
adroit and succinct manner.[1] By any standard, it is a remarkable
tour de force: it represents the first real innovation in Marxist theory
vis-à-vis the theory of ideology, insofar as it shifts the conceptual
terrain away from an epistemological preoccupation with cognitive
distortion and vague notions like 'world-view' or 'belief system'
towards a concern with semiotic and linguistic processes. As a
prefatory remark, it is worth noting that the Circle's theories of
ideology and language were primarily developed through an

extensive critique of competing positions within such existing disciplines as linguistics, literary theory and philosophy. An integral aspect of this critical strategy is the interrogation of two diametrically opposed views on a given theoretical problem, followed by an attempt to overcome the shortcomings of each through a series of dialectical negations and syntheses. In *Marxism and the Philosophy of Language* the two main *dramatis personae* are, firstly, the 'abstract objectivism' of the Swiss linguist Saussure, who is generally acknowledged as the forerunner of modern structuralism and semiotics; and secondly, the 'individualistic subjectivism' of Dilthey, Vossler, and Croce, which can be characterized as a form of idealist hermeneutics. There are other intellectual traditions that Voloshinov also considers here – such as 'vulgar' Marxism, which he castigates for its economic reductionism and its failure to account for the specificity of ideological and linguistic processes. However, these minor commentaries exist as a kind of critical subtext alongside the main arguments, and I will not include them in the following discussion.

These two opposing schools of thought have dealt with the delineation of language as a distinct object of study in very different ways. For the 'subjectivists', speech-acts were best understood as stylistically unreproducible utterances which resulted from the 'creative externalization' of the thoughts, emotions or intentions of the individual mind. Hence, the historicity of language was its essential feature – language was synonymous with the continuous and creative renovation of linguistic form by particular human beings. For Saussure and the other 'objectivists', by contrast, the goal was to conceptualize language as a fixed system comprising certain phonetic, grammatical and lexical forms. For this school, the given language system of a particular community constituted a discrete whole – what Saussure termed *langue* – which could be distinguished from the contingent and unique utterances of particular individuals – characterized as *parole*. But because *parole* was too random and effusive to be accounted for in terms of a rational philosophy of language, the position of objectivism was that only language understood as a self-contained system was amenable to systematic analysis. In short, *langue* was seen as a definite structure comprising a series of binary phonetic oppositions and rules of grammatical and syntactic combination which stood apart from individual speech-acts as an 'inviolable, incontestable norm'.

In considering objectivism first, Voloshinov decisively rejects the suggestion that language can be understood as a system of 'self-identical linguistic norms', insofar as language is a dynamic process, a 'ceaseless flow of becoming'. Therefore, language *qua* system is only a useful abstraction constructed by the theorist, a heuristic device that does not in fact exist in real historical time and space. As a corollary to this, Voloshinov argues that individual speakers do not relate to language as an external 'object' or a fixed, normative structure. Language competence is not simply a matter of the production of grammatically-correct sentences, but rather indicates the creative and reflexive adaptation of a given speech-act by particular social agents to fluid and changing social situations.[2] A language system does not, therefore, enforce a particular usage regardless of the social context involved. This system is brought into line with the concrete socio-historical conditions within which it is produced through a continuous process of 'linguistic praxis'. Because objectivism insisted on the unmediated reality of the language system, it was guilty of projecting language as a hypostatized, free-floating entity, a 'transcendental structure'. Voloshinov argues that, genealogically speaking, the essential precursor of objectivism was the philological study of dead or alien languages. Because European linguistics had traditionally been preoccupied with the analysis of written texts from no longer existing or geographically-distant civilizations, the primary object of study was taken to be the 'finished, monologic utterance'. For Voloshinov, this served to legitimate the empiricist/positivist account of knowledge as a form of passive understanding. More importantly, it meant that objectivism lacked the necessary conceptual tools to examine the meaning or 'value' of living speech as it was 'actually and continuously generated', to enter reflexively into the 'living, dynamic reality of language and its social functions' (1973: 82) as an active participant.[3]

Subjectivism, by contrast, is linked by Voloshinov to the Romantic movement. Romanticism spurned the neo-classical obsession with the alien word, and concentrated on the question of how particular national languages constituted the 'experiential medium' through which one's thoughts and emotions were produced. Thus, whereas objectivism focused on the systematicity and 'object-ness' of *langue*, subjectivism insisted on the primacy of the creative subject. Despite the apparent gulf that separates these two schools of thought, Voloshinov asserts that both take the monologic utterance to be the *locus classicus* of language. Hence, whilst subjectivism is correct (*contra* objectivism) in that individual utterances do constitute a crucial aspect of language, and that human speech therefore displays 'creative value', it errs because it mistakenly locates the ideological or meaningful nature of the word in the individual psyche rather than in society. In contradistinction to both subjectivism and objectivism, Voloshinov maintains that the continuous flow of verbal interaction in particular social contexts – and not the abstract system of *langue* or the creativity of the inner psyche – is the fundamental reality of the phenomenon of language.

For Voloshinov, the linchpin of this communicative process is the dialogic interaction between concrete utterances, a phenomenon which involves all forms of semiosis and not just face-to-face speech acts. Every utterance, he suggests, is produced by a concrete addresser and is oriented towards a (real or presumed) addressee. Both interlocutors occupy a precise location within wider social relations (kinship, social class, gender, and ethnicity). Voloshinov argues that these are hierarchically organized in terms of asymmetrical power-resources (political, cultural, symbolic) and antagonistic social interests. As the sociopolitical order is internally and 'ecologically' stratified, so too is the organization of verbal interaction. Individuals, being competent, knowledgeable agents, learn to tailor their utterances (with varying degrees of success) to conform to the demands of the immediate social situation – what the French sociologist Pierre Bourdieu (1977c) has appositely termed the 'linguistic market'. Thus, in Voloshinov's view, popular communicative forms are marginalized, and speakers from subordinate social groups are motivated to defer to the authoritative language. Nevertheless, such an acquiescence to the conventions of 'official' language is not invariant across all possible social contexts. For, as Bakhtin in particular was concerned to illustrate, the oppressed can draw upon discernible symbolic and cultural resources which are at least partially successful in resisting the dictates of the official language and its concomitant ideological forms.[4] None the less, Voloshinov argues that insofar as each of us occupies a precise location within a series of overlapping discursive and cultural fields, we are disposed towards a distinct 'social purview' which structures the ideological orientation of our thoughts, utterances and actions.

Another reason Voloshinov rejects subjectivism is because it

posits a radical disjuncture between the 'inner world' of the individual mind and the outer world of linguistic communication.
Such a dualism is for Voloshinov untenable, because the inner and
outer features of expression are composed of the 'raw material' of
the sign. The implications of Voloshinov's comments on 'inner
speech' or cognitive semiosis for a theory of the subject and
psychology are significant, but will not be discussed in any detail
here.[5] Suffice it to say that, for Voloshinov, the tendency for idealistic and psychologistic approaches to reduce ideology to individual
consciousness deprives the material and social character of ideology of 'any support in reality'. Accordingly, he strongly argues that
human consciousness and its symbolic objectifications can only be
defined in sociological terms. These are constituted in and
through the material of signs, which are themselves the product of
actual social groups engaged in the practices of everyday life: 'I
give myself verbal shape from another point of view, ultimately,
from the point of view of the community to which I belong' (1973:
86).

Whilst nowhere in *Marxism and the Philosophy of Language* does
Voloshinov advance an explicit definition of ideology, by paying
careful attention to his texts it is possible to reconstruct a schematic outline of a theory of ideology that accords with his general
views on the dialogic nature of language and social interaction. For
Voloshinov, 'ideology' basically refers to the process whereby
meaning or 'value' is conferred on the natural and social worlds.
Ideologies are also 'material', not only because all possible forms
of human action and cognition are embodied in some kind of
semiotic sign (e.g. words, gestures, facial expressions, and so on),
but because such signs elicit real effects in society.[6] Insofar as
ideology is grounded in a myriad of social and cultural practices, it
is not epiphenomenal or merely ideational but 'an objective fact
and a tremendous social force'. However, the phenomenon of
ideology in Voloshinov's mind exhibits one additional feature – it
'reflects and refracts' an external reality: 'Everything ideological
possesses *meaning*: it represents, depicts or stands for something
lying outside itself. In other words, it is a *sign*. *Without signs there is
no ideology*' (1973: 9). Anything produced or utilized by human
beings (tools, foodstuffs, etc.) can be converted into a sign with a
meaning that goes beyond the 'particularity' of the object itself.
Hence, the sign has the potential to distort the reality it represents,
or be true to it, or to see it from another perspective. However, the

sphere of ideological signs is not a monolithic whole. On the contrary, Voloshinov suggests that each particular 'field' of cultural and artistic activity refracts reality in different ways, in terms of its general role and function in social life. Nevertheless, all such fields possess a unifying and distinctive feature – they all utilize the common material of the sign: 'The domain of ideology coincides with the domain of signs. They equate with one another. Whenever a sign is present, ideology is present, too' (1973: 10). Given that ideology can only be expressed through the medium of social communication ('the existence of the sign is nothing but the materialization of that communication'), language constitutes the site of ideological phenomena *par excellence.* As such, the study of the word reveals the 'general-ideological forms of semiotic communication' in sharp relief. It is the most sensitive possible index of wider social processes and antagonisms.

For Voloshinov, the objective reality of such social signs corresponds to general laws of semiotic communication, which are themselves determined by the 'total aggregate of social and economic laws' upon which the ideological superstructure rests. Hence, the productive relations of a particular society and the sociopolitical order conditioned by these relations determine the 'forms and means' of verbal communication – which, in turn, provides the structural context (or generic basis) for the forms and themes of actual speech performances. Voloshinov suggests that these speech performances can be conceptualized in terms of a loose typology of 'speech genres' which, in turn, are bound up with other forms of semiotic communication and interchange (gesturing, clothing style, body stance, and so on). Although Voloshinov does not supply us with a detailed categorization of these speech genres, he does note that every social group and historical period has its own repertoire of speech forms which facilitates distinct modes of ideological communication within what he terms 'behavioral genres'.

Voloshinov's account of 'speech genres' concerns the social organization of verbal communication as structured 'events' or performances. Yet he also feels that a proper understanding of the content or 'value' of social signs is of equal importance. Voloshinov argues that the issue of linguistic or semiotic meaning has generally been ignored within the discipline of linguistics, chiefly because of an uncritical adherence to a positivist epistemology combined with a monologic conception of language-use. He rejects this atomistic conception of language (in which a solitary word directly signifies an external object through the intentions of an autonomous subject) as an anachronistic legacy of Cartesian rationalism, and insists that 'ideological significance' is something that belongs to the utterance as a whole. To grasp this utterance-level significance (or 'theme'), an understanding of the syntactic and morphological structure of the utterance is necessary but not sufficient. Extra-verbal (contextual or 'situational') factors also must be taken into account: 'Only an utterance taken in its full, concrete scope as a historical phenomenon possesses a theme' (1973: 100). As such, Voloshinov argues that the comprehension of an utterance's 'theme' must be active in order to grasp language as a 'generative process'. As discussed above, this involves a cognizance of the appropriate context within which a given utterance is produced. But more than this: in attempting to comprehend a given utterance, we must be capable of responding to it by producing our own. Thus, the understanding of concrete language-use is only possible in the dialogic space between active, responsive agents and, therefore, the 'meaningfulness' of an utterance does not reside in either the word or sentence (conceived of in the formal or dictionary sense) or the psyche of the listener. This condition – what Clarke and Holquist (1984a) have termed 'answerability' – explains Voloshinov's assertion that 'Any true understanding is dialogic in nature' (1973: 102).

Furthermore, Voloshinov argues that a word produced within a given speech complex possesses not only theme and meaning; it also expresses a particular value judgement or 'evaluative accent'.[7] He suggests that this process of accentuation is primarily a matter of the 'evaluative context' within which a particular utterance is enunciated. This implies, amongst other things, that the meaning of the 'same' word can radically differ depending on the cultural and discursive field within which it is articulated. Precisely how the sign is so accentuated is ultimately dependent upon the shared values, beliefs and perspectives adhered to by particular social groups. These beliefs and values are not static but dynamic, determined by the historically-evolving mode of existence characteristic of given communities. Nor are such values wholly consensual or uniform; rather, the persistence of divergent social interests in class-divided societies guarantees a general struggle of accents in each semantic domain. This is why, in Voloshinov's view, meaning is inherently polysemic and unstable. Formal-linguistic meaning is continually 'subsumed under theme and torn apart by theme's living contradictions so as to return in the shape of a new meaning with a fixity and self-identity only for the while' (1973: 106).

It is at this point where Voloshinov's philosophy of language acquires a particular relevance for the project of *Ideologiekritik.* Because social and psychical life is inevitably refracted through the prism of class struggle, a given sign community is constituted by contradictory and competing social interests. Although different classes may use the 'same' formal sign-system, given signs are in fact subject to divergent ideological accents depending on the specific context of their usage – what he terms the multi-accentuality of the social sign. The dominant class is motivated to ensure the fixity of meaning and arrest the flux of the sign, insofar as the establishment of a monolithic or 'official' language facilitates the sociopolitical unification of society. However, Voloshinov feels that this Orwellian desire is continually thwarted by the irrepressible and decentralizing forces of popular speech and culture. This continual 'clash of accents' means that modern society is marked by a plethora of antagonistic discursive forms, by a 'struggle over the sign' which gives language its dynamic and fluid character. Indeed, it explains the very historicity of language itself, and why the sign is the richest and most sensitive indicator of cultural and political social conflict, a kind of semiotic litmus paper. I quote at length what is perhaps the most important passage in *Marxism and the Philosophy of Language*, at least from the standpoint of the theory of ideology:

> Existence reflected in the sign is not merely reflected but *refracted.* How is this refraction of existence of the ideological sign determined? By an intersecting of differently oriented social interests within one and the same sign community, i.e., *by the class struggle.* Class does not coincide with the sign community, i.e., with the community which is the totality of users of the same set of signs for ideological communication. Thus various classes will use one and the same language. As a result, differently oriented accents intersect in every ideological sign. Sign becomes an arena of class struggle. This social *multi-accentuality* of the ideological sign is a very crucial aspect. [...] The ruling class strives to impart a supraclass, eternal character to the ideological sign, to extinguish or drive inward the struggle between social value judgments which occurs in it, to

make the sign uniaccentual. In actual fact, each living ideological sign has two faces, like Janus. Any current curse word can
become a word of praise, any current truth must inevitably
sound to many other people as the greatest lie. This *inner
dialectical quality* of the sign comes out fully in the open only in
times of social crises or revolutionary changes. In the ordinary
conditions of life, the contradiction embedded in every
ideological sign cannot emerge fully because the ideological
sign in an established, dominant ideology is always somewhat
reactionary and tries, as it were, to stabilize the preceding factor
in the dialectical flux of the social generative process, so ac-
centuating yesterday's truth as to make it appear today's. And
that is what is responsible for the refracting and distorting
peculiarity of the ideological sign within the dominant ideology.

(1973: 23–4)

This quotation explains why Voloshinov felt that Saussure failed to
grasp the full political significance of the arbitrariness of the sign.
That the relation between signifier and signified is 'arbitrary' does
not mean that this connection is completely random or accidental.
As Raymond Williams (1977: 37) correctly notes, this would imply
that signifying processes are totally removed from the exigencies
of history and the class struggle. But this is precisely the conclusion
that Voloshinov wants to avoid. Instead, he continually stresses that
signification does not take place in some neutral space, in some
Archimedean point beyond the social. Rather, the word is always
the site of a struggle between multiple and intersecting meanings
which, in turn, reflects wider social conflicts. The attempt by the
dominant class to fix meaning and neutralize semantic flux is a
specifically political act – it represents the perennial authoritarian
desire hegemonically to secure an inseparable fusion between
signifier and signified, between form and meaning. Signification is
itself inherently ideological. The struggle over meaning in the
communicative sphere cannot be accounted for by the existing
precepts of linguistic science, but only through a broader translinguistics which conceptualizes actual language use in relation to
the continuous struggle over scarce forms of economic, political
and cultural capital. From the perspective of the development of a
critical theory of language and ideology, *Marxism and the Philosophy
of Language* is therefore one of the richest and most evocative texts
bequeathed to us by the Bakhtin Circle.

P. N. MEDVEDEV AND THE CRITIQUE OF RUSSIAN FORMALISM

In this section I will examine Pavel N. Medvedev's critical assessment of Russian Formalism in his *The Formal Method in Literary Scholarship* (1985)[8] and his attempt to develop a Marxian-influenced sociological poetics of literary works.[9] Any discussion of *The Formal Method* must logically begin with a consideration of the 'formal method' itself. Russian Formalism as an intellectual movement first emerged in Petrograd in the period just preceding the outbreak of the First World War. It can be described as the first sophisticated attempt to develop a theory of literature based on the close textual-linguistic analysis of literary works.[10] In the immediate post-revolutionary years (roughly from about 1921 to 1926), when theoretical innovation was tolerated and even encouraged in the USSR, the Formalists came to dominate the language section of the prestigious Leningrad division of the State Institute for the History of Arts and exercised a considerable degree of influence over Soviet literary theory. Formalism thereafter fell into disrepute but, in its heyday, it generated a great deal of interest and fuelled a long-standing controversy in Soviet literary and cultural circles.[11] Because of its wide-spread appeal and polemical style, and because it espoused a position that (in certain respects) was almost diametrically opposed to that of Bakhtin and his followers, particular members of the Bakhtin Circle were compelled to assess the relative merits of the Formalist doctrine.[12] None the less, *The Formal Method* remains the most sustained and systematic response to the challenge of Formalism, one that seeks a *rapprochement* between the most plausible elements of the Formalist doctrine and an advanced Marxist theory of ideological superstructures.

At the heart of the Formalist doctrine was an attempt to delineate the quality of 'literariness' and to define the phenomenon of literature as an object of scientific study. The question of what made a particular text 'literary' could only be answered by reference to the functioning of language within the poetic text. For the Formalists, what was of importance in analysing a given text was not the socio-historical conditions of its production, and still less the biography of the author in question,[13] but rather the hierarchical system of objective formal 'devices' (plot digression, phonetic repetition, the speed of the action, etc.). Together, such devices (or 'phonetic phonemes') constituted the 'building blocks' of artistic construction, which operated to generate a particular apperceptive effect. To neglect their detailed examination meant that no feature of plot, narrative or style could be properly understood.[14] This attempt to delimit the theoretical object of 'literature' was premised upon a fundamental distinction between 'poetic' and 'practical' language. In everyday speech-acts or non-literary texts, asserted the Formalists, the practical-communicative or referential function of language tended to predominate. Moreover, it was argued that practical language was characterized by a process of perceptual habitualization or 'automatization'. It had become part of the 'common sense' of a particular linguistic community and was thus rendered impervious to the recuperative processes of a reflexive knowledge. Poetic language, on the other hand, was not motivated by such external pragmatic considerations: it had an inherent value and constituted an end in itself (hence the Kantian-inspired notion of the 'self-valuable' word). Moreover, it was suggested that poetic language had an innate capacity to focus the reader's attention upon the principles of the text's linguistic and narrative constitution – the 'laying bare of the device'. This is referred to by Tzvetan Todorov (1987: 12) as the 'autotelic function' of the poetic word: a perceptual exposure of the constructive principles of the text, which serves to demarcate the operation of poetic language from the taken-for-granted referential or mimetic function of practical language. More specifically, it was felt that these habitualized forms of signification were 'made strange' or deautomatized by the gamut of poetic devices within the literary work (and particularly the *avant-garde* work), involving such phenomena as the subversion of established perceptions of time and space, the use of disorienting oxymorons and unexpected phonetic repetitions, and many others. This 'revolt against meaning' which, suggests Medvedev, can in fact be traced to the interrelationship between Formalism and the literary and artistic trend known as Futurism,[15] found its fullest expression in the Formalist doctrine that poetic language was 'trans-rational' and the celebration of the 'whimsical interplay of the word's potential meanings' (Erlich 1981: 46). As Shklovsky suggested, the aesthetic function of art was to make objects 'unfamiliar', to 'increase the difficulty and length of perception. [...] *Art is a way of experiencing the artfulness of an object; the object is not important*' (1965a: 11).

Medvedev's specific response to the Formalist challenge warrants close attention, insofar as it departed significantly from the typical Soviet Marxist line.[16] Whilst somewhat sympathetic to the Formalist approach, he does identify many problematic aspects which he uses as a conceptual springboard whence to develop an alternative sociological poetics. One of his main objections was that whilst certain Formalists (such as Shklovsky and Tynyanov) did not expressly deny that sociological factors could influence the literary milieu, they consistently rejected the notion that there could be any direct causal linkage between socio-historical factors and literary forms. Any relationship between them could only be based on the principle of 'interaction' or 'conditionality' – that is, contingent and external rather than necessary and internal.[17] By contrast, Medvedev insisted that the connection between the literary and the social was guaranteed by their common location in the ideological superstructure and, more importantly, by the fact that literature was bound up with the same semiotic processes that governed the ideological environment as a whole.

Insofar as Medvedev's comments on ideology and the sign wholly conform to the general position sketched out by Voloshinov, it will not receive any attention here. Instead, I turn to Medvedev's methodological and substantive objections to Formalism. In particular, he rejects the opposition between poetic and practical language, which in his opinion represents Formalism's most grievous error. He suggests that the concept of 'poetic language' is a neo-Platonic abstraction which (like Saussure's *langue*) manifestly fails to grasp the connection between language and the 'unity of social life'. Formalism ignores the 'organizational forms of concrete utterances and their socio-ideological functions' and is therefore indifferent to issues of 'cognitive truth, poetic beauty, [and] political correctness'. Hence, the Formalist doctrine severs the ideological plane 'from the real social conditions of its realization. Within the work an empty game is played with material with no regard for its meaning' (1985: 41).

By contrast, Medvedev asserts that there is no *prima facie* reason to maintain such an ontological dualism in the sphere of semiotic or linguistic analysis, insofar as the constructive principles of poetic language do not radically differ from those principles which regulate even the most mundane and prosaic forms of verbal interaction. Accordingly, the constructive functions of any language-form can only be grasped through a rigorous analysis of the 'various types of speech performance and the corresponding forms of utterance from all spheres of practical interchange and practice'. This in turn must involve an interpretive understanding of the 'social characteristics of the communicating groups and all the concrete complexity of the ideological horizon [within which] each practical utterance is formed' (1985: 93). Formalist analysis is certainly useful, suggests Medvedev, but ultimately incomplete. A knowledge of the linguistic minutiae of literary texts must be supplemented with a comprehension of the wider dialogic context which binds author, reader and text into a complexly structured whole. Thus, whilst Medvedev finds broad agreement with the Formalist desire to specify the phenomenon of 'literature' as a viable object of study and to investigate the 'laws of motion' which pertain to the constitution of any literary work, he equally affirms the need to ascertain the text's 'fullness, generality, and breadth of meaning'.

In order to overcome the Formalist emphasis on pure form, Medvedev asserts that the essential task of a sociological poetics is to uncover that aspect of the literary work which mediates between the 'depth and generality of meaning' on the one hand with the 'uniqueness of the articulated sound' on the other. Only then can we ascertain the connection between external form and inner ideological significance. For Medvedev, this mediating factor is the phenomenon of social evaluation, which (as for Voloshinov) is indissolubly linked to the production of concrete, social utterances in any medium of semiotic communication. The process of social evaluation (encompassing expressive intonation, inflection, and so on) makes meaning 'concrete and individual', and it determines 'the historical physiognomy of every action and every utterance, its individual, class and epochal physiognomy'. We can only comprehend a given utterance if we are attuned to the ideological values embedded within it: 'It is necessary to understand the meaning of the utterance, the content of the act, and its historical reality, and to do so, moreover, in their concrete inner unity. Without such an understanding, meaning is dead' (Medvedev 1985: 121–2). In terms of the literary text per se, social evaluation makes possible an 'inseparable unity of meaning and reality' within the poetic work; it forms a linkage between the work and the 'general canvass of the social life of a given historical period and a given social group'. Only by rejecting a Formalist textualism and embracing a contextually-sensitive discourse-centred model of semiotic communication, argues Medvedev, can the creative production of novel meanings and significances in language and literature be conceptualized.

Of particular interest is Medvedev's suggestion that the apprehension of social or natural reality through any given semiotic medium – and here the literary occupies a privileged place – is organized in terms of specific generic forms, each of which 'possesses definite principles of selection, definite forms for seeing and conceptualizing reality, and a definite scope and depth of penetration' (1985: 131). Hence, they constitute a kind of ideological framework or cultural grid through which the 'substantial, objective, [and] thematic' features of the text coalesce into particular forms. Such literary genres also enrich our inner speech with new 'devices' which transform our awareness and conceptualization of external reality. He speculates that the emergence of new literary forms (and corresponding systems of representation) enable individuals to perceive and visualize aspects of reality in unexpected and novel ways (the dual meaning of the word 'novel' being perfectly appropriate in this case). Through the mediation of literary forms, both artists and readers can understand 'the unity and inner logic of an entire epoch' and 'master new aspects of reality'. This is a highly suggestive insight, but unfortunately Medvedev does not develop it in any great detail.

It is worth noting in conclusion that contemporary critics are divided as to the overall success of Medvedev's critique of Formalism.[18] For instance, it is often remarked that *The Formal Method* is too polemical and not broad-minded enough (although this style typified much intellectual debate in the USSR during that period), and that Medvedev ignores the 'sociological turn' of the Formalists in the mid- to late 1920s. Nevertheless, it remains a valuable work, if only because it convincingly attacks the Formalist obsession with linguistic structure and sketches out an alternative poetics which focuses on the intersubjective semiotic environment linking text, author and recipient. Accordingly, whatever its ultimate success or failure, Medvedev's tentative steps towards a discourse-centred model of communication which seeks to overcome the recurrent opposition between form and content represent an important step in the maturation of the Bakhtin Circle's critical project.

BAKHTIN AND DOSTOEVSKY'S POLYPHONIC UNIVERSE

Originally published in 1929 under the title *Problems of the Works of Dostoevsky*, *Problems of Dostoevsky's Poetics* has since undergone various reworkings, deletions and additions.[19] In many respects, the original sections of the book are sometimes more 'formalist' than many of the Formalists' own critical writings.[20] If this emphasis on formal categories of discourse was to be at least partially superseded by the more historical and sociological thrust of the 'mature' Bakhtin, *Problems of Dostoevsky's Poetics* remains significant in that it strives to carve out a radically new way of looking at language and intertextuality in both literature and everyday life. The primary concepts that emerged from this text were to remain central to Bakhtin's philosophical project until his death in 1975, despite various theoretical shifts in orientation and emphasis. As such, they are of more than passing interest vis-à-vis the understanding of the nature of ideology and the dynamics of discursive struggle in society, and to much contemporary writing in sociology, communications theory, literary criticism, and linguistics which are only now 'catching up' to the themes and problematics sketched out by Bakhtin and his colleagues decades earlier.

As Tzvetan Todorov (1987: 70) correctly notes, the edition which is now familiar to Bakhtin scholars is roughly divided up into three almost self-sufficient essays. The first examines Dostoevsky's 'novelistic universe' using broad philosophical categories which owe much to the tradition of German idealist philosophy (particular that of Kant as well as the neo-Kantians Ernst Cassirer and Hermann Cohen) and the Romantic aesthetic in general. The second section represents Bakhtin's attempt to situate Dostoevsky in relation to a particular literary/cultural tradition which he designated as the 'carnivalesque'. He felt that this particular generic tradition could be ultimately traced to Socratic dialogue and Menippean satire through to the popular carnivals of the Middle Ages and early Renaissance, and he insisted that Dostoevsky's (like Rabelais's) work could not be adequately comprehended unless this ancient folk-carnival basis was fully acknowledged and appreciated. The third part is concerned with detailed stylistic analyses of selected passages from Dostoevsky's novels and short stories, organized in terms of a complex typology of discourse-types.[21] These are designed to illuminate and support his general theses with respect to the nature of language and textuality and their role in literary and social life. Given the thematic orientation of this study, however, I will restrict my commentary to the initial, more philosophical section which opens this treatise.

For Bakhtin, Dostoevsky was the first genuine exponent of the 'fully polyphonic novel' which, as both a description of literary form and an ethical ideal, had hitherto been only partially realized in particular, marginalized genres within European literary history. The crux of this 'polyphony' is the suggestion that Dostoevsky's novels contain a plurality of unmerged consciousnesses, a mixture of 'valid voices' which are not completely subordinated to authorial intentions or the heavy hand of the omniscient authorial voice/narrational voice. That is, the character's voice is equally as important and 'fully weighted' as the author's own, and the former cannot be simply viewed as an appendage of the latter. In Dostoevsky's novels, that is, the hero's word 'possesses extraordinary independence in the structure of the work; it sounds, as it were, *alongside* the author's word and with the full and equally valid voices of other characters' (Bakhtin 1984: 7). This construction of a series of autonomous yet interacting ideological worlds (as embodied by particular characters) within the text affects every element of the novel itself – plot, narration, style, imagery, or the portrayal of time and space (the chronotope). For Bakhtin, the subordination of such elements of the novel to the interaction of consciousnesses was the essence of Dostoevsky's artistic genius:

> Dostoevsky, like Goethe's Prometheus, creates not voiceless slaves (as does Zeus), but *free* people, capable of standing *alongside* their creator, capable of not agreeing with him and even of rebelling against him. *A plurality of independent and unmerged voices and consciousnesses, a genuine polyphony of fully valid voices is in fact the chief characteristic of Dostoevsky's novels.* What unfolds in his works is not a multitude of characters and fates in a single objective world, illuminated by a single authorial consciousness; rather a *plurality of consciousnesses, with equal rights and each with its own world,* combine but are not merged in the unity of the event. Dostoevsky's major heroes are, by the very nature of his creative design, *not only objects of authorial discourse but also subjects of their own directly signifying discourse.* [. . .] The consciousness of a character is given as *someone else's* consciousness, another

consciousness, yet at the same time it is not turned into an object, is not closed, does not become a simple object of the author's consciousness.

(1984: 6–7)

Bakhtin stresses that such a multiplicity of interacting consciousnesses is a necessary but not a sufficient characteristic of a genuine polyphony. The author's affirmation of a character's right to be treated as a subject and not as an object must also constitute the guiding artistic principle behind the verbal structuring of the novel as a whole and the world beyond the text it projects – in other words, it must form the basis of a fully-fledged dialogic world-view. Bakhtin suggests that the maintenance of this dialogical principle can be accomplished through the use of particular artistic 'devices' which 'predestines the character for freedom (a relative freedom, of course), and incorporates him into the strict and carefully calculated plan of the whole' (1984: 13). Such devices aim at the rupturing and dislocation of the seamless whole of the monologic world of objects, events and consciousnesses through the introduction of heterogeneous and multiform 'materials' into the text. In the polyphonic novel, elements of plot, characterization and so forth are all 'structured to make dialogic opposition inescapable'. The result is an endless clash of 'unmerged souls', the construction of a multiplicity of diverse yet interconnecting ideological worlds. Bakhtin refers to this as the 'great dialogue', and he feels it is a principle which inheres in every element of the polyphonic text – indeed, in all of social life itself:

> To be means to communicate dialogically. When dialogue ends, everything ends. Thus dialogue, by its very essence, cannot and must not come to an end. [. . .] Everything in Dostoevsky's novels tends toward dialogue, toward a dialogic opposition, as if tending toward its center. All else is means; dialogue is the end. A single voice ends nothing and resolves nothing. Two voices is the minimum for life, the minimum for existence.
>
> (1984: 252)

Dostoevsky's characters are therefore ideologists in the fullest sense of the word. They express a coherent *Weltanschauung,* what Bakhtin calls an 'integral ideational position'. Dostoevsky's artistic goal is therefore not mimesis, the faithful reproduction of an external 'reality', but rather the representation of how this reality appears to the hero's self-consciousness. In Dostoevsky's writings, then, we are not privileged to see who the hero is, but rather '*how* he is conscious of himself'; our act of artistic visualization occurs not before the reality of the hero, but before a pure function of his awareness of that reality' (1984: 48). Accordingly, Dostoevsky's most significant heroes – such as Ivan Karamazov, Raskolnikov, and Prince Myshkin – cannot be understood as amalgams of fixed, static traits; nor are their actions and thoughts wholly predictable. They not only react but act; sensitized to their own surroundings and to their situation, they are existential beings who are fully responsible for their own deeds and words. Hence, Dostoevsky's primary artistic strategy is oriented toward the expression and 'fine-tuning' of a character's discourse, a discourse which is designed to galvanize characters, provoke them, make them respond dialogically, thereby 'laying bare [their] own final word as it interacts intensely with other consciousnesses' (Bakhtin 1984: 54). Dostoevsky's heroes are imbued with the 'power to signify' because they are privileged with a 'fully weighted semantic position'. If polyphony is to be fully realized, then this 'direct and unmediated power to mean' cannot be restricted to the author. And it is precisely Dostoevsky's approach which, according to Bakhtin, represents a 'new and integral authorial position' which allows for an unprecedented method of visualizing the human being in the sphere of art.[22]

For Bakhtin, Dostoevsky's utilization of self-consciousness as a pivotal artistic device is the centrepiece of a dialogical principle which manages to subvert the monologic point of view of traditional thought and literature. Monologism, for Bakhtin, describes a condition wherein the matrix of ideological values, signifying practices, and creative impulses which constitute the living reality of language are subordinated to the hegemony of a single, unified consciousness or perspective. Whatever cannot be subsumed under this transcendent consciousness is regarded as extraneous or superfluous. In other words, monologism denies the 'equal rights of consciousness vis-à-vis truth (understood abstractly and systematically)' (1984: 285), thereby ignoring or reifying the individual's capacity to produce autonomous meaning. Significantly, Bakhtin argues that this monologic principle, which permeates all ideological spheres within society and not simply those of literature or philosophy, was encouraged by the 'cult of unified and exclusive reason' promulgated by European rationalism and Enlightenment thought. In an appendix to the *Dostoevsky* text which was added to the 1963 Soviet edition (entitled 'Towards a Reworking of the Dostoevsky Book'), Bakhtin provides what is probably the most succinct characterization of the concept of monologism:

> Monologism, at its extreme, denies the existence outside itself of another consciousness with equal rights and equal responsibilities, another *I* with equal rights (*thou*). With a monologic approach (in its extreme or pure form) *another person* remains wholly and merely an *object* of consciousness, and not another consciousness. No response is expected from it that could change everything in the world of my consciousness. Monologue is finalized and deaf to the other's response, does not expect it and does not acknowledge in it any *decisive* force. Monologue manages without the other, and therefore to some degree materializes all reality. Monologue pretends to be the *ultimate word*. It closes down the represented world and represented persons.
>
> (1984: 292–3)

In the monologic or 'homophonic' text, all aspects of plot, dialogue and characterization are subordinated to the monologic will of the author. Characters are static and predetermined, and they lack any vestige of autonomous creativity and free will. Instead, their *raison d'être* is to function as a mouthpiece for the transmission of the author's own ideological viewpoint. Accordingly, the latter enjoys an enormous 'surplus of vision' with respect to the former: 'A monologic artistic world does not recognize someone else's thought, someone else's idea, as an object of representation' (1984: 79). The authorial idea alone visualizes and illuminates the world contained in the novel, which results in the featureless and 'single-toned' quality of the monologic work. The monologic text may well represent ideas, even opposed and contradictory ones, but only in a disembodied and 'dematerialized' fashion. By restricting dialogue to the abstract collision of ideas on a rarefied plane of pure consciousness, Bakhtin claims that the living dialogic interaction between autonomous beings is transformed into a lifeless 'philosophical monologue', a *dialogue des sourds*. Free, untrammelled dialogue is therefore subordinated to the dictates of a monolithic, objectified world which is ultimately controlled by

a unitary, transcendental authorial (and authoritarian) consciousness. While Bakhtin does not deny the importance of the interaction of ideas in the novel, he argues that such abstract, logical
interconnections between ideas are secondary to the embodiment
of ideologies in distinct characters and personalities which is a
central characteristic of the polyphonic text.

It is not surprising that Bakhtin has scant regard for the monologic position – at one point, he refers to artistic finalization as a
form of 'violence', although it should be noted that he also feels
that some degree of finalization or 'consummation' is necessary to
produce an aesthetically-viable artistic whole.[23] Methodologically,
Bakhtin feels that monologism is suspect simply because it fails
adequately to capture the exigencies of heterodox discursive
practices in the social world as well as the inherently dialogic
orientation of all signifying practices. Ethically, of course, monologism objectifies and quantifies human subjectivity and robs
individual creativity of any real significance. In either case, Bakhtin
holds up Dostoevsky's novels as exemplars of how the dialogic
nature of human existence can be artistically represented. To
grasp what he has in mind here requires a brief digression with
respect to his phenomenology of consciousness and a more extended examination of what he means by 'dialogism'. For Bakhtin,
human consciousness is not a unified whole, but always exists in a
tensile, conflict-ridden relationship with other consciousnesses, in
a constant alterity between self and other. In fact, a fully self-
sufficient and isolated consciousness cannot possibly exist: the very
process of acquiring self-consciousness from birth to maturity is, in
Bakhtin's eyes, utterly dependent upon discursive interaction with
another 'I'.[24] Separation from the other can only result in the loss
of self: '*To be means to communicate*. Absolute death (non-being) is
the state of being unheard, unrecognized' (1984: 287). Every
aspect of consciousness and every signifying practice a subject
engages in is therefore constituted dialogically, through the ebb
and flow of a multitude of continuous and inherently responsive
communicative acts. Unlike the monologic word, which always
'gravitates towards itself and its referential object', the dialogic
word is locked into an intense relationship with the word of
another. It is always addressed to someone – a witness, a judge or
simply a listener – and it is accompanied by the keen anticipation
of another's response. Nor is the dialogic word a passive vehicle of
neutral description or information: because it is designed to

provoke a response, to initiate dialogue, it is an 'arena of battle between two voices' and is charged with polemic, parody, evaluation and so on. This is what Bakhtin means when he refers to the dialogic utterance as being 'double-voiced', 'vari-directional', and 'multiaccented'.

Bakhtin holds that Dostoevsky does not seek to subordinate or suppress these pervasive vari-directional accents and double-voiced discourses that characterize the natural milieu of living language; rather, he aims to enhance and encourage this 'dialogically-charged atmosphere' in the context of the novel form. In Dostoevsky's novels, the dialogic principle can be found in the interaction between the hero and the author, the series of 'micro-dialogues' that takes place between the various characters, and even the 'inner speech' that occurs within the hero's own self-consciousness (insofar as introspection itself is merely another example of 'internal dialogue'). And it is only within the polyphonic novel that artistic justice can be done to the 'objective complexity, contradictoriness and multi-voicedness' of the social world as a whole. The thoughts of Dostoevsky's characters, then, are like the rejoinders within an eternal, unending dialogue. Because of their resistance to closure, their refusal to submit to unambiguous and unequivocal expression, these thoughts and words fail to congeal into a fixed 'monologic whole'. The Dostoevskian hero's words always live 'a tense life on the borders of someone else's thought, someone else's consciousness' (1984: 32). In a crucial passage, Bakhtin writes:

> . . . a consciousness in Dostoevsky's world is presented not on the path of its own evolution and growth, that is, not historically, but rather *alongside* other consciousnesses, it cannot concentrate on itself and its own idea, on the immanent logical development of that idea; instead, it is pulled into interaction with other consciousnesses. In Dostoevsky, consciousness never gravitates towards itself but is always found in intense relationship with another consciousnesses. Every experience, every thought of a character is internally dialogic, adorned with polemic, filled with struggle, or is on the contrary open to inspiration from outside itself – but it is not in any case concentrated simply on its own object; it is accompanied by a continual sideways glance at another person. It could be said that Dostoevsky offers, in artistic form, something like a

sociology of consciousness – to be sure, only on the level of coexistence. But even so, Dostoevsky as an artist does arrive at an *objective* mode for visualizing the life of consciousness and the forms of their living coexistence, and thus offers material that is valuable for the sociologist as well.

(1984: 32)

This quotation highlights a number of crucial features pertaining to Bakhtin's dialogic reading of Dostoevsky. Firstly, he argues that while the 'idea' is an important object of representation in Dostoevsky's novels, it is never the 'hero' as such. Rather, the 'hero' is always a concrete personality who embodies and lives out the idea in question. If the idea is extracted from this interaction of consciousnesses and subjected to a process of reification, then it is 'forced into a systematically monologic context' and lapses into a sterile solipsism. By empowering the character with the independent capacity to signify, and by making the dialogic principle the 'artistic dominant' of the polyphonic text, Dostoevsky's works are much more 'objective' than their monologic counterparts in the sense that they transcend the blinkered ideological perspective of the author. This is what Bakhtin refers to as a specifically dialogical form of literary realism, which he contrasts with the idealistic and subjectivistic tendencies of 'monologic realism'. Secondly, Dostoevsky escapes Bakhtin's ethical invective against monologism because he always treats human relations in a dialogical rather than a mechanistic fashion. Because he does not represent autonomous subjects as objects, Dostoevsky avoids the quantification of his heroes and does not supply them with 'finalizing authorial words'.[25] As such, Dostoevsky is faithful to Bakhtin's vision of the human condition: namely, that humankind is essentially indeterminate and 'eternally unfinalizable'. Subjects continually strive to resist the constraints placed upon them by 'externalizing secondhand definitions', which seek to curtail and 'deaden' their thoughts and actions. Bakhtin passionately argues that there is something within a concrete individual that can only be revealed in a 'free act of self-consciousness and discourse', an act of self-revelation which cannot be known or predicted beforehand. Thus, through the artistic design of the polyphonic novel, Dostoevsky seeks to liberate and de-reify the human being, to reveal those sides of humanity which cannot be shown by the traditional monologic novel.[26]

What emerges from this discussion is the realization that, for Bakhtin, dialogism is not simply a textual or even an intertextual phenomenon: it reaches beyond the text as such to embrace the social world as a whole. Bakhtin argues that the attempt to study not only Dostoevsky's poetics but dialogical relations of any kind cannot be satisfied with the utilization of received linguistic categories and definitions. Linguistics can tell us about the formal structure of language, its 'dead husk', but it can reveal very little about language as a 'living concrete totality'. As such, existing theories of language and language-use are invariably monologic, and are guilty of perpetrating a form of violence on humanity. As Bakhtin puts it:

> The single adequate form for *verbally expressing* authentic human life is the *open-ended dialogue*. Life by its very nature is dialogic. To live means to participate in dialogue: to ask questions, to heed, to respond, to agree, and so forth. In this dialogue a person participates wholly and throughout his whole life: with his eyes, lips, hands, soul, spirit, with his whole body and deeds. He invests his entire self in discourse, and this discourse enters into the dialogic fabric of human life, into the world symposium. Reified (materializing, objectified) images are profoundly inadequate for life and for discourse. A reified model of the world is now being replaced by a dialogic model. Every thought and every life merges in the open-ended dialogue. Also impermissible is any materialization of the word: its nature is also dialogic.

> (1984: 293)

Hence, the examination of dialogism in life and art can only be accomplished through the development of a new theoretical approach – what Bakhtin refers to as 'metalinguistics' or 'translinguistics'. Such a translinguistics studies not 'texts' or 'systems of language' in isolation but the entire sphere of dialogic interaction itself, where 'discourse lives an authentic life'. This general research programme was destined to monopolize Bakhtin's attention until the end of his life. In the essays written in the 1930s and later collected as *The Dialogic Imagination* and in *Rabelais and His World*, Bakhtin shifted his attention away from a strict preoccupation with polyphony in the literary text to embrace the wider dynamics of heteroglossia and discursive struggle in the socio-historical world. It is this aspect of Bakhtin's legacy which I will examine in the following chapter.

Chapter 2

The 1930s and 1940s writings

In the dream in which every epoch sees in images the epoch which is to succeed it, the latter appears coupled with elements of prehistory – that is to say of a classless society. The experiences of this society, which have their store-place in the collective unconsciousness, interact with the new to give birth to a thousand configurations of life, from permanent buildings to ephemeral fashions.

Walter Benjamin

INTRODUCTION

Not long after the publication of his study of Dostoevsky, Bakhtin was arrested for 'anti-Soviet' activities and sentenced to five years' internal exile in the remote province of Kazakhstan, eventually ending up in a Moscow suburb in 1940. Yet despite such personal vicissitudes and hardships, this period was a remarkably fertile and productive one in Bakhtin's intellectual career. In general, this phase of Bakhtin's studies marks a shift away from the phenomenological orientation of the *Dostoevsky* book and the earlier 'architectonic' essays towards what Todorov (1987: 83) has succinctly described as an 'historico-literary' one. In this section I will discuss this period, starting with the four essays which have been collected in *The Dialogic Imagination* (1981). Particular emphasis will be placed on the lengthy essay 'Discourse in the Novel' which concludes this volume, a complex and extremely suggestive treatise which arguably contains some of Bakhtin's most cogent and insightful observations on the dynamics of discursive struggle in contemporary society. Next, I turn to a consideration of Bakhtin's *Rabelais and His World* (1968), which extends and intensifies his interest in the socially-transgressive qualities of popular culture. In this chapter, I will argue that a thorough understanding of Bakhtin's intellectual output during this period is of critical importance in the appropriation of Bakhtinian themes and concepts for the task of reconstructing the theory of ideology.

HETEROGLOSSIA IN/AND THE NOVEL

The essays in *The Dialogic Imagination* are thematically organized along two major lines of inquiry: (i) a theorization of how heteroglossia operates in the novel and the social world, in terms of what could be termed the *longue durée*[1] of cultural-artistic and linguistic evolution; and (ii) the elaboration of an intricate model of the poetics of prose discourse, concentrating on the stylistic features of the particular sub-genres of the novel, encompassing detailed textual analyses of numerous examples of novelistic prose (e.g. Dickens, Turgenev, and Sterne). However, since the latter is more properly concerned with literary theory and therefore lies outside the remit of this study, I will concentrate on the former. One of my central aims in what follows will be to argue that underlying Bakhtin's conceptualization of heteroglossia in/and the novel is another, less obvious interest: to critique various theoretical and artistic positions which serve to buttress and legitimate the centralization and hierarchization of what he terms the 'verbal-ideological' sphere. This necessitates an exploration of his understanding of the dynamics of heteroglossia in the social world and how this phenomenon is articulated with the novel form.

Bakhtin argues that when we confront the novel 'as a whole', we are presented with an undeniable fact: it is 'multiform in style and variform in speech and voice'. Accordingly, the novel is best understood as a diversity of 'social speech types' or languages which are organized in terms of a 'structured artistic system'. Particular combinations of such socio-linguistic forms (and the time-space coordinates or chronotopes[2] they embody) result in different literary genres. Hence, the 'concrete social context' of discourse must be revealed before the dialogic nature of the novel can itself be comprehended. Whilst this multi-voiced quality of the novel has long been recognized, traditional approaches have generally been satisfied with a description of the stylistic idiosyncrasies of a given author or literary school. In Bakhtin's view, this can be faulted because it assumes that the author is responsible for all ideological creativity and constitutes the epicentre of linguistic meaning. He dismisses this as a vestige of bourgeois egoism, and argues that the creativity of the author is secondary to the syncretic incorporation of social heteroglossia into the novel form.[3] This fetishization of the author has other, more ominous ramifications: for Bakhtin, it is nothing less than an ideological expression of forces which strive hegemonically to unify the social world. Such a conceptualization of the literary text as a closed system – that is, as a self-sufficient authorial monologue – is the literary counterpart of the theoretical or ideological construal of language as a stable, monolithic entity. For Bakhtin, a myriad of philosophical, literary and linguistic movements from Aristotle's poetics to Saussure's structuralism and beyond can be implicated in this reifying and centralizing process. Far from being innocent examples of 'pure scholarship', these traditions have actively contributed to the consolidation of a 'unified language' throughout European history. This official language takes its cue from the conversational and literary generic forms characteristic of the educated elites. The language of this elite defines itself in contradistinction to the 'low' speech types found in the street, in the marketplace, and so on. It attempts to stamp a fixed order on these heteroglot languages, to introduce a canonical style to which the latter must submit in order to 'preserve the socially sealed-off quality of a privileged community' and solidify the boundary between 'legitimate' and 'illegitimate' language use. Nevertheless, argues Bakhtin, this drive to unify the verbal-ideological world is never completely successful. Accompanying this centripetal tendency towards integration are (more or less powerful) centrifugal processes which continue unabated. The latter – which Bakhtin identifies as the folk-festive genres of the people – operate to ensure the subversion and disunification of the officially-sanctioned language system from within. The natural environment of the utterance is hence a 'dialogized heteroglossia', which imparts to it a specific ideological value and content. Accordingly, Bakhtin views the communicative sphere as the terrain of a ceaseless battle between the forces of stasis and fixity on the one hand, and movement, change and diversification on the other, a struggle which is ultimately responsible for the continual emergence of new meanings and significances in the verbal-ideological world.

Bakhtin argues that, historically speaking, social formations which are characterized by a monolithic linguistic-ideological system tend to display predominantly magical or mythological forms of consciousness. Mythical thought encourages a relatively stable fusion between a particular meaning and a corresponding linguistic expression, which reflects and strengthens the world-view of the secular and religious elite. Hence, a mythological consciousness fetters the free, unhindered development of dialogic intercourse and dampens the word's capacity for greater 'expressiveness'. Yet Bakhtin speculated that this situation of monoglossia could not hold sway for long. This rupturing of a hierarchical and mythologized image of the past can be traced to a particular moment in European history: the 'heteroglossization' of an isolated and 'culturally deaf semipatriarchal society' due to a myriad of cultural and linguistic influences. Bakhtin suggests that the emergence of the novel form and the liberation of consciousness that it makes possible is ultimately dependent upon the 'active polyglossia of the new world, the new culture and its creative literary consciousness' (1981: 12). When the period of sealed-off national languages came to an end (dating roughly from the Hellenic period), Bakhtin asserts that there occurred a process of 'active, mutual cause and effect and interillumination' between different dialects and languages. He argues that languages and literary forms were effectively 'reborn' in this milieu, resulting in a plurality of different (and often contradictory) ideological worlds and the birth of a new cultural consciousness.

Bakhtin is never entirely clear on precisely why and how this decentring and subversion of official discourse occurred when it did, although he seems to suggest that this is inevitable when a given society opens itself up to a multiplicity of linguistic and artistic influences.[4] However, he is certainly in no doubt as to the overwhelming significance of such an event. For the proliferation of socio-ideological points of view effectively ends the hegemony of a single and unitary official language, and it frees a plurality of 'cultural-semantic and emotional intentions' from the one-dimensional constraints of mythical thought. This truly revolutionary change (akin to a Kuhnian 'paradigm shift') encourages not only a sensitivity toward alien languages but also the 'alien' or heteroglot qualities of one's own language. In Formalist terms, the ideological and verbal 'decentring' of language from its mythological moorings 'makes strange' or defamiliarizes our own language

because it allows us to view the world from the perspective of a
different language and world-view, which in turn promotes more
reflexive and self-critical forms of consciousness:

> The internal speech diversity of a literary dialect and of its
> surrounding extraliterary environment [. . .] undermines the
> authority of custom and of whatever traditions still fetter
> linguistic consciousness; it erodes that system of national myth
> that is organically fused with language, in effect destroying once
> and for all a mythic and magical attitude to language and the
> word. A deeply involved participation in alien cultures and
> languages (one is impossible without the other) inevitably leads
> to an awareness of the disassociation between language and
> intention, language and thought, language and expression.
>
> (Bakhtin 1981: 368–9)

For Bakhtin, then, language is unitary only 'in the abstract', only if
it is viewed as a reified 'grammatical system of normative forms'.
When language is examined in terms of its actual utilization in the
social world, it becomes apparent that there exists an irreducible
plurality of 'verbal-ideological and social belief systems'. Within
any overarching cultural formation, which corresponds to a
particular 'socio-ideological conceptual horizon', there can exist a
number of distinct national languages. Yet internal to any such
'national language' are always present two or more 'social
languages', which Bakhtin describes as 'a concrete socio-linguistic
belief system that defines a distinct identity for itself within the
boundaries of a [national] language' (1981: 356). Such a social
language is distinguished by particular semantic shifts and lexical
choices that can be made within the national language in question,
and which can be correlated with certain formal linguistic textures
and ideological motifs. Bakhtin argues that this internal
diversification of a national language can be best understood
through the construction of a typology of various 'speech genres'
(including oratory or journalistic forms, the language of the
marketplace, rural dialects, and so on), each such genre
incorporating different modes of intentionality, intonation and
social evaluation. Some forms of 'semantic stratification' are
relatively enduring and widespread, whilst others live only a brief
'socio-ideological life' before disappearing altogether. But they all
have something in common: all such heteroglot languages express
a particular point of view on the world, a relatively coherent system

of values, meanings, and time-space indices. These languages enter into struggle, invest and animate human consciousness with specific patterns of motivation and action, co-exist and interrelate dialogically:

> . . . at any given moment of its historical existence, language is heteroglot from top to bottom: it represents the co-existence of socio-ideological contradictions between the present and the past, between differing epochs of the past, between different socio-ideological groups in the present, between tendencies, schools, circles and so forth, all given a bodily form. These 'languages' of heteroglossia intersect each other in a variety of ways, forming new socially typifying 'languages'.
>
> (1981: 291)

Bakhtin suggests that all such heteroglot social languages and speech genres are animated by a form of internal or 'primordial' dialogism, by which he means the intrinsic orientation of all discourse to the utterances of others. Whereas in traditional stylistics the word is treated as a self-contained entity which signifies the external world 'directly', Bakhtin insists that between the word and its object is interposed an 'elastic environment' of other, alien words which also refer to the same object and theme and which enter into a 'process of living interaction'. That is, meaning is always brought to the object from outside, through the 'social accentuation of the word'. But this social accentuation is itself always stratified and heteroglot. The object to be signified is plunged into an oscillating play of light and shadow; some elements are illuminated, while others are obscured. The semantic and stylistic features of the word are formed inside this intersecting network of light and darkness, wherein each voice projects a different socio-verbal 'image' onto the object. It is within this milieu of dialogic harmony and dissonance that the word acquires its particular 'stylistic profile and tone'. Hence, only a 'mythical Adam' could approach the object to be signified in an untouched, pristine state; for the rest of us, language-use is always infused from within by multiform paths of social consciousness. A failure to grasp this inescapably dialogical quality of the word can only result in the hypostatization of language into a 'dead, thing-like shell' or a 'naked corpse'. Utilizing a series of provocative visual metaphors, Bakhtin writes:

If we imagine the *intention* of a [word] in the form of a ray of light, then the living and unrepeatable play of colours and light on the facets of the image that it constructs can be explained as the spectral dispersion of the ray-word, not within the object itself (as would be the case in the play of an image-as-trope, in poetic speech taken in the narrow sense, in an 'autotelic word'), but rather as its spectral dispersion in an atmosphere filled with alien words, value judgements and accents through which the ray passes on its way toward the object; the social atmosphere of the word, the atmosphere that surrounds the object, makes the facets of the image sparkle.

(1981: 277)

Of particular importance in this regard is the means by which the speech of others is transmitted and evaluated, given that the alien word is such a pervasive aspect of our own speech. Bakhtin suggests that all living discourse is concerned with the representation and transmission of the speech of others, which also involves assessing these words, judging them as to veracity or accuracy, or arguing with them. Our speech is continually criss-crossed with references to others' speech: 'Everybody says . . . ', 'she or he said . . . ', 'I heard . . . ', 'This book I read said . . . ', and so on. Typically, we do not transmit information or opinions in a direct form as our own, but by reference to 'some indefinite and general source'. We constantly monitor, interpret and respond to the words and meanings of others in the context of everyday social interaction, which means that 'no less than half (on the average) of all the words uttered by [a given individual] will be someone else's words (consciously someone else's) transmitted with varying degrees of precision and impartiality (or more precisely, partiality)' (1981: 339). What this implies is that the act of understanding and interpreting the alien word requires a kind of hermeneutics of the quotidian micro-world of the word. In other words, Bakhtin continually stresses the dynamic role of consciousness in the apprehension and understanding of social being as mediated through language: 'Responsive understanding is a fundamental force, one that participates in the formulation of discourse, and it is moreover an *active* understanding, one that discourse senses as resistance or support enriching the discourse' (1981: 280–1). Each participant in dialogue always brings pre-existing expectations and 'frames of meaning' to bear on the comprehension of concrete discourse. Therefore, the crux of an 'active and engaged under-standing' is the act of incorporating the word of the other into one's own conceptual system, thereby imbuing the word with an entirely new range of inflections and evaluative nuances. It is this feature of linguistic interaction that makes genuine dialogue possible, and it facilitates the introduction of new meanings into language. Any speaker is tacitly aware of this process and orients his or her utterances to resonate with the listener's own apperceptive system in a Gadamerian 'fusion of horizons':

> . . . [the speaker's] orientation toward the listener is an orientation toward a specific conceptual horizon, toward the specific world of the listener; it introduces totally new elements into his discourse; it is in this way, after all, that various points of view, conceptual horizons, systems for providing expressive accents, various social 'languages' come to interact with one another. The speaker strives to get a reading on his own word, and on his own conceptual system that determines this word, within the alien conceptual system of the understanding receiver; he enters into dialogical relationships with certain aspects of this system. The speaker breaks through the alien conceptual horizon of the listener, constructs his own utterance on alien territory, against his, the listener's, apperceptive background.
>
> (1981: 282)

As the preceding discussion indicates, Bakhtin feels that this dialogic interaction between self and other and the incorporation of the latter's conceptual horizon to one's own perspective is a vital stage in the maturation of an individual's self-consciousness: 'The ideological becoming of a human being [. . .] is the process of selectively assimilating the words of others' (1981: 341). This 'authoring' of the self necessarily involves a 'projection' into the consciousness of the other. After this moment of projection, one can return to one's own ideological horizon and situate oneself socially, temporally and spatially in relation to other subjects in the social world. The other, therefore, exists in a dialectical relation to one's own consciousness as both subject and object, and is therefore an inseparable component of our being-in-the-world.[5] Nevertheless, this process is not always the free and spontaneous act of human self-development that Bakhtin obviously feels that it should be. He suggests that there are two very different relations that a subject can have vis-à-vis the discourse of the other: the alien word can either operate in an 'authoritative' or else an 'internally persuasive' fashion. The former unambiguously demarcates itself apart from other utterances and projects itself as an inert, thing-like object, whilst the latter is 'unfinished' and semantically inexhaustible, and therefore open to a free dialogic interaction with our own consciousness. Our own word thus enters into a continuous struggle with both internally persuasive and authoritative discourses, each vying for supremacy. As we attain psycho-social maturity through reflection and social interaction, we can learn to 'experimentally objectify' the coercive discourse of the other and adopt those alien words which are most in concert with our values and experiences: 'An independent, responsible and active discourse is *the* fundamental indication of an ethical, legal and political human being' (1981: 349–50). Moreover, internally persuasive discourse (unlike authoritative discourse) can become an artistic object of representation. It can be translated into the speech of characters and can also constitute part of the unresolved dialogue between the author and hero.

This brief examination of the 'internally persuasive word' and its relation to the literary sphere constitutes a convenient point of departure into a more detailed discussion of Bakhtin's theory of the novel and its relation to social heteroglossia. Again, Bakhtin suggests there is a kind of synchronicity or 'uninterrupted mutual interaction' between discourse in life and discourse in art. It is this capacity of the novel to assimilate such a variety of genres and speech-types that makes it an important site through which wider discursive struggles are condensed and refracted: 'co-existence and becoming are here fused into an indissoluble concrete unity that is contradictory, multi-speeched and heterogeneous (1981: 365). Hence, because the novel has an enhanced capacity to represent a diversity of linguistic forms – that is, it is a meta-language of the highest order – Bakhtin feels that it merits special attention. By carving artistic images of social languages out of the raw material of heteroglossia, the novel constitutes a privileged vantage-point whence to grasp the 'great dialogue' of the age: 'It is precisely thanks to the novel that languages are able to illuminate each other mutually; literary language becomes a dialogue of languages that both know about and understand each other' (1981: 400). In this way, the novel is radically influenced by and fully partakes of the contradictory forces that exist in the verbal-ideological world. Social heteroglossia can enter the novel either through the speech of specific characters, each bringing their own ideological orientation [*ideologeme*] to the text or, more significantly, as a wider 'dialogizing background' which interacts with the form and content of the work as a whole. The latter refers to the general dialogical relation between text and context, an underlying and primordial social heteroglossia which saturates the words and thoughts of characters and author alike with a 'fundamental speech diversity'. This internal dialogism is never subject to ultimate resolution or closure; nor can it be reduced to mere conversation or extant dialogue. Hence, social heteroglossia enters the novel under the aegis of a 'unique artistic system'; that is, through a number of thematic and stylistic strategies (parody, 'character zones', indirect speech, 'hybridization', incorporated genres, etc.) which serve to

> . . . permit language to be used in ways that are indirect, conditional, distanced. They all signify a relativizing of linguistic consciousness in the perception of language borders – borders created by history and society, and even the most fundamental borders (i.e., those between languages as such) – and permit expression of a feeling for the materiality of language that defines such a relativized consciousness. [. . .] Prose consciousness feels cramped when it is confined to only *one* out of a multitude of heteroglot languages, for only one linguistic timbre is inadequate to it.
>
> (Bakhtin 1981: 323–4)

The essential point that must be grasped is that language in the novel is not unitary, but rather 'contested, contestable and contesting', riven with a multitude of voices and opposing points of view. Yet the novel is also festive and playful: it contains a utopian promise of the full emancipation of human thought and creativity. However, the carnivalization of the word effected by the novel is subject to the same kind of centralizing pressures that can be found in other ideological domains. Indeed, Bakhtin suggests that there are literary analogues to the centripetal tendencies which can be found in the verbal-ideological world of 'official language'. These are the various poetic genres, in which the internal dialogization of discourse does not enter into the 'aesthetic object' of the artistic work as it does in prose writing. Here, the autonomy of the alien word is not respected. Instead, it is torn away and discarded – it is decontextualized, stripped of its previous meanings and connotations, and subordinated to the will of direct authorial intention. As a result, the poetic genres are 'authoritarian, dogmatic and conservative', sealed off from the energizing and liberating influence of extra-literary social languages. An awareness of the historically- and culturally-situated nature of language is not encouraged in poetry by virtue of its very form, and therefore a critical distancing from one's own socio-linguistic perspective is effectively negated. Bakhtin argues that the notion of a special or sacred 'poetic language' – exemplified by the genre of the epic[6] – has been fostered by the advocates of officialdom throughout the ages: 'The language of the poetic genre is a unitary and singular Ptolemaic world outside of which nothing exists and nothing else is needed. The concept of many worlds of language, all equal in their ability to conceptualize and be expressive, is organically denied to poetic style' (1981: 285–6).

In the 'rich soil' of novelistic prose, by contrast, the dialogized ambiguity of double-voicedness takes root in a 'fundamental, socio-linguistic speech diversity and multi-languagedness'. The prose writer therefore does not attempt to expunge heteroglossia from the work or to manage and contain it, but strives to nourish verbal-ideological diversity. Discourse in the novel cannot help expressing heteroglossia, because it 'inevitably accompanies the social, contradictory historical becoming of language'. Unlike the reified, artificial language of the poetic genres, the novel is 'still warm from the struggle and hostility' of the world of social existence; it is 'born of the new world and in total affinity with it' (Bakhtin 1981: 7). The novel resists the canonization which typifies other genres, and exposes the linguistic and formal conventionality of the 'official' genres. That is, in its self-appointed role as the *enfant terrible* of the literary world, the novel assumes a parodic stance towards its literary rivals in a manner which enhances its own self-consciousness. The novel is also self-critical in that it is not adverse to the parodization of its own antecedent forms and the 'novelization' of official genres, with the result that these lifeless canonical genres become more 'free and flexible', more imbued with elements of laughter and self-parody, and more predisposed toward a semantic open-endedness and the influences of an extra-literary heteroglossia. Thus, in Clarke and Holquist's (1984a: 276) phrase, Bakhtin views the novel as an anti-genre, as a 'kind of epistemological outlaw, a Robin Hood of texts'. In this capacity, the novel contributes to a reflexive understanding of the social world and of one's location within it, and it encourages a transcendence of the perceived threat of 'otherness': 'The novel demands a broadening and deepening of the language horizon, a sharpening in our perception of socio-linguistic representations' (1981: 365–6).

Hence, it is important to realize the kind of pervasive social power Bakhtin is attributing to the epic and related genres and, conversely, to the counter-hegemonic or liberating potential of the novel form. In his opinion, literary genres are not 'just' fictional texts designed for leisure or entertainment. Rather, they have an enormous capacity to shape the contours of mass consciousness, and they can play a decisive role in the organization (and the subversion) of ideological hegemony. More specifically, Bakhtin argues that the epic and similar genres are wedded to a doom-laden eschatology, an apocalyptic vision of the future which functions to legitimate the 'dominant force and truth' in society. Consequently, the destruction of the zone of absolute distancing perpetrated by the official genres is of epochal significance. The novel therefore represents the 'vanguard' of literature and culture within human history.[7] It has a unique and special relationship with extra-literary genres (particularly the popular folk-festive genres which he claims can be traced to antiquity, including satires, mimes, etc.). And, because it is capable of anticipating the development of literature as a whole, it can draw non-novelistic genres into its 'orbit' and imbue them with its spirit. Of course, this ideological shift has a number of important artistic ramifications as well. For instance, the puncturing of 'epic distance' implies that we can now enter into the 'world of the text' and relate this fictional world to our everyday existence. Furthermore, continuous changes in the nature of heteroglossia in the social world make possible a corresponding re-accentuation of images and languages within the novel. Thus, the 'meaning' of a particular novel is never fixed or stable: 'Each age re-accentuates in its own way the works of its most immediate past' (Bakhtin 1981: 421). Finally, as Bakhtin stressed in *Problems of Dostoevsky's Poetics*, the evolution of the novel form has crucial implications for the aesthetic relationship between author and fictional hero. To conclude:

The novel is the expression of a Galilean perception of language, one that denies the absolutism of a single and unitary language – that is, that refuses to acknowledge its own language as the sole verbal and semantic centre of the ideological world. It is a perception that has been made conscious of the vast plentitude of national and, more to the point, social languages – all of which are equally capable of being 'languages of truth,' but, since such is the case, all of which are merely the languages of social groups, professions and other cross-sections of everyday life. The novel begins by presuming a verbal and semantic decentering of the ideological world, a certain linguistic homelessness of literary consciousness, which no longer possesses a sacrosanct and unitary linguistic medium for containing ideological thought.

(1981: 366–7)

BAKHTIN AND RABELAIS'S WORLD

Whilst visiting Rome in 1788, Johann Wolfgang Goethe had the opportunity to witness a New Year carnival, an event which did not leave an 'altogether agreeable impression'.[8] Despite his personal ambivalence about what he witnessed, he tells his readers that he will strive to record the festivities as accurately as possible. Goethe begins by noting that the carnival is not an occasion of state – rather, it is something that the people 'give themselves'. Beginning with a seemingly endless number of noisy and colourful processions, horse races, and impromptu concerts, the tolling of the city's church bells signals the advent of complete licence. In the carnival proper, everything (except violence) is permissible: it is, he writes, as if all existing differences between the social orders had been temporarily obliterated. Members of all social strata mix, joke and cavort in a mood of carefree abandon and 'universal good humour' and a tolerant acceptance of all acts of buffoonery and 'torrential merriment'. Young men and women, each dressed in the clothes of the opposite sex, interact in a scandalous and provocative manner. Mock officials parade through the crowd, accusing people of horrible crimes and threatening them with arrest and punishment, which only elicits howls of laughter from the populace. A panoply of elaborate costumes, satirical masks, clowns and fools, musical instruments of every description, ridiculous props (such as giant foodstuffs), and banners completes the scene. Public drunkenness and licentiousness, he mentions with some disdain, are rife. But one cannot really describe carnival, or translate them into words on the page, concludes Goethe: such a 'tumult of people, things and movements' can only be experienced firsthand.

For Bakhtin, Goethe's eyewitness account is valuable because it succinctly sums up the central features of carnival and the complex relations connecting popular culture, history, and the novel. This new direction came to fruition in a work completed in 1940 and (unsuccessfully) submitted as a doctoral dissertation but not published in the Soviet Union until 1965: *Rabelais and His World*.[9] Without wishing to lapse into hyperbole, *Rabelais and His World* constitutes Bakhtin's masterwork. It represents his most sustained attempt to think through the analytical categories and philosophical concepts developed earlier in his career and substantiate them through a wealth of historical, cultural and literary examples. In this study, Bakhtin focuses on the cultural dynamics of a particular historical moment – the collapse of medievalism and the emergence of a more secularized, humanistic society – particularly as reflected in the novels of François Rabelais, a figure who for Bakhtin epitomizes the spirit of the Renaissance. *Rabelais and His World* is not a work of literary criticism in any standard sense – for example, it contains little of the detailed textual-linguistic analysis which marked his Dostoevsky period. Nor are the startling and controversial insights this study generates only relevant for an historical understanding of a bygone era. Bakhtin uses Rabelais as a kind of sounding board through which to interrogate his real subject: the 'thousand year old development of popular culture', which he feels has energized the most significant forms of European literature and culture since pre-classical times and which continues to be a potent force even today. 'Carnival' is Bakhtin's term for a bewildering constellation of rituals, games, symbols, and various carnal excesses which together constitute an alternative 'social space' of freedom, abundance and equality.

For Bakhtin, carnival is 'one of the most complex and most interesting problems in the history of culture' (1984: 112). Far from being a mere amalgamation of 'festive events', it is a 'syncretic pageantry of a ritualistic sort' which expresses a 'general world outlook'. It is often difficult to disentangle what Bakhtin takes to be some of the more salient features of carnival, insofar as it constitutes a complexly interconnected and 'organic' whole. Nevertheless, we can single out the following: (i) 'eccentricity', an almost Sartrean refusal to accept the constraints of fixed, pre-given social roles. This not only facilitates a free and familiar contact between people, it permits 'the latent sides of human nature to reveal and express themselves'.[10] (ii) Related to this 'familiarization' or de-alienation of social life is the phenomenon of 'carnivalistic *mésalliances*' – the free and spontaneous combination of formerly self-enclosed and fixed categories. Carnival 'brings together, unifies, weds, and combines the sacred with the profane, the lofty with the low, the great with the insignificant, the wise with the stupid' (1984: 123). (iii) Yet another common trait of the carnivalesque genres is their indissoluble link to 'gay time', a heightened consciousness of the relativity of history: 'Time itself abuses and praises, beats and decorates, kills and gives birth; this time is simultaneously ironic and gay, it is the "playing boy" of Heraclitus, who wields supreme power in the universe' (Bakhtin 1968: 435). Carnivalesque images tie together a number of contradictory events and images into a more complex and ambivalent unity, an 'indissoluble grotesque whole' which underscores the inevitability of change and transformation. (iv) There is also 'profanation', the blasphemic degrading of the official world-view through the parodization of sacred texts and rituals, the inversion of received social categories, and so on. Carnival transgresses the usual norms and rules that govern everyday life; it represents 'life turned inside out'. (v) This highlights the crucial importance of carnival laughter, which will be discussed in more detail later. Deeply ambivalent ('ridicule fused with rejoicing'), like all features of the carnivalesque, it is directed towards the profanation of higher authority and is connected with the symbolism of reproductive force. In the typical carnival image we find the 'pathos of shifts and changes, of death and renewal', an 'all-annihilating and all-renewing' force worked out in special carnival time which celebrates the 'joyful relativity' of all hierarchical, authoritarian structures. As such, all genuine carnival images are profoundly dualistic, and contain within themselves 'both poles of change and crises': birth with death, youth and old age, and praise with abuse. Such symbolic strategies are designed to facilitate the 'violation of the usual and the generally accepted', which David Carroll characterizes as a '*momentary*, "aesthetic" break with the structures, laws, and dogmatically imposed "truths" which determine *the place* of "the people" under normal conditions' (1983: 80).

Perhaps one of the most essential aspects of the carnivalesque is the 'material bodily principle', which is connected to the aesthetic of 'grotesque realism'. This can be characterized as the incorporation of images depicting the material functions of the human body (eating and drinking, defecation, copulation) into cultural or artistic texts. As Clarke and Holquist put it, the grotesque 'incorporates what are [Bakhtin's] primary values: incompleteness, becoming, ambiguity, indefinability, non-canonicalism – indeed, all that jolts us out of our normal expectations and epistemological complacency' (1984a: 312). The term 'grotesque' itself usually conjures up notions of distortion or deformity, usually for the purposes of caricature or irony. For Bakhtin, however, the tendency towards extreme exaggeration in the grotesque is not simply a satirical device, which would fail to explain the ambivalence and unexpected richness and complexity of such images and their connection to seemingly disparate events and phenomena. When infused with grotesque imagery, objects transcend their own 'natural' boundaries and become fused or linked with other things. From this is derived their pregnant and two-sided nature, the quality of 'unfinished becoming' which is anathema to officialdom. Not surprisingly, Bakhtin asserts that this hyperbole and anamorphosis is positive and affirmative. The primary guiding image is one of abundance, growth and fertility, which supplants the drabness and routinization of everyday life with a celebration of gaiety and festivity and an awareness of the immortal 'collective body'. Repudiating the asceticism and other-worldly spirituality of medievalism, the grotesque stresses the sensual, bodily aspects of human existence. All that is abstract and idealized is degraded and 'lowered' by the transferral of these images and symbols to the material, profane level, which represents the 'indissoluble unity' of earth and body. Grotesque realism acts to 'degrade, bring down to earth, turn their subject into flesh' (1968: 20). Upwards and downwards acquire a cosmic, typographical quality in folk images: 'down' is earth, the body, which devours and gives birth (the belly, genital organs, buttocks, etc.), while 'up' is the sky, spirit, the head. To degrade is to swallow and consume, to materialize by bringing things into contact with the earth, to kill and give birth simultaneously.[11]

Accordingly, acts of defecation, birth, eating, and conception play a major symbolic role in folkloric texts and practices. Bakhtin refers to the images of excrement and urine in folk culture as simultaneously degrading and renewing, substances which 'familiarize' matter, the world and the universe. This also explains why abusive language figures prominently in grotesque imagery, particularly with regard to symbolic degradation and the 'bringing down to earth' of lofty sentiments and ideas. Such debasement is profoundly ambivalent: the act of being inundated by urine or excrement is complemented by a connection to the procreative genital organs, which represent the locus of birth and fertility. Excrement is linked to regeneration and renewal: it is a 'gay matter' that occupies a space between earth and body while simultaneously relating one to the other. 'To degrade an object', Bakhtin writes, 'does not imply merely hurling into the void of nonexistence, into absolute destruction, but to hurl it down to the reproductive lower stratum, the zone in which conception and a new birth take place' (1968: 21). The crux of the grotesque aesthetic therefore lies in its portrayal of transformation and temporal change, of the contradictory yet interconnected processes of death and birth, ending and becoming. The symbolism of grotesque realism thus explicitly denies the possibility of completion, of ending, of finality. Instead, it historicizes what is generally taken to be immutable and eternal. By relativizing abstract claims to eternal truth, it releases humankind from Marx's 'dull compulsion of economic necessity' and encourages a recrudescence of repressed potentialities and creative energies:

> Necessity, in every concept which prevails at any time, is always one-piece, serious, unconditional, and indisputable. But historically the idea of necessity is relative and variable. The principle of laughter and the carnival spirit on which grotesque is based destroys this limited seriousness and all pretense of an extratemporal meaning and unconditional value of necessity.
>
> (1968: 49)

Rabelais and His World is unique in a number of respects, not least because it treats the human body itself as a semiotic medium, as an 'open' signifier which is inscribed and 'made meaningful' through the operation of contesting signifying practices. Accordingly, as the Soviet academician V. V. Ivanov (1974) has astutely pointed out, one implication of Bakhtin's pan-semiotic theory is that there can be no strict demarcation between the human body and the sphere of culture. For instance, the body as depicted in grotesque realism is not an autonomous, self-sufficient object, but rather an indivisible unity, a collective or 'cosmic' representation of the people which is 'grandiose, exaggerated, immeasurable'. The grotesque body always supersedes its apparent boundaries, particularly those parts of the body which directly interact with the external world: the nose, the mouth, the anus, and the sexual organs. Such a body merges with the external world and with the other beings, objects and animals that populate it. Bakhtin claims that the system of images associated with the grotesque body takes innumerable forms in the rituals, language and artefacts of folk culture: in the colloquial oaths and curses of 'marketplace speech' and the symbolic oppositions of praise/abuse and crowning/uncrowning, in folklore and myth (such as tales of giants and griffins, harpies and demons), in diableries and mystery plays, the bodily relics of saints, the circuses and comic performers of the marketplace, and even in the popular cosmology of the Middle Ages, wherein the earth is conceptualized as a form of grotesque body. It is highly significant, for example, that carnival was often personified in medieval festivals in the form of a fat, boisterous man, garlanded with sausages and wild fowl, who devoured impossible quantities of food and wine.[12]

At least two other central elements of the 'carnival sense of the world' require further elucidation: folk laughter and marketplace speech. To begin with the former, Bakhtin stresses that laughter in this 'festive-comic' sense cannot be understood as a form of trivial ribaldry or light-hearted jesting. Rather, folk laughter expresses a distinctive ideological viewpoint which is diametrically opposed to the 'monolithically serious' world of officialdom: it is 'universal', it heals and regenerates, and it is linked to essential philosophical questions. Whilst in ancient society, the comic and the official co-existed in an environment of mutual tolerance, when the feudal system became consolidated these comic forms came under attack as a form of heretical paganism. Folk culture was driven underground, where it came to be marked by an 'exceptional radicalism, freedom, and ruthlessness'.[13] None the less, it continued to have a significant impact upon the life of the market-place and the public square, and achieved special prominence during the many carnivals, feasts, and festivities which punctuated the social calendar of the Middle Ages. Laughter had an 'in-dissoluble and essential relation' to the realm of freedom: during such popular feasts and festivals 'life came out of its usual, legal-ized and consecrated furrows and entered the sphere of útopian freedom. The very brevity of this freedom increased its fantastic nature and utopian radicalism, born in the festive atmosphere of images' (Bakhtin 1968: 89). For Bakhtin, the world of folk laughter was literally 'boundless', involving humorous rites and cults, fools and giants, clowns and jugglers, agricultural festivals and various genres of verbal and literary parody, many of which were trans-formed into the sophisticated satires and rhetorics of high scholas-tic culture.[14]

Closely connected to folk laughter was the phenomenon of marketplace speech or 'billingsgate language'. Bakhtin maintains that folk culture was characterized by a system of speech genres which were very different from those of the church and the ruling classes. During carnival and major feast days, the 'elemental force' of this popular orality penetrated every sector of feudal society. It could be found in the hawker's cry, which parodied and travestied ecclesiastical forms of address through comic pledges and oaths; in billingsgate abuses, which oscillated between extreme praise and exaggerated derision in rapid succession; and in many other popular oral forms. Such colloquial oaths and profanities were for Bakhtin a codified form of verbal protest, a repudiation of officialdom through the violation of sanctioned verbal forms of expression. In thematic terms, these oaths often involved the symbolic rending of the body, particularly the Lord's body, and references to the bodily relics of saints and holy persons, and to diseases (especially venereal afflictions) and organs of the lower material stratum were commonplace. Such popular speech genres were therefore unofficial in both tone (laughter) and content (the lower material stratum), and they had a tremendous capacity for parody, debasing, and travesty. They waged a relentless battle against the 'stabilizing tendencies of the official monotone':

Abuses, curses, profanities, and improprieties are the unofficial elements of speech. They were and are still conceived as a breach of the established norms of verbal address; they refuse to conform to conventions, to etiquette, civility, respectability. These elements of freedom, if present in sufficient numbers and with a precise intention, exercise a strong influence on the entire contents of speech, transferring it to another sphere beyond the limits of conventional language. Such speech forms, liberated from norms, hierarchies, and prohibitions of established idiom, become themselves a peculiar argot and create a special collectivity, a group of people initiated in familiar intercourse, who are frank and free in expressing themselves verbally. The marketplace crowd was such a collectivity, especially the festive, carnivalesque crowd at the fair.

(1968: 187–8)

Together, these carnivalesque rituals, symbols and practices aimed at the destruction of the 'medieval hierarchic picture of the world'. The ideology of medievalism portrayed society as a stable and unchanging order sanctioned by God and governed by a complex system of immutable social distinctions. Everything in the social and natural worlds occupied a fixed position in an all-embracing cosmology. This culture was intolerant of change and dissent: it was ascetic, intimidatory and oppressive. Moreover, the world was viewed as alienating and terrible, poised on the brink of cosmic destruction and eternal damnation – an attitude exemplified by the concept of *Götterdämmerung* (the twilight of the world), wherein escape could only occur through mystical transcendence.[15] Bakhtin asserts that this fear of the elemental and destructive forces of nature and the supernatural 'penetrated to the very basis of language, imagery, and thought' in medieval society. Such a 'cosmic terror' was exploited by the theocracy in order to subdue the populace and dampen a critical consciousness, to legitimate the existing social hierarchy and the system of taboos and prohibitions which reinforced it. Yet, claims Bakhtin, the forces of officialdom could not entirely destroy the centrifugal impulses of folk culture. Folk-festive culture had evolved specifically to combat this dread, and to bolster a 'true human fearlessness' via a celebration of the immortal, collective human body. Through folk laughter and symbolic degradation and renewal, the abstract terror of the unknown was 'made flesh', transformed into a 'grotesque monster' that was to be laughed at and overcome. Utilizing a constantly recurring metaphor, Bakhtin argues that popular festivals and rituals carved out a 'second life' for the people within the womb of the old society, a world where the normal rules of social conduct were (at least temporarily) suspended and life was 'shaped according to a certain pattern of play'. Hence, the deconstructive thrust of folk culture was not simply negative or dismissive – rather, it held out the promise of a renewal of humankind on a more egalitarian and radically democratic basis, through the creation of a utopian sphere of abundance and freedom. Carnival effectively broke down the formalities of hierarchy and the inherited differences between different social classes, ages and castes, replacing established traditions and canons with a 'free and familiar' social interaction based on the principles of mutual cooperation, solidarity and equality.

Carnival, in short, is 'the only feast people offer to themselves', and there is no barrier between actors or performers and those who witness it. As a 'symbol of communal performance', it can only occur in the streets and the public square, wherein social relations are 'free and unrestricted, full of ambivalent laughter, blasphemy, the profanation of everything sacred, full of debasing and obscenities, familiar contact with everyone and everything' (Bakhtin 1984: 129–30). Such spectacles are not passively consumed; rather, they are lived, experienced, and transformed into life itself.[16] In carnival, the individual is fused into a 'mass body' which is continually and collectively renewed: bodies are 'exchanged' both symbolically (through the changing of masks and costumes, the inversion of social ranks, etc.) and materially (the sexual act, consumption of food and drink, various bodily functions). Carnival generates an intense feeling of unity and solidarity, wherein the collectivity becomes acutely aware of its 'uninterrupted continuity within time, of its relative historic immortality [...] of the unfinished metamorphosis of death and renewal. [...] Carnival with all its images, indecencies, and curses affirms the people's immortal, indestructible character' (Bakhtin 1968: 255–6). Official ceremonies were mocked, lampooned, and subjected to comic ridicule and profanation. Indeed, Bakhtin suggests that almost every religious ritual and event had its carnivalesque counterpart.[17]

Bakhtin felt there existed an especially important relation between carnival and time. According to the logic of the carnivalesque, all that was new (springtime vegetation, the phases of sun and moon, agricultural cycles, etc.) was portrayed as regenerative and positive. Folk-festive culture promised a better and happier future, one characterized by material abundance, equality and freedom – a distinctly utopian vision epitomized by the myth of the 'Land of Cockaigne'. This mythical land, immortalized by Breughel's famous painting (and once referred to by Walter Benjamin as a 'primal wish symbol'[18]), depicted a place where work was unknown, where rivers ran with milk and roast pigs ran about with forks stuck in them, literally begging to be eaten. Because medievalism privileged stasis and valorized a mythical past, its institutions and proscriptions were subjected to mockery and derision. In an attempt to generate an entirely new chronotope which was inimical to official conceptions of time and space, the traditions of folk-festive culture 'opposed the protective, timeless stability, the unchanging established order and ideology, and stressed the element of change and renewal' (1968: 81). This relation between folk humour and time had special affinities with the system of images associated with the material bodily stratum. Established hierarchies were reversed through the appointment of mock pontiffs and nobles, feudal social relations were travestied and 'made strange', and normal topographical logic was turned inside out or upside down (clothes worn inside out, fools presiding over the royal court instead of kings). Bakhtin contends these carnivalesque images were 'Janus-faced', ambivalent dualities which were 'deeply immersed in the triumphant theme of bodily regeneration and renewal. It was "man's second nature" that was laughing, the lower bodily stratum which could not express itself in official cult and ideology' (1968: 75). Those 'sombre hypocrites and slanderers' which are the target of such abuse represent those remnants of the dying order that stubbornly resist the inevitable and regenerative process of change. Such 'agelasts' refuse to glimpse at the 'mirror of time' and accept their irrelevance. Instead, they remain pompous, grim and finally pathetic: they are, as Marx himself said, 'mere comedians of the world order whose real heroes have already died'. To summarize:

> The serious aspects of class culture are official and authoritarian; they are combined with violence, prohibitions, limitations and always contain an element of fear and intimidation. These elements prevailed in the Middle Ages. Laughter, on the contrary, overcomes fear, for it knows no inhibitions, no limitations. Its idiom is never used by violence and authority. It was the victory of laughter over fear that most impressed Medieval man. It was not only a victory over the awe

inspired by the forces of nature, and most of all over the oppression and guilt related to all that was consecrated and forbidden ('mana' and 'taboo'). It was the defeat of divine and human power, of authoritarian commandments and prohibitions, of death and punishment after death, hell and all that is more terrifying than the earth itself. [. . .] Medieval laughter, when it triumphed over the fear inspired by the mystery of the world and by power, boldly unveiled the truth about both. It resisted praise, flattery, hypocrisy. This laughing truth, expressed in curses and abusive words, degraded power.

(1968: 90–3)

Bakhtin claims that this 'cultural schizophrenia' was reflected in all aspects of medieval life. Yet because the unofficial was marginalized and continually subject to officially-sponsored repression, it could not fully reveal or realize its utopian promise. Bakhtin contends that in the late Middle Ages and early Renaissance, this division between the official and the unofficial was gradually erased, mainly because of the decline of the absolute hegemony of the Catholic Church and of Latin as the authoritative language of church and state.[19] That is, Bakhtin holds that the late 15th and early 16th century was marked by a dramatic linguistic and ideological transformation. As the medieval order began to collapse, there occurred an 'intense interorientation, interaction, and mutual clarification' between various national languages and dialects, which fostered a deep awareness of the relativity of languages and their social and historical constitution. Whereas medieval Latin 'levelled all things' and projected an 'eternal, unchanging world', the interaction of classical Latin, medieval Latin, and marketplace speech promoted a deep awareness of 'historic space': 'The modern time became conscious of itself. It too could reflect its face in the "mirror of comedy" (1968: 468).

This development signalled the end of the cultural-linguistic dualism that had pervaded feudal life and the beginning of what Carlo Ginzburg has succinctly characterized as a 'circular, reciprocal relationship between the cultures of [the] subordinate and ruling classes' (1980: xvii). The irruption of popular linguistic-literary genres into 'high' culture introduced a system of moral and political values which decisively challenged the 'century-old linguistic dogmatism' of medievalism. But why did humanistically-inclined writers and thinkers turn to popular culture to further their cause? As a partial answer, Bakhtin suggests that unlike the traditions of classicism or monastic scholasticism, folk culture was the only significant cultural form which had not already been extensively 'colonized' by officialdom to prop up the feudal order. Insofar as this popular culture had always used festive comic images to express the people's 'criticism, their deep distrust of official truth, and their highest hopes and aspirations' (1968: 268–9), it was perhaps inevitable that this 'thousand-year-old language of fearlessness' would constitute a vital source of inspiration for great writers of the Renaissance era:

> Medieval laughter became at the Renaissance stage of its development the expression of a new free and critical *historical* consciousness. It could acquire this character only because the buds and shoots of new potentialities had been prepared in the Medieval period. [. . .] Thus had the new awareness been initiated and had found its most radical expression in laughter. [. . .] These images, saturated with time and the utopian future, reflecting the people's hopes and strivings, now became the expression of the general gay funeral of a dying era, of the old power and the old truth.
>
> (1968: 73, 99)

As elements of the 'lower' or popular genres began to appear in even the 'highest' literary spheres, argues Bakhtin, folk culture began to play a vital role in the work of Cervantes, Boccaccio, Grimmelschausen, and many others. For Bakhtin, however, it was the French novelist and humanist François Rabelais (1495–1553) and his masterpiece *Gargantua and Pantagruel* that represented the apex of this development. Rabelais's name has become synonymous with excess, with fantastic exaggeration, and with crude, bawdy humour. Yet he was also a learned monk with a doctorate in medicine who caricatured and parodied the stubborn anachronisms of medieval society, and who earned the respect of progressive scholars and the masses alike. Of all the major Renaissance figures, Rabelais is for Bakhtin the most radically democratic, in that his work is intimately linked to an inexhaustible well-spring of both literary and extra-literary popular sources. These had a profound influence on Rabelais's written work, in terms of the system of images he devised and his artistic and political viewpoint on the world. Indeed, *Gargantua and Pantagruel* is an 'encyclopedia of folk culture', wherein the heterogeneous elements of this culture 'emerge with extra-ordinary clarity'. Whilst Rabelais's contemporaries were intimately familiar with this folk culture, with the passage of time this essential connection has been forgotten or only dimly realized. Hence, Bakhtin argues that any attempt to understand the work of Rabelais must come to terms with the traditions, practices and imagery contained within folk-festive culture.

As discussed above, Rabelais's time was marked by the rapid disintegration of the feudal order. This vertically-organized and extratemporal world was being replaced by a new chronotope and value-system which privileged horizonal movement on the plane of real space and historical time. The emerging scope and importance of Renaissance science and humanistic culture were reflected in Rabelais's encyclopedic knowledge of philosophy, science, and medicine. Rabelais was a champion of humanism in all these spheres, and an implacable foe of the Gothic age. Yet while he recognized and supported far-sighted initiatives by particular members of the nobility, his true sympathies (or so Bakhtin claims) lay with the common people and their 'gay, free, absolutely sober word'. However serious Rabelais may have been in his quest to combat 'Gothic darkness', his use of popular-festive imagery always left him a 'gay loophole' which lent 'an aspect of ridicule to the relative progressiveness and relative truth accessible to the present or to the immediate future' (Bakhtin 1968: 454). Rabelais's critique was undeniably utopian, but it never lost sight of the ordinary people's inspirations and ideals and the realities of everyday life. In this pitched battle between two diametrically-opposed world-views, Rabelais's use of the 'carnivalesque spirit' constituted a powerful weapon against the dogmas of medievalism:

> Rabelais's basic goal was to destroy the official picture of events. He strove to take a new look at them, to interpret the tragedy or comedy they represented from the point of view of the laughing chorus of the marketplace. He summoned all the resources of popular sober imagery in order to break up official lies and the narrow seriousness dictated by the ruling classes. [. . .] While destroying the official conception of his time and of contemporary events, Rabelais did not seek, of course, to submit them to a scholarly analysis. He did not speak in the conceptual language but in the tongue of popular comic images. While breaking up false seriousness, false historic

pathos, he prepared the soil for a new seriousness and for a new historic pathos.

(Bakhtin 1968: 439)

Yet, as Bakhtin is at pains to point out, this critical strategy was not merely destructive: it also incorporated the positive pole of popular-festive imagery. This form of 'positive negation' lacks the formal, abstract quality of idealist dialectics. It is concrete and tangible, drawing on experiential, sensuous knowledge, and it is grounded in historical rather than mythological time.[20] Positive negation does not entail nihilism, but the inversion of what is denied, the 'carnivalesque upside down'. Thus, Rabelais's 'new, free, and sober seriousness' reaffirmed the emphasis on change and renewal that for Bakhtin was an essential element of folk-festive culture. Rabelais's game was a 'gay and free play', but one that sought to dispel 'a gloomy and false seriousness enveloping the world and its phenomena, to lend it a different look, to render it more material, closer to man and his body, more understandable, and lighter in the bodily sense' (Bakhtin 1968: 380). Folk laughter gave Rabelais the ideological weaponry to rescue human consciousness from the stultifying conceptual framework in which it had been imprisoned since the Dark Ages, to help prevent what Benjamin once called the 'paralysis of the imagination'. Even Rabelais's language, suggests Bakhtin, drew on popular oral sources and reinvested tired clichés and platitudes with new meanings by placing them in unexpected and often disturbing contexts. Under Rabelais's tutelage, words became involved in a 'carnival game of negation' which was enlisted to 'serve utopian tendencies'.

To conclude this discussion, it is worth noting that toward the end of *Rabelais and His World*, Bakhtin also traces the decline of the carnivalesque after the 16th century. He suggests that the carnival promise of the early Renaissance eventually degenerated into the absolute monarchy of the *ancien régime*, wherein rationalism and neo-classicism held sway. While certainly very different from feudalism, they shared an authoritarian and overly serious tone. The grotesque survived, but in a truncated form, and in such secondary and marginal genres as children's fables or the burlesque. As such, folk laughter began to deteriorate into trivia and erotic frivolity, and the utopian spirit and historical consciousness of popular culture began to fade. From the 17th century onwards, laughter ceased to be seen in a universal and philosophical form but was subject to a process of increasing rationalization.[21] Carnival was severed from its folk basis and from its communal performance in the carnival square, and its characteristic symbols, gestures and speech-genres became merely decorative or narrowly farcical. Yet despite the emasculation of carnival since the Renaissance, Bakhtin argues that popular-festive culture remains 'indestructible', and it continues to celebrate invention, human creativity, and the liberation of human consciousness from the dictates of official truth in a manner which encourages a 'completely new order of things'. Bakhtin is quite explicit about the utopian possibilities of carnival: in a strikingly Benjaminesque refrain, he writes that carnival

> . . . discloses the potentiality of an entirely different world, of another order, another way of life. It leads men out of the confines of the apparent (false) unity, of the indisputable and stable. Born of folk humor, it always represents in one form or another, through these or other means, the return of Saturn's golden age to earth – the living possibility of its return. [The] utopian element, the 'golden age', was disclosed in the pre-Romantic period not for the sake of abstract thought or of inner experience; it is lived by the whole man, in thought and body. This bodily participation in the potentiality of another world has an immense importance for the grotesque.
>
> (1968: 48)

Chapter 3

The Bakhtin Circle and the theory of ideology

We have thought too much in terms of a will which submits and not enough in terms of an imagination which opens up.

Paul Ricoeur

INTRODUCTION

Raymond Williams has cogently argued that, given the tortuous history of the concept 'ideology' and the manifest complexity of the social processes that the term is meant to elucidate, one must conclude that 'there can be no question of establishing, except in polemics, a single "correct" Marxist definition of ideology' (1977: 56). Whilst the discussion that follows may contain a number of polemical elements, it does not seek to defend a unitary version of ideology against all possible 'deviations'. Rather, I seek to explore the contours of a particular interpretation – a semiotic or, better, a 'dialogic' theory of ideology – and to establish it as both a viable and a significant contribution to current debates vis-à-vis the nature of the text, ideology and power. Accordingly, this chapter will investigate the writings of Mikhail Bakhtin and the Bakhtin Circle with respect to the classical Marxian theory of ideology and the general project of *Ideologiekritik*.[1]

THE CLASSICAL PROBLEMATIC AND ITS CRITIQUE

Any attempt to assess Voloshinov, Medvedev and Bakhtin's voluminous (if ambiguous) pronouncements on ideology in the light of the classical Marxist account is complicated by the fact that neither Marx nor the Bakhtin Circle managed to delineate in any systematic fashion what the term 'ideology' was meant to designate or how it was supposed to operate in the social world.[2] The similarities and differences are (relatively) straightforward if we choose to restrict ourselves to Marx and Engels's characterization in *The German Ideology*, which identifies ideology as a form of cognitive distortion, a false or illusory representation of the real. For Marx, this category of distortion primarily resulted from the (structurally-induced) tendency in capitalist society for social agents to attribute the determination of history to ideas and the philosophical or religious systems that corresponded to these ideas. Thus, Marx posited a close, even necessary connection between ideology and philosophical idealism. But ideology in this sense is not simply a kind of logical error resulting from a sense of misplaced priorities about cause and effect, a failure to grasp the precise nature of the relationship between the material and the immaterial. For such idealist propositions were expressed within grand philosophical systems which operated as *post-facto* rationalizations of the age, as powerful (if mythical) legitimations which buttressed the prevailing class system. Marx's reaction to this duplicity was to connect particular ideological forms – for instance, Malthus's justification of *laissez-faire* capitalism by conjuring up the spectre of rampant over-population – to dominant material interests and the exploitation of the labouring masses. In exposing the underlying cynicism which tainted any ideological system, Marx not only called into question the pretence of these systems to objectivity and universality; he also criticized the social role performed by the various intellectual strata who functioned as apologists for the capitalist order. As György Márkus has written:

> In these polemical contexts, Marx employs a genetic method of critique of ideologies, the essence of which consists in the reduction of systems of thought to the conscious or unconscious social interests which they express. [. . .] By transforming definite social interests into the requirements of human reason as such, these systems of thought contribute to the stabilization of the given relations of social domination: the fixation of belief becomes a mode of legitimation.
>
> (1983: 86)

This conception of ideological analysis as a kind of 'unmasking' or 'exposure' (what Paul Ricoeur has referred to as the 'hermeneutics of suspicion') has obvious foundations in the

Enlightenment critique of the metaphysical illusions perpetrated by church and state in pre-modern Europe.[3] What is less often acknowledged, as Márkus is at pains to emphasize, is that Marx was also highly critical of the Enlightenment tradition inasmuch as he felt that it was inappropriate to reject ideological bias from the standpoint of abstract 'reason' or a Feuerbachian 'human essence'. As an example, one could mention Marx's castigation of the Young Hegelians for failing to realize that any critique worth the appellation 'radical' (in the original sense of grasping things by the root) could not remain on the level of rarefied philosophical debate, but had to be conjoined with both a concrete understanding of the material conditions which in fact engendered 'consciousness and its products' in the first place and forms of appropriate collective action designed to alter these conditions. In other words, Marx simultaneously affirmed the Enlightenment stress on dispelling the fog of illusion encouraged by idealist thought whilst making this ideological critique contingent upon the practical transcendence of the material conditions of class domination.

If we momentarily 'bracket off' the countervailing tendencies elsewhere in the writings of Marx and Engels vis-à-vis alternative formulations of the concept of ideology (and these are significant), it is clear that the account sketched out above has little in common with the concept of 'ideology' utilized by the Bakhtin Circle. At the risk of drastic simplification, we could characterize Marx's construal of ideology as a structural or historical condition wherein the actual circumstances of men and women engaged in productive social intercourse spontaneously appear as if in a *camera obscura* – that is, inverted, and hence distorting or illusory. This general principle – based on the Hegelian distinction between 'real relations' and 'phenomenal forms' – is arguably recapitulated in the chapter on 'fetishism' in *Capital*, which for some constitutes the *locus classicus* for a Marxist theory of ideology.[4] This cognitive dislocation plays a functional role in the legitimation of class domination, since it shifts attention away from the real terrain of social life toward the fanciful abstractions of idealist thought (which represent a more systematic 'working up' of the spontaneous illusions projected by fetishized social relations).[5] As such, the capacity for individuals to perceive the truth about their real conditions of existence is blocked or occluded. The 'cure' for such a pathology is similar to

Marx's treatment of Hegel's philosophy of spirit: since it is now standing on its head, it must be returned to its feet. That is, the supposed autonomy of ideas and ideological systems must be decisively rejected, and replaced with empirical historiographic research into the production and reproduction of social life through human praxis within particular historical circumstances – what Marx referred to as the 'study of actuality'. The material conception of history, wrote Marx and Engels in *The German Ideology*, 'remains constantly on the real *ground* of history; it does not explain practice from the idea but explains the formation of ideas from material practice' (cited in McLellan 1971: 129).

Given the virtually unchallenged domination of idealist philosophies amongst the European intelligentsia in the mid-19th century, Marx's stance was wholly appropriate and indeed necessary at the time, and as a research programme it arguably remains the guiding tenet of much valuable contemporary Marxist writing in history and politics. Nevertheless, the reflection metaphor itself and the abstract base–superstructure schema that is its necessary corollary have come under increasing attack and today claim very few adherents – and, in any event, as an explanatory framework it was never compatible with the realignment toward cultural and aesthetic themes in the work of Lukács, Gramsci, Adorno, and others. The philosophical complexities of these debates are difficult indeed; here, I restrict myself to a brief discussion of the trenchant critique of orthodox Marxism developed by Raymond Williams in his *Marxism and Literature* (1977), which remains a central text in the recent revitalization of what is today known as 'cultural studies'. The crux of Williams's position is that the reflectionist model of ideology and consciousness developed by Marx in *The German Ideology* represents a form of mechanical materialism, insofar as it posits an elemental ontological division between 'mind' and 'matter'. This metaphysical dualism, which is uncomfortably close to the 17th- and 18th-century materialism of Hobbes, La Mettrie and d'Holbach, was contradicted elsewhere in Marx's writings (most notably in the *Theses on Feuerbach* and parts of *Capital*, such as the famous passage about the role of imagination in human labour). In general, however, Williams claims that the overall thrust of Marx's theory with respect to superstructural phenomena was overly simplistic and reductionistic. Such a position was reinforced in Engels's later writings (such as the *Anti-Dühring* and *Dialectics of*

Nature), which sought to codify Marx's thought into a general philosophical world-view with pronounced scientistic and naturalistic overtones. It also received subsequent elaboration in Lenin's *Philosophical Notebooks* and *Materialism and Empirio-Criticism*, which guaranteed its incorporation into the Soviet version of dialectical materialism or *Diamat*. The net result was two-fold: first, Marxism was increasingly transformed into a self-validating body of 'scientific' knowledge; and secondly, that so-called superstructural phenomena were undervalued or even ignored as being irrelevant to an objective understanding of the inexorable laws of history culminating in the victory of the proletariat and, eventually, communism.

It is worth stressing at this juncture that Williams is not suggesting that the appearance of what Albrecht Wellmer (1971) has termed a 'latent positivism' in *The German Ideology* and elsewhere is an essential feature of the Marxian world-view, but is largely explicable by reference to contingent factors. For instance, *The German Ideology* was a polemical, almost journalistic piece, intended to distance Marx and Engels's emerging method of socio-historical investigation from that of their idealist contemporaries and predecessors in no uncertain terms, which (as Engels himself was later to acknowledge) led them to overemphasize the causal efficacy of the economic and to neglect the impact of 'various ideological spheres' upon history. Moreover, given that it was an early and therefore formative text, Marx had not been able to describe consciousness, ideology, and so on in terms of a theoretical vocabulary other than that derived from an older (and cruder) philosophical materialism.[6] It could also be mentioned that Marx's later work was almost exclusively concerned with the mapping out of the complex inner workings of the capitalist mode of production and its likely future tendencies – a strategy that was hardly conducive to the articulation of a sophisticated theory of cultural or ideological production. Despite these provisos, however, Williams is adamant that there remains a strong undercurrent in *The German Ideology* and elsewhere which encourages the reification of 'consciousness and its products' as something secondary and derivative. The simple reversal of the Hegelian dictum that 'consciousness determines life' may have made for a nifty slogan, but it could scarcely have solved the immensely complex philosophical questions that it raised at a stroke. In order to counteract this positivist drift in the Marxist tradition, Williams asserts that it is necessary to stress that ideology, consciousness, and so on are indissoluble parts of what he refers to as the 'material social process'. In other words, ideology must be considered as an integral element of the general social process by which men and women produce (and reproduce) their social life through the medium of conscious human praxis. Such a position affirms the active role of consciousness in the appropriation and construction of external reality through what the 'humanistic' Marx called 'practical, human-sensuous activity', a form of praxis which simultaneously changes both subject and object. More specifically, ideology enters into this process insofar as it is centrally implicated in the symbolic constitution of human thought and action. Hence, consciousness, ideas, conceptions – as embodied in human cultural and ideological relations understood as material social practices – are necessary aspects of the socio-historical development of human society as a whole. As Williams writes:

> . . . 'consciousness and its products' are always, though in variable forms, parts of the material social process itself: whether as what Marx called the necessary element of 'imagination' in the labour process; or as the necessary conditions of associated labour, in language and in practical ideas of relationships; or, which is so often and significantly forgotten, in the real processes – all of which are physical and material, most of them manifestly so – which are masked and idealized as 'consciousness and its products', but which, when seen without illusions, are themselves necessary social material activities. [. . .] To exclude these material social processes from *the* material social process is the same error as to reduce all material social processes to mere technical means for some other abstracted 'life'.
>
> (1977: 62)

Williams's position here is indicative of a broader conceptual shift in the theoretical discourse of Western Marxism away from a strict emphasis on political economy towards questions of culture, aesthetics, and language. The reasons for this sea-change are complex and manifold yet none the less historically discernible, as the work of Perry Anderson (amongst others) has demonstrated.[7] Focusing on the sphere of cultural/ideological critique, it is possible to distinguish some of the major implications of this shift vis-à-vis the classical theory of ideology:

(i) A rejection of abstract determining base/determined superstructure held to be indicative of economistic versions of Marxism, in order better to account for the specificity and (at least partial) independence of cultural/ideological phenomena from the dictates of the infrastructure.[8]

(ii) A renunciation of a series of metaphysical dualities – subject/object, symbolic/real, science/ideology, and so on – which are now believed to be unhelpful and indeed debilitating. This is accompanied by a concomitant stress on ideology as a material force with a practical efficacy to shape and influence social relations, and on the inescapably symbolic dimension of all human activity, cognition and perception. Paul Ricoeur characterizes this position as follows: 'Action is immediately ruled by cultural patterns which provide templates or blueprints for the organization of social and psychological processes, perhaps just as genetic codes [. . .] provide such templates for the organization of biological processes' (1986: 12).

(iii) A new stress on the way ideology relates to the constitution of subjectivity and social identity, which was widely considered to be a major deficiency of the orthodox theory of ideology. Ideology is now understood as 'that aspect of the human condition under which human beings live their life as conscious actors in a world that makes sense to them in various ways. [To] conceive of a text as ideology is to focus on the way it operates in the formation and transformation of human subjectivity' (Therborn 1980: 2).

(iv) A rejection of ideology as a form of 'false consciousness', a system of purely illusory or false representations. Such an emphasis on ideology as an epistemological category, as a type of 'cognitive error', is believed to be inherently psychologistic, and it shifts attention away from ideology as an irreducibly social process. Any ideology, as Gramsci stressed, is a mixture of true and false beliefs; what is of interest is not ideology's alleged epistemological status (which unproblematically assumes the possibility of a non-ideological form of knowledge), but rather the role it plays in the hegemonic organization of the social world. As Alex Callinicos puts it: 'Explaining why an individual holds ideological beliefs is a matter of analyzing *social* processes, not of diagnosing individual error or individual pathology. Ideology is social consciousness' (1987: 139).[9]

(v) Ideology is no longer viewed as a simple imposition of particular values and beliefs 'downward', in order to incorporate the masses into the prevailing normative structure – what has come to be known as the 'dominant ideology thesis' after Abercrombie *et al.*'s (1980) seminal research. Rather, ideology is increasingly seen as the site or 'terrain' of symbolic-cultural struggle, as the primary medium through which social conflicts are registered. Nor does ideology necessarily benefit the dominant class; ideological constructs (e.g. aspects of liberalism or nationalism) have no 'necessary class belongingness' and may be turned against the status quo given particular socio-historical circumstances and a favourable constellation of class forces. As a corollary to this, ideology is not conceived of as a highly systematic or axiomatic 'belief-system', but as a disparate, contradictory and stratified complex of practices and symbols, which are pitched at different levels of coherence and social effectivity and which are subject to continual contestation and negotiation.[10]

(vi) If the category of ideology can no longer be conveniently contrasted with non-ideological or scientific knowledge, then the Mannheimian objection of how the observer is able magically to escape the pernicious effects of ideology loses its force. Instead, the emphasis is now upon what could be termed a 'second-order' or meta-critique of ideology, which involves not only an exposure of the unacknowledged ideological presuppositions of others but also a reflexive understanding of our own prejudicial and limited beliefs and values. As Culler (1975: 254) says: 'Rather than try and get outside ideology we must remain resolutely within it, for both the conventions to be analysed and the notions of understanding lie within. If circle there be, it is the circle of culture itself'.[11]

Of course, we could extend this list at some length, but at least we are now in a better position to identify and understand some of the theoretical contributions of Bakhtin and company vis-à-vis the theory of ideology. To facilitate this exploration, however, perhaps it would be useful to isolate a series of central propositions from the preceding discussion: (a) ideology is not a passive (and distorting) reflection of the 'real'; it is a formidable material force in its own right. (b) Ideology is significant as a material power not least because it is (at least partially) constitutive of the symbolic dimension of social relations, which is an inescapable element of any human activity and indeed 'subjectivity' itself. (c) Ideology plays this role because it is centrally implicated in the process of signification, in semiosis. (d) If ideology is primarily a semiotic phenomenon, a product of textuality (understood broadly), then to grasp the essential nature of ideology is to understand its imbrication with language or, more precisely, with its concrete instantiation in forms of oral or written discourse. Alex Callinicos puts the matter as follows:

> . . . ideologies are practices which function symbolically, usually through the generation of utterances, subject to definite norms and constraints. Very often these norms and constraints derive from the prevailing structure of class power. [Once] we accept that thought and language are interdependent, then the study of ideologies must involve an analysis of the system of signs through which they are expressed. [Such an] analysis presupposes some general account of how signification itself occurs, what analytical philosophers call a theory of meaning.
>
> (1983: 135–6)

THE VITEBSK OPTION

It is my contention in this study that the points raised above characterize precisely the theoretical space staked out by Voloshinov, Medvedev and Bakhtin in their 1920s texts on language, psychology, and literary theory. What is remarkable is not so much the manifest similarities between such recent innovations in the theory of ideology and the central writings of the Bakhtin Circle, but rather that the Circle formulated its general position on these and related matters some forty years before they emerged in the West under the impetus of the structuralist problematic.[12] The preoccupation of the Bakhtin Circle with the signifying function of ideology, and with the nature of linguistic phenomena in general, grew out of the intense debates amongst the Russian intelligentsia on the role of language in cultural and political life which occurred immediately before and after the October Revolution in 1917. Of course, a concern with the formal properties of language (and related types of semiosis) – that is, with the significance and plasticity of linguistic form as an expressive medium rather than with its referential function – has long been recognized as a central characteristic of the modernist *avant-garde*. Nevertheless, such a stress on the centrality of language in social and cultural life had a particularly strong resonance in the Russian (and later Soviet) milieu, as

Phillips (1986) has recently demonstrated. Russian Symbolism, for instance, rejected the Romanticist emphasis on individual creativity and stressed the objective, *sui generis* capacity of poetic language to generate meaning. This shift had a decisive influence on many of the Russian *avant-gardes*, including Acmeism, Futurism and early Constructivism, although the more politicized of these movements rejected the mystical *cum* religious elements of the Symbolist aesthetic. It also received theoretical elaboration in the Formalist writing of Shklovsky and Eichenbaum, which had allied itself to the Futurist poetry of Mayakovsky and Khlebnikov. As mentioned in chapter one, Medvedev himself chronicled some of these developments in his 1928 book *The Formal Method*, but it will none the less prove worthwhile briefly to examine the main elements of this conjuncture and to situate the writings of the Bakhtin Circle on ideology in relation to it.

The crux of this debate centred around the nature of the text. For the Formalists, textuality was a matter of the structural organization of particular stylistic devices, and ideological or social factors only existed in a text in order to sustain or 'motivate' form in a purely technical sense. Not surprisingly, this anti-mimetic refusal of content was anathema to the Marxists, who condemned Formalism as a politically-suspect intellectual dandyism (if only because the Formalists refused to view literary criticism in terms of political partisanship). The standard Marxist objection was two-fold: firstly, the notion of 'device' excluded extra-literary factors from the art-work (class structures, social institutions, ideologies, and so on); secondly, the Formalist doctrine of the 'autonomy of the word' (ultimately traceable to Futurist 'trans-sense' poetry) contradicted the materialist insistence on the causal primacy of social being and could therefore be dismissed as a philosophical idealism. Yet, as Peter Zima (1981b: 104) has pointed out, neither antagonist adequately understood textuality – and hence the sphere of ideology – as a specifically social phenomenon. The Formalists, of course, were guilty of denying any social or ideological significance behind the signifier (a stance reminiscent of Derrida's poststructuralism). Yet the Marxists were not exactly above reproach insofar as they conceived of the text in Hegelian terms, as a transparent medium for the transmission of an underlying, univocal meaning. This interpretation not only ignored the specificity of the text (which the Formalists could not be legitimately accused of); it could not account for the social constitution of textuality or signification. It was the Bakhtin Circle's declared intention to overcome this duality of 'form' and 'content' by stressing that the formal organization of discourse was itself essentially a social construction, and that the signifying medium influenced the production and reception of ideological messages as much as overt thematic content. This explains why we find Medvedev in *The Formal Method* castigating Formalism (despite its productivist rhetoric) for failing to account for the social and historical character of ideological phenomena – thereby assuming an 'eternal contemporaneity' – whilst simultaneously accusing the Marxists of reducing the 'concrete unity, variety, and importance of the ideological' to the immediate or empirically-given conditions of the socio-economic environment (1985: 15). In his 1924 work *Literature and Revolution*, Trotsky condemned the Formalists for maintaining a barely-disguised religiosity, because of their tacit acceptance of St John's credo that 'In the beginning was the Word'. As good Marxists and materialists, he suggested, we should unhesitatingly adopt Goethe's version: 'In the beginning was the Deed'. One might construe Medvedev/Bakhtin's possible response to this dilemma as a characteristically synthetic one: 'In the Beginning was the Deed of the Word'.[13]

THE CONCEPT OF 'IDEOLOGY' IN MEDVEDEV AND VOLOSHINOV

With this brief foray into the fertile (and certainly prescient) debates on language and signification that dominated Soviet intellectual circles in the first decade following the Russian Revolution, I turn to an exploration of the concept of 'ideology' as it was utilized by Voloshinov and Medvedev in their central writings of the 1920s.[14] Firstly, it is worth stressing that the Bakhtin Circle did not use the term ideology in an overtly pejorative sense, as an epistemological category denoting falsity or cognitive error. Voloshinov and Medvedev studiously avoided any such psychologistic overtones: ideology for them was an irreducibly social phenomenon, although it none the less played a crucial role in the constitution of subjectivity and consciousness. Whilst they continued to use much of the vocabulary of orthodox Marxism, including the metaphor of 'reflection' (though whether out of political expediency or because of the lack of an appropriate terminology is difficult to ascertain), it must be emphasized that their approach is at some distance from the theory of reflection worked out by Marx and Engels in *The German Ideology*. Ideology for the members of the Bakhtin Circle could indeed 'reflect' external reality, but it did not necessarily do so: it could also refract it in the sense of producing an altered or mediated representation of 'the real'. Moreover, Voloshinov and Medvedev suggested that there were different domains or regions of ideological production (science, literature, everyday speech genres) and that each reflected or refracted reality (and other such ideological spheres) in particular ways depending on the semiotic material involved and their general location in the social totality. According to the Bakhtinian perspective, therefore, ideological signs were not simply empty forms ('dead husks') which obligingly conveyed a unitary representation of a pre-existent reality, whether in a distorting or a faithful manner. Rather, the Circle sought to problematize the very notion of referentiality itself by conceiving of the sign as the terrain of contestation and struggle, resulting in a deep-rooted semantic ambivalence [*ambivalentnost'*] which could be ultimately traced to systemic social contradictions and antagonistic material or class interests. In other words, the operation of ideology in actual social contexts shattered the sign's pretence to a self-evident, unitary meaning; any such unity was a contingent and transient one, dependent upon the prevailing state of interacting and opposed class forces and the wider historical context.[15]

It could be said, therefore, that the Bakhtin Circle utilized what Larrain (1982 and 1983) has termed a 'positive' account of ideology, in that it refers to the 'totality of forms of social consciousness' (albeit inscribed in some semiotic medium, particularly language) in a manner which implied no necessary epistemological significance.[16] This stance can be contrasted with Marx's original 'negative' categorization of ideology as a form of distortion or mystifying illusion which he sought to supersede through the development of a precise – and by definition non-ideological – knowledge of socio-historical processes. Precisely why Voloshinov *et al.* did not employ a similarly negative interpretation is an important question, one for which there is no simple answer.[17] Yet if this conception seems to be at odds with that developed by Marx and Engels, neither can it be confused with other, vaguer notions of ideology (for example, established political doctrines such as communism, liberalism or, more generally, a system of thought or world-view). Rather, the term 'ideology' [*ideologija*] is rather loosely employed by Voloshinov and company to designate any signifying practice or meaning-endowing activity.[18] Such a practice or (following Kenneth Burke) symbolic action is an integral element of any human endeavour in the sciences or humanities, in the arts, or in everyday life.

IDEOLOGY AND THE CONSTITUTION OF THE SUBJECT

Ideology for the Bakhtin Circle is therefore not significant for what it 'represents' or reflects, but for how it functions as an effective force in the social world with the capacity to shape socio-historical processes in important ways. Insofar as ideology operates as a material segment of 'reality', there can be no absolute ontological gap between base and superstructure, and any distinction between them remains a purely analytical one. Ideology in their view had no *sui generis* existence: it had to be embodied in some signifying practice or semiotic material (words, gestures, etc.) if these ideas or beliefs were to have any social efficacy whatever. For Bakhtin (not unlike the later Foucault), even the body itself was the site of ideological inscription, and *Rabelais and His World* can in fact be read as an extended treatise on the semiotics of the body – a 'somatic semiotics' (or bawdy language) which reverses the traditional hermeneutic emphasis on the interpretation of texts of a written or oral nature. This leads us to the issue of the relation between ideological signs and the constitution of consciousness or subjectivity. A frequently-voiced objection to classical Marxism (one that is not without some justification) is that it does not have a viable theory of the subject and that, as a result, its account of ideology is seriously deficient.[19] This perceived shortcoming prompted Althusser and his followers to appropriate the Freudian conception of the unconsciousness (or, more precisely, Lacan's structuralist reworking of psychoanalysis) in order to explain the construction of subjectivity through a process of 'hailing' or ideological interpellation.[20] What is noteworthy is that the Bakhtin Circle developed an alternative model of subjectivity which is in many respects antithetical to the Lacanian approach favoured by the Althusserians (and later the Feminist-Lacanians), yet which does not rely on Cartesian or rationalist assumptions vis-à-vis the subject.[21] Here, I confine my comments to a few basic points. To begin with, it is important to stress that the Circle does break with the conception of the subject as an integral totality which had dominated Western philosophy since the 17th century up until the triple-onslaught of Heidegger's demolition of Husserlian phenomenology, Saussure's dismissal of atomistic theories of language, and Freud's decentring of the rational *cogito* – though how decisively is still an open question, given that Bakhtin *et al.* continued to utilize much of the theoretical baggage of the German philosophical tradition.

At the risk of oversimplification, we can characterize the orthodox humanist view as the position that, as Kate Soper has put it, takes 'history to be a product of human thought and action, and thus claims that the categories of "consciousness", "agency", "choice", "responsibility", "moral value", etc. are indispensable to its understanding' (1986: 12). Thus, the individual is seen to be the primary agent through which social relations, history, and even meaning are constituted – and, moreover, the intentions, purposes and capacities of this agent are held to be transparent to itself (because they can be recuperated to consciousness through an act of contemplation or reflection). In other words, experience is 'given' directly to the subject, who can ascertain the nature of this experience because language is a transparent medium for describing and understanding the external world. It is not necessary at this point to rehearse the (by now well known) structuralist and poststructuralist objections to the postulation of the subject as a central analytical or philosophical category, a stance which has received ever more subtle and complex justifications since Lévi-Strauss argued that 'I believe the ultimate goal of the human sciences to be not to constitute, but to dissolve man'.[22] Suffice it to say that for the members of the Bakhtin Circle, consciousness (subjectivity, the 'psyche') is not a self-sufficient, pre-constituted entity, but is formed through the dialogic struggle between contending 'voices' or discourses. In fact, Bakhtin's project can be interpreted as a sustained attack on the epistemological and moral precepts of bourgeois individualism, which he roundly condemns for its decadence and solipsism (he refers to it as a 'culture of essential and inescapable solitude'), and he continually stresses that the entire gamut of social and cultural phenomena are profoundly intersubjective or dialogic in nature. This continuous dialogue with the 'other', with oneself (inner speech), and with the external world – which involves the active construction of relations between diverse phenomena (a process generally denoted as 'architectonics') – is constitutive of human subjectivity as such and represents an inescapable component of any possible creative thought or deed. As Bakhtin's biographers, Clarke and Holquist, have written:

> . . . the self, conceived by Bakhtin, is not a presence wherein is lodged the ultimate guarantor of unified meaning. The Bakhtinian self is never whole, since it can only exist dialogically. It is not a substance or essence in its own right but exists in a tensile relationship with all that is other and, most importantly, with other selves.
>
> (1984a: 65)

Tracing the phenomenological dynamics of this self/other relation in the sphere of literary discourse was one of Bakhtin's central concerns in his first major work, *Problems of Dostoevsky's Poetics*, wherein he argued that Dostoevsky's distinctiveness lay in his uncommon refusal to merge a plurality of interacting consciousnesses into a higher unity. It was also a theme which he returned to in his later philosophical and methodological fragments, which have been collected in the volume *Speech Genres and Other Late Essays*. Voloshinov and Medvedev, on the other hand, gave the theme of the dialogic constitution of subjectivity a more overtly semiotic emphasis. They argued that the subject could have no 'pure' or direct experience of reality, insofar as any experiential relation to the external world was always mediated by the various modes of representations, speech genres and sign-systems through which we become conscious beings in the first place: 'It is true that no distinct or clear consciousness of the world is possible outside the word' (Medvedev 1985: 133).[23] These representational systems, discourses, narratives and so on always pre-exist us; accordingly, any possible form of cognition or activity is therefore a semiotic process, one that is socially and historically determined: 'the content of the "individual" psyche is by its very nature just as social as is ideology, and the very degree of consciousness of one's individuality and its inner rights and privileges is ideological, historical, and wholly conditioned by sociological factors' (Voloshinov 1973: 34). Of course, these pre-existing narratives, representations and ideologies are not static but historically dynamic or 'generative' – and, moreover, any social formation contains a plurality of (albeit hierarchically ordered) speech genres and signifying systems which are in a state of constant interaction and competition for supremacy.[24]

Inasmuch as they conceive of the subjective states of individual actors as only explicable by reference to the 'objective social logic' which defines their experiences and modes of inner and outer speech, the Bakhtin Circle departs substantially from the traditional Marxist position that ideology is a primarily psychological phenomenon, as beliefs or values which are located inside people's heads. Evoking and then cleverly inverting Marx's famous dictum that it was social being that determined consciousness and not the reverse, Voloshinov asserts that 'It is not experience that organizes expression, but the other way around – *expression organizes experience.* Expression is what first gives experience its form and specificity of direction' (1973: 85). This directly contradicts Marx and Engels's statement in *The German Ideology* that a genuinely materialist approach to the study of history and society cannot involve 'men as narrated, thought of, imagined, conceived' – if, that is, one wants to examine 'men in the flesh' rather than the echoes and phantoms that accompany the real life-process. The Bakhtinian position, by contrast, would be that it is specifically through such discursive and ideological phenomena that men and women 'in the flesh' can (and indeed must) be conceptualized. To believe otherwise is, as Williams (1977: 60) astutely puts it, an 'objectivist fantasy'.

The upshot of this preceding discussion is that, for the Bakhtin Circle, the subject is an internally complex and socially-constituted entity which bears little similarity to the fully autonomous, rational and curiously incorporeal being postulated by Descartes or Kant: 'A single consciousness is *contradicto in adjecto.* Consciousness is in essence multiple. *Pluralia tantum*' (Bakhtin 1984: 228). This is not, however, to suggest that Bakhtin and company fully subscribe to all aspects of the poststructuralist decentring of the subject. For, as Voloshinov in particular stresses, the subject does have a (relative) biographical and biological unity – a unity-in-difference, it could be said – which is derived from both the nature of the biological organism and the relevant socio-historical conditions. Like Marx, in other words, the members of the Circle do seem to subscribe to something called 'human nature' – not a fixed or static 'essence', but an historically-mutable and socially-embedded complex of qualities, capacities and powers. This is obviously at odds with the poststructuralist view of Foucault or Deleuze and Guattari that the subject is an infinitely malleable and contingent constellation of forces, a temporary nodal point in the endless flux of discourses and signifying processes. Thus, as Allon White (1987–8) has recently argued, Bakhtin *et al.* remain 'humanists' in the sense that they retain an interest in freedom, the fulfilment of human potentiality, and the cessation of oppression, but also in the more technical sense that they continue to ascribe importance to the category of 'agency' – that is, a belief in the creative or active role of collective human praxis vis-à-vis the making of history. The conception of 'history' maintained by the individual members of the Bakhtin Circle is not, however, teleologically inscribed or inexorable: it is 'open', a horizon of unfulfilled possibilities which is 'capable of death and renewal, transcending itself, that is, exceeding its own boundaries' (Bakhtin 1986: 135).

It must be stressed that Bakhtin *et al.* retain such a conviction in the efficacy of human agency despite (or rather because of) their acknowledgement of the structural constraints effected by existing social institutions, ideological formations, speech genres, and so on. In fact, they consider the reflexive understanding of the contours and parameters of such inevitable structural limitations to be one of the crucial pre-conditions for the exercise of freedom and moral responsibility. Echoing Engels's famous statement in his *Anti-Dühring*, Bakhtin writes that the 'better a person understands the degree to which he is externally determined [. . .] the closer to home he comes to understanding and exercising his real freedom' (1986: 139).[25] Language, insofar as it is organized into particular conventional or generic forms, cannot be generated *ex nihilo* by individual speakers – this is precisely the crux of Voloshinov's critique of 'individualistic subjectivism' in *Marxism and the Philosophy of Language*, and it is a point often overlooked by those commentators on Bakhtin who perhaps tend to overemphasize his libertarian ethos, his 'ethics of dialogism'. Nevertheless, this does not preclude the possibility that the subject can relate to these structures and conventions in an active, reflexive and dialectically-constitutive fashion.[26] To conclude, Bakhtin strongly believed that the relation between subjects, being dialogic, could never be fully predictable or quantifiable: 'the subject can never become a concept (he himself speaks and responds)' (1986: 169).[27] This position helps to explain his undying admiration for Dostoevsky, whom Bakhtin felt always maintained a strong belief in the unfinalizability [*nezavershennyj*] and heterogeneity of humanity. The thoughts and actions of Dostoevsky's characters, he believed, could never be fully 'explained' by reference to external factors. There was always a 'last word' capable of being spoken, a 'surplus of vision' or a 'sideways glance' that enabled an existentialist-like or anarchistic refusal on the part of the subject to acquiesce totally in received social roles, to proffered definitions and predictions: 'man is free, and can therefore violate any regulating norms that can be thrust upon him' (Bakhtin 1984: 59).[28]

MARX AND BAKHTIN

With these issues in mind, I wish to turn to some of the other points of difference and convergence between the Bakhtin Circle and classical Marxism with respect to the theory of ideology. To begin with, it can be plausibly argued that there is a latent functionalism in Marx's original account of ideology, one that was certainly encouraged by many of his later followers. For the Marx and Engels of *The German Ideology*, ideology was interpreted as a symptom of idealism which involved a misapprehension of the actual historical constitution of the social world. Such a failure to grasp the true nature of the real served to mask existing social contradictions, particularly the class antagonism between labour and capital, what Engels referred to as the 'supreme contradiction'. This resulted in the substitution of bogus 'universal' interests for sectional or class-specific ones which 'solved' real social contradictions in thought and encouraged the integration of the natural enemies of capitalism into the reigning social order. Following Marx, 'ideology' generally came to mean the world-view of the ruling class, propagated by the apologists of capital through various channels (e.g. the mass media, the family, church, etc.) and which kindled a 'false consciousness' amongst the exploited masses by occluding genuine class interests.[29] Yet this particular interpretation, which has come to be known as the 'dominant ideology thesis' (hereafter DIT) runs up against the powerful criticisms levelled at it by N. Abercrombie *et al.* (1980) and supported by the writings of Swingewood (1977), Williams (1977) and Callinicos (1987), amongst others.[30] Briefly, Abercrombie *et al.*'s objections to the DIT can be summarized as follows: (i) the postulation of the existence of a coherent dominant ideology and its effects upon the subordinate social classes is an *a priori* theoretical presumption that is never empirically demonstrated; (ii) it typically fails to characterize its (assumed or real) effects upon the dominant as opposed to the subordinate classes; (iii) it rarely identifies or analyses the institutions and apparatuses through which the beliefs and values of the dominant class are transmitted and distributed in any depth; and (iv) it assumes that the presence of the DIT can be explained by the role it plays in maintaining the integrity and coherence of the capitalist system as a whole. In blunter terms, the DIT is idealist, ignoring more important processes of political and economic domination; it maintains a functionalist view of society as a homogeneous and smoothly-functioning system; empirically vacuous, in that substantial evidence exists which indicates that the subordinate classes do not readily adhere to the beliefs and values of the dominant groups; and finally, it is elitist: whilst the 'masses' are more or less unproblematically lulled into accepting the bourgeois myths foisted upon them, Marxist intellectuals are magically exempt from this process.

Does the work of the Bakhtin Circle fall prey to these criticisms? I think not, for a number of reasons. First, 'ideology' for the Bakhtin Circle does not represent a seamless whole or a highly systematic world-view, but rather a disparate and heteroglot complex of meanings, discourses and symbols which are culled from a wide range of textual sources, historical periods and social experiences. Ideologies, according to this conception, have no necessary coherence or systematicity but are stratified in relation to the prevailing system of social organization and range from the most inchoate and fragmentary (inner speech) to the great scientific or religious ideologies of the age. Second, they do not suggest that a 'dominant ideology' is imposed by the ruling class on a pliant mass. Rather, they stress that ideology represents the terrain of semiotic contestation and struggle. As Susan Stewart has cogently written, ideology is viewed by the Circle 'as an arena of conflict: one's speech both reveals *and produces* one's position in class society, in such a way, moreover, as to set into dialogue the relations between classes' (1986: 52). This brings us to the problem of the standpoint whence the critique of ideology might be conducted. The traditional Marxist position on this question – or at least the stance taken by what Ernst Bloch once termed the 'cold stream' of Marxist thought – is that insofar as the critique of ideology is grounded in a 'language of real life' or represents a form of scientific knowledge, it can escape the charge that it is itself ideological. Yet this runs up against a number of important objections, especially what could be termed 'Mannheim's paradox'. In his 1936 *Ideology and Utopia*, Karl Mannheim argued that if ideology represented a particular, limited perspective, which could be traced to the existential situation of a given social group, then any theory about ideology also represented a specific viewpoint which was not itself exempt from the social determination of ideas. By thereby denying the possibility of an 'absolute onlooker', Mannheim was able to extend the analysis of ideology to include the analyst. On the basis of this insight, Mannheim advocated moving away from a self-legitimating *parti pris* Marxism in order to reconstitute the theory of ideology as a self-reflexive sociology of knowledge based on the *Verstehen* perspective of Dilthey and Windelband.

Yet the writings of the Bakhtin Circle on ideology manage to avoid the main thrust of such Mannheimian objections. The primary reason for this is that they do not subscribe to the *post-hoc* justification of this ideological critique on epistemological or scientistic grounds. If ideology is not necessarily a misrepresentation of the real, then the admission that one's own thoughts, beliefs, utterances, etc. are (at least partially) ideologically-determined is not a particularly damaging one. The clearest indication of this self-reflexive approach to ideological analysis is to be found in an oft-overlooked passage in *Freudianism: A Marxist Critique*, wherein Voloshinov asserts that Marxism (even considered as a purely 'technical-scientific' method) cannot be completely 'neutral' or dispassionate. Any theory, he suggests, necessarily incorporates an implicit ideological stance which goes beyond its own stated goals and methods, regardless of the theory's internal consistency or its object of knowledge. As Alan Swingewood (1977) has convincingly argued, knowledge-systems or ideologies are always 'practical-social' no less than 'theoretical' – a particular theory or world-view claims adherents not simply because of its alleged 'objectivity' or truth-status (as Lenin once claimed of Marxism), but because it 'makes sense' of people's everyday social existence, and thereby provides the conceptual framework for the enactment of particular forms of social practice and cognition.[31] Voloshinov's position here would seem to invalidate any attempt to legitimate Marxism's scientific credentials on the basis of a dogmatic science/ideology distinction (which was, incidentally, common practice in 1920s Soviet Marxism), and it also casts into doubt some of his more positivistic pronouncements on the issue of method which have been duly criticized elsewhere. To quote the passage in question:

> . . . if a thought is powerful, convincing, significant, then obviously it has succeeded in contacting *essential* aspects of the life of the social group in question, succeeded in making a connection between itself and the basic position of that group in the *class struggle*, despite the fact that the creator of that thought might himself be wholly unaware of having done so. [. . .] Human thought never reflects merely the object under scrutiny. It also reflects, along with that object, the being of the scrutinizing subject, his concrete social existence. Thought is a two-sided mirror, and both sides can and should be clear and unobscured.
>
> (Voloshinov 1976: 25–6)

At first glance, therefore, it may appear that the Bakhtin Circle's linguistically-based or semiotic account of ideological processes bears little affinity to the Marxian construal of ideology as a weapon in the class struggle. Upon closer inspection, however, it is apparent that the Circle does indeed retain a critical interest in delineating the discursive mechanisms of class domination. This is because they continually emphasize that the ideological sign – indeed, the general process of semiosis itself – is not autonomous but ultimately connected to wider social contradictions and the dynamics of revolutionary historical change. The convergence between Bakhtin *et al.* and Marx on this issue can be underscored if we choose to prioritize not *The German Ideology* (circa 1845–6) but Marx's famous 'Preface' to *A Contribution to the Critique of Political Economy*, written during 1859. Here, Marx is less concerned with the epistemological status of ideology as a distorted reflection of the 'real' than with conceptualizing it as the terrain of more inclusive social, political and cultural struggles, as the dimension through which individuals become conscious social actors and act to realize their material interests. This version places a much-needed stress on the social constitution of ideology, its hegemonic function, and the role it plays vis-à-vis the formation of subjectivity – factors which are all lacking in 'false consciousness' or *camera obscura* accounts of ideological phenomenon. There are other manifest similarities and congruities which could also be mentioned at this stage. For example, both Marx and the Bakhtin Circle are exceedingly hostile towards idealism, the notion that history and society are the product of the 'idea' or transcendent spirit. For Marx, this illusion could only be rectified through a Feuerbachian inversion of the terms spirit/real life (i.e., substituting a practical materialism for an historical idealism). Likewise, Bakhtin and company argued that ideological signs were not a product of an isolated, disembodied consciousness, but rather determined through dialogic interaction in the context of practical social intercourse: 'The idea is a *live event*, played out in the point of dialogic meeting between two or several consciousnesses' (Bakhtin 1984: 88).

Moreover, both parties were cognizant of the political and theoretical dangers which could potentially result from the abstraction of thought from concrete material reality. In certain of Marx's writings, this is the *locus classicus* of ideology; for the Bakhtin Circle, it was symptomatic of the reification and monolithic centralization of social life which they sought to combat at all costs.[32] In *Problems of Dostoevsky's Poetics*, for example, Bakhtin draws a strong connection between what he terms 'ideological monologism' and idealist philosophy. Idealism for Bakhtin is guilty of transforming 'consciousness' into a single, transcendent and metaphysical unity: 'absolute spirit' or 'consciousness in general'. Accordingly, actual empirical consciousnesses are considered superfluous and irrelevant – and, as a result, idealism refuses to acknowledge Bakhtin's cherished principle of diversity, his emphatic insistence on the irreducible integrity of each individual consciousness: 'In the ideal a single consciousness and a single mouth are sufficient for maximally full cognition; there is no need for a multitude of consciousnesses, and no basis for it' (1984: 81). Under the aegis of a philosophical idealism, then, an interaction of consciousnesses and, by implication, a genuine dialogue is not possible. Finally, Bakhtin's emphasis on struggle, on the Heraclitean clash of opposites that he clearly feels is necessary if linguistic-cultural creativity and dynamism is to flourish (he speaks, for instance, of a 'primal artistic struggle' between the 'gnostic ethical inclination of life' and a 'semiotic life-force') is arguably not too far removed from Marx's injunction that history is constituted through class struggle – although Bakhtin never implies that these dialectical skirmishes will ever be reconciled into a higher unity, which helps to explain his pronounced hostility toward the arid abstractions of formal dialectical thought.

THE CONCEPT OF SPEECH GENRES

Given the manifestly political stance taken by the members of the Bakhtin Circle, how do they conceptualize the interconnection of ideological and linguistic processes with forms of power, class-based or otherwise? There are at least two facets of the Circle's metalinguistics that are of interest in this regard: firstly, what could be termed the generic structuration of speech performances; secondly, and related to this, the intrinsically 'value-laden' character of any sign. As I discussed above, it is important to reiterate that, while any utterance is inherently dialogic in nature (in that it is responsively oriented toward past, present and potential future utterances and therefore only 'one link in a continuous series of speech performances'), this does not mean that dialogic interaction is totally free or unconstrained by social and institutional factors. Rather, any actual discourse is organized into particular structured forms, what Voloshinov *et al.* generally refer to as 'speech genres'.

One of Bakhtin's later essays, translated as 'The Problem of Speech Genres' (1986), contains what is perhaps the Circle's most concise and developed statement on this topic. In this text, Bakhtin suggests that speech genres are relatively stable types of utterance (with respect to content, linguistic style, and compositional structure), which in turn correspond to particular kinds of social activity. There are the simple (or 'primary') genres of everyday life — of the street, conversations about the weather, market transactions, and so forth — which are familiar, informal and relatively flexible. There are also more complex, secondary genres which incorporate or 'ingest' the former — the entire gamut of judicial, scientific, or philosophical discourses. These tend to represent the genres of officialdom, and are therefore much more rigid and hierarchical. Together, such genres mediate between sociopolitical and economic life on the one hand and language on the other; they represent, as Bakhtin puts it, the 'drive belts between the history of society [and] the history of language' (1986: 65). Not unlike Foucault's 'orders of discourse' (1977a), genres regulate what can and cannot be said in given situations, by facilitating certain forms of communication within proscribed limits and suppressing others. A tacit understanding of these generic forms is, of course, not innate but learned; it is acquired like any other cultural knowledge through socialization into a particular socio-cultural environment. As reflexive social actors we eventually master (with greater or lesser degrees of success) a repertoire of practical skills pertaining to the production and consumption of a vast array of signs and messages. It would indeed be difficult to imagine any form of effective communication which did not depend upon the mutual comprehension of a specific set of linguistic and cultural codes. Such a communicative competence (described variously by Bakhtin as 'apperceptive background', 'dialogizing background' or 'social purview') enables us to tailor a given 'speech plan' in response to the relevant generic constraints and varidirectional social contexts. As Voloshinov puts it in his brief but important essay 'Discourse in Life and Discourse in Art':

> ... the behavioral utterance always joins the participants in the situation together as *co-participants* who know, understand, and evaluate the situation in like manner. *The utterance, consequently, depends on their real, material appurtenance to one and the same segment of being and gives this material commonness ideological expression and further ideological development.*
>
> (1976: 100)

Most of the points raised in the preceding discussion have now attained widespread acceptance and are relatively uncontroversial. Indeed, as a general theoretical and methodological position, it constitutes the starting-point of any viable post-Saussurean semiology (see Eco's work on the 'role of the reader') or socio-linguistics (the writings of Halliday *et al.*). It also has obvious affinities with the various 'sociology of everyday life' approaches, including the ethnomethodology of Goffman (1959) or the more phenomenological method of Berger and Luckmann (1966). However, Bakhtin gives it a much more radical inflection than most of these contemporary interpretive sociologists would be comfortable with. For one thing, Bakhtin suggests that we are typically unaware that we possess such a tacit or practical knowledge of the social-generic structures which shape our thoughts and utterances. Accordingly, we tend to believe that our (spoken or written) utterances are completely spontaneous and unconstrained, and that we are the undisputed masters of the words and phrases we utilize. More importantly, Bakhtin asserts that we fail to recognize that such speech genres are hierarchically stratified in tandem with the sociopolitical organization of society as a whole, that our utterances unwittingly reflect and reproduce the existing framework of asymmetrical power-relations.[33] It is even suggested that these generic systems represent an underlying 'cultural grammar' or preferred code which, as Medvedev puts it, unconsciously 'defines the deep structural aspects' of the utterance. Of course, the effects of this 'form-shaping ideology' are not necessarily pernicious. For example, Bakhtin continually stresses that without the various carnivalesque genres operating as a kind of background 'cultural memory', the great novels of Rabelais and Dostoevsky could never have been bequeathed to humanity. Nevertheless, it is apparent that the opaque workings of such generic forms are fraught with undesirable political ramifications, and Bakhtin himself clearly prioritizes the 'free and familiar' forms of dialogic interaction to be found within the informal speech genres.

Take, for example, the notion of 'community' vis-à-vis the constitution of language-systems. In the section entitled 'Two Trends of Thought' in *Marxism and the Philosophy of Language*, Voloshinov makes a point of acknowledging Saussure's recognition of the importance of the linguistic community with respect to the development of *langue*, as against the extreme asocial perspective maintained by the 'individualistic subjectivists' (e.g. Dilthey, Wundt, Vossler). Yet 'society' for Saussure was an abstract, stable system of norms, whereas for Voloshinov it represented a dynamic totality containing a complex of interacting and conflictual forces. In other words, whilst the Bakhtin Circle was certainly aware of the role played by the speech community in the structuration of a given cultural-linguistic field – 'I give myself verbal shape from another's point of view, from the point of view of the community to which I belong. A word is a bridge thrown between myself and another' (Voloshinov 1973: 86) – they unequivocally rejected the notion that such communities were undifferentiated, organic wholes. Rather – at least in the context of industrial-bureaucratic societies – such communities were characterized by class antagonisms and sectional interests, and were only artificially unified through a hegemonic combination of force and ideologically-wrought 'consent'. As the social world is hierarchically stratified, so too is the linguistic-ideological domain, which means the latter continually devolves into opposed, heteroglot discursive forms. This position helps to explain why Bakhtin *et al.* place so much stress on the vital part played by the 'concrete addressee' in the communicative act. This addressee must have a particular class affiliation and social identity, one that the addresser may not necessarily share. It is the specific function of the various speech genres to proscribe the relevant lexical and syntactic choices that can be made during the speech-act in a manner which coincides with the interlocutor's social position(s). In Bakhtin's view, popular linguistic forms (dialects, argot, patois, etc.) were marginalized, and speakers from subordinate social groups were encouraged (through various symbolic and material pressures) to defer to the authoritative or 'official' language in situations of social inequality – in other words, to conform to the dictates of what Bourdieu (1977c) has referred to as the 'linguistic market'.[34] This structural isomorphism between the form of language-use and extant power-relations – which is primarily effected through the canonization of the speech practices of elites and the concomitant devaluation of the 'low' or vernacular languages[35] – is succinctly characterized by Bakhtin in his seminal essay 'Discourse in the Novel' as follows:

> Unitary language constitutes the theoretical expression of the historical processes of linguistic unification and centralization, an expression of the centripetal forces of language. A unitary language is not something given [*dan*] but is always in essence posited [*zadan*] – and at every moment of its linguistic life it is opposed to the realities of this heteroglossia. [It is] a force for overcoming this heteroglossia, imposing specific limits to it, guaranteeing a certain maximum of mutual understanding and crystalizing into a real, although still relative unity – the unity of the reigning conversational (everyday) and literary language, 'correct language'.
>
> (1981: 270)

Thus far I have examined how genres can structure the grammatical properties of an utterance. But genres are not relevant simply with respect to the formal organization of speech-acts. They are equally oriented 'in' social life, in that they are inescapably intertwined with the entire range of affective, moral, and emotive values and beliefs which accompany all forms of social interaction. More specifically, they encourage the communication of a particular set of pre-established 'themes' through the regulation or selection of pertinent topics in discourse, by specifying a given range of appropriate questions and answers, by organizing the perception of time and space, and so on. To clarify this point, perhaps some background discussion would prove useful. For the members of the Bakhtin Circle, language conceived of as a social practice (or, better, a symbolic action) only existed by virtue of its material instantiation in oral or written discourse, as articulated by particular social agents acting within a given social formation. In order to be socially efficacious (to elicit a response, to motivate, etc.), that is, the abstract system of *langue* had to be 'concretized' – transformed from a purely mechanical signal-system with a potential for meaning into a 'changeable and adaptable sign'. To imbue the sign with meaning meant that it had to be invested with the existing complex of living social values and ideologies which already permeated the life-world, which were themselves ultimately traceable to the various 'behavioral genres' bound up with everyday social practice. The theoretical alternative – to ascribe an 'essential' meaning to phonetic/grammatical forms – not only implied the hypo-statization of discourse into a transcendental structure, but also reinforced the notion of language as a 'fixed monologic utterance' and thereby facilitated the ideological-linguistic centralization of society. The Bakhtin Circle was, of course, concerned to subvert these forces of stability and closure by emphasizing the desirability of multiplicity and openness, a stance which was reinforced by their critique of any theory which functioned to reify or fetishize linguistic form at the expense of its ideological meaning or performative force. An important aspect of this critical stance was the emphatic insistence that the sign was not 'neutral', but always inscribed with a range of ethical, cognitive, aesthetic, and affective values: 'Every utterance makes a claim to justice, beauty, and truthfulness (a model utterance) and so forth' (Bakhtin 1986: 123). As such, it represented a distinct perspective, a unique 'semantic whole' incorporating a 'particular referentio-semantic and evaluative horizon': 'all languages of heteroglossia [. . .] are specific points of view on the world, forms for conceptualizing the world in words, specific world views, each characterized by its own objects, meanings and values' (Bakhtin 1981: 292).

BAKHTIN'S ANTI-ESSENTIALISM

Bakhtin and company therefore decisively rejected what could be termed an 'essentialist' theory of language – i.e., that meaning or value is an inherent property of a word or sentence (grammatically defined) or else an expression of the subjective intentions of the individual language-user. Yet they viewed with equal animosity Saussure's anti-subjectivist (and anti-realist) solution to this problem: that language was best understood as *langue*, as a system of pure differences which lacked any 'positive' content whatsoever. The alternative approach of the Bakhtin Circle to the problem of semantics is not immediately obvious – different texts stress certain elements of the communicative act as being the most important in this regard. Nevertheless, perhaps the most complete response to this issue can be found in a brief fragment written by Bakhtin entitled 'The Problem of the Text' (1986). Here, three key factors are identified vis-à-vis the generation of meaning: (i) the 'various forms of relations to reality' – by which he seems to imply the referential status of the word, its context; (ii) the dialogic relation of the word to other 'alien utterances' – that is, the semantic and stylistic interaction between the various meanings and significances which circulate endlessly throughout the social universe; and (iii) the enunciative agent – the (relative) biological and biographical unity generally denoted as the 'subject', which is (in the final analysis) constituted through a particular set of dialogical relations to the other, to language, and to the world. Thus, Bakhtin neither reduces the word to its referential or denotative function (a naive realism), to the intertextual dimension of the utterance (a poststructuralist textualism), or to the consciousness of the individual (a form of subjectivism or idealism). Each such 'moment' retains its own specificity and integrity, and thereby constitutes a vital element of the dialogic process as a whole.

I have dealt with (iii) – the Bakhtinian account of the subject – at length earlier. To reiterate briefly, Bakhtin *et al.* clearly reject the notion of the 'self-present subject' – i.e., that reality is directly available to the sensory apparatus of the subject (without the *a priori* mediation of symbolic structures) – a version of naive empiricism – and that this subject is an autonomous, rational entity and the epicentre of meaning because it is directly constitutive of language – a legacy of 17th- and 18th-century philosophical rationalism. By contrast, the Circle takes the position that the conscious subject is itself dialogically constructed, and can therefore only exist through its materialization in social or intersubjective signs: 'Individual consciousness is not the architect of the ideological superstructure, but only a tenant lodging in the social edifice of ideological signs' (Voloshinov 1973: 13). I shall examine (i) and (ii) in more detail. Following Alex Callinicos (1985), I refer to (i) as the 'thesis of contextualism' – i.e., that our talk has an extra-discursive referent, and that communication as such is unintelligible without grasping the character of this non-linguistic referent or context. In line with this, Bakhtin and company acknowledge that all texts, all forms of semiotic communication incorporate a mutually-understood stratum of linguistic signs. Such a formal sign-system stands 'behind' the text; it is the structural framework on which communication itself depends. Yet this is only a partial concession to Saussure's concept of *langue*, for the members of the Bakhtin Circle also argue that at the heart of any textual material is an elemental contradiction, a tension between two 'poles' – between, that is, the formal sign-system (which is repeatable and reproducible) and the actual implementation or enactment of a particular utterance in a concrete social space and historical time (which is singular and unrepeatable). This latter pole (which is a property of discourse and not 'language') only emerges in response to the relevant context. It is an index of the sensitivity any addressee must display in the act of enunciation with respect to both the immediate social situation (whether one is making a speech, requesting information about train timetables, or involved in a domestic dispute – i.e., what the speech performance is about and to whom it is being addressed) and wider socio-historical circumstances (the more inclusive economic, political and cultural environment). For an utterance to have 'significance' or socio-ideological force – that is, if it is to be invested with such emotive or evaluative indices as 'intention', 'purpose' or 'value' – it must be related to the demands and requirements posed by the nature of the situation and thereby constitute the basis for actual choices and decisions to be made in the realm of everyday social existence: 'Only that which has acquired social value can enter the world of ideology, take shape, and establish itself there' (Voloshinov 1973: 22). Accordingly, any utterance must enter the social purview or value-horizon [*krugozor*] of a given social group or class, which is itself determined by 'aggregate sociohistorical conditions'. Again quoting from Bakhtin's 'Discourse in the Novel':

> When we seek to understand a word, what matters is not the direct meaning the word gives to objects and emotions – this is the false front of the word; what matters is rather the actual and always self-interested *use* to which this meaning is put and the way it is expressed by the speaker, a use determined by the speaker's position (profession, social class, etc.) and by the concrete situation. *Who* speaks and under what conditions he speaks: this is what determines the word's actual meaning. All direct meanings and direct expressions are false, and this is especially true of emotional meanings and expressions.
>
> (1981: 401)

However, 'context' in Bakhtin's usage is not exhausted by this pragmatist (and almost Nietzschean) stress on the exigencies of the extra-linguistic situation, however that is to be defined. Acknowledging the pioneering work of the French neo-structuralist Julia Kristeva (1986) on Bakhtin, (ii) above could be termed the 'thesis of intertextuality': the proposition that the utterance is not a self-contained monad, but is at least partially dependent on a network of other, equally unique utterances (past and present) for its significance – not unlike the analytical philosopher W. V. Quine's (1960) notion of the 'fabric of sentences' that binds a language-system into a meaningful whole. Between the word and the object or event is interposed a 'dialogically agitated and tension filled environment' of alien words, each with their own values and accents. No utterance is able to avoid coming into contact and interacting with this volatile atmosphere of alien words, and must therefore become an 'active participant in social dialogue'. This kind of interaction – which is dialogic (a 'contact of personalities') to the core – accounts for the utterance's range of potential meanings, its multiple and polysemic layers of semantic depth. It also helps to explain the remarkable capacity of the word continually to generate new significances and connotations. Bakhtin's stress on the creative, productive side of language-use [*slovonost'*] in both the linguistic and literary spheres vindicates his reluctance to equate 'language' with either formal structure or its referentiality. That is, since language can generate new meanings which did not exist previously, it cannot be said to be a mere reflection of a pre-existing reality. In short, any text is an inter-text, part of a wider con-text which 'is but one link in a continuous chain of speech performances' and therefore inexhaustible and potentially infinite, like a mirror reflecting back on itself. This accounts for Bakhtin's stress on the need for a 'living hermeneutics', for a responsive understanding to grasp the plurality of dialogic meanings found in the social world: 'I live in a world of others' words. And my entire life is an orientation in this world, a reaction to others' words' (Bakhtin 1986: 143). Thus, for Bakhtin and company, there can be no direct relation between the utterance and the external world, but only a mediated or inter-discursive one. This continual interaction between a profusion of words and accents implies that the utterance is not autonomous or self-contained, but that particular utterances are only momentary objectifications within a wider semiotic stream or 'chain of meaning' which itself has no beginning and no end: 'No one utterance can be either the first or the last. Each is only a link in the chain, and none can be studied outside this chain' (1986: 136).

THE STRUGGLE OVER THE SIGN

If meaning is indeed a function of context (however defined) rather than some 'natural essence' inhering in the word itself, then it is possible for two grammatically-identical utterances to have an entirely different meaning or significance, depending on the social situation in which they are located and the intonational accents they receive. The transposition of a word from one evaluative context to another, that is to say, results in a re-evaluation, and therefore a shift in meaning. These utterances could be said to occupy divergent semantic universes. Such values and accents – which represent the link between the (unspoken) evaluative horizon and the articulated word – are produced through such phenomena as expressive intonation, style, inflection, *skaz* (the Russian term for the imitation or parody of narrated speech-patterns), and the various 'framing' devices of indirect speech. This differential accentuation of the sign by particular social groups with divergent interests and experiences results in what Voloshinov has described as the 'struggle over the sign'. Or, as the American critic Fredric Jameson wrote in his *The Political Unconsciousness* (1981: 84): 'the dialogue of class struggle is one in which two opposed discourses fight it out within the general unity of the shared code'. Hence, the fusion between meaning and form, between signifier and signified, is not a natural one – there is no 'transcendental signified' in the Bakhtinian schema. Rather, it is the result of specific socio-historical conditions and determinations. This connection can be relatively stable – such as when there is mass adherence to a given social order and there exists a substantial degree of what Gramsci called 'moral and intellectual unity' with respect to the ruling social group. In this situation, the union between linguistic form and value judgements is 'a matter of dogmatic belief, something taken for granted and not subject to discussion' (Voloshinov 1976: 101). Like Gramsci's 'common sense' or Anthony Giddens's 'practical consciousness', these preferred codes are only rarely brought to a state of verbalized awareness. Yet signification can also be fragile and precarious, as during any period of social or political unrest, wherein even the most ingrained and commonsensical meanings are contested and the full 'dialectical flux' of language once again returns to the fore. This is the crux of ideological phenomena in the negative or critical sense for the Bakhtin Circle: that any ruling class, concomitant with its general interest in centralizing and unifying the social world (in all of its economic, political and cultural manifestations), attempts to fix meaning and univocalize the sign, and thereby to effect a form of ideological closure or homophony. Any discursive practice is therefore ideological in this negative sense if it projects itself as nature and not culture, if it effaces its own socially-constructed character and aspires to the status of an 'objective referential meaning' – in short, if it legitimates one symbolic-system as the only possible or rational one. Given the close symbiosis between language and cognition, this dissimulation imparts the illusion that our relationship to reality is unmediated or direct and, therefore, our own perceptions and experiences appear to us as spontaneous, self-evident and eminently commonsensical. This process – what Stuart Hall (1985a) has termed the 'reality effect' – is one of the most significant features of ideological hegemony for the Bakhtin Circle. As Voloshinov wrote in his essay 'Literary Stylistics':

> The ruling class strives to lend the ideological sign a supraclass, external character, to extinguish or exhaust the struggle of class relations that occurs within it, to make it the expression of only one, solid and immutable view. Any living abuse may become

praise, any living truth is bound to sound to many like the greatest lie. This *internal dialectical character* of the sign unfolds finally only in an epoch of social crises and revolutionary displacements. In the normal conditions of social life the contradiction with which every ideological sign is invested cannot completely unfold because the ideological sign in the prevalent ruling ideology is somewhat reactionary and, as it were, attempts to arrest, to render immobile the *preceding moment* in the dialectical flow of social coming-to-be, to mark and fix *yesterday's* as *today's* truth.

(1983: 147)

This attempt to inject the sign with a 'supraclass, external character' is designated by Bakhtin and company by a range of different appellations: the 'authoritative word', the 'sacred word', the 'poetic word', or the 'direct word'. All, however, conform to more or less the same basic principle: the authoritarian desire to silence the 'dialogical echoes' found in the sphere of living heteroglossia. The dialogic word always exceeds the formal boundaries of any 'text' within which it is found; it manifests a 'living impulse' toward the object and toward variable contexts, whence it derives its semantic richness, its manifold complexity and natural 'infinitude and bottomlessness'. The authoritative word, on the other hand, refuses any such dialogizing contact; it recoils in horror from the alien word. It assumes that it represents the 'last word', one that cannot be responded to, ironized, or challenged. It is a 'word mummy', as Bakhtin puts it, in that it strives to reify or naturalize these dialogic relations, to de-personalize them, to accept only one possible context for its (univocal) meaning to be registered. Ideology (in the negative sense) – that is, ideology as monologism – therefore de-problematizes representation by fixing one mode of signification as fully adequate to the comprehension of the object:

Because of its sacrosanct, impenetrable boundaries, this ['sacred' or 'authoritative'] word is inert, and it has limited possibilities of contacts and combinations. This is the word that retards and freezes thought. The word that demands reverent repetition and not further development, corrections and additions. The word removed from dialogue: it can only be cited amid rejoinders; it cannot itself become a rejoinder among equally privileged rejoinders. This word has spread everywhere, limiting, directing, and retarding both thought and live experience of life.

(Bakhtin 1986: 133)

THE DECONSTRUCTION OF REPRESENTATION

None the less, Bakhtin is relatively optimistic that the reifying proclivities of the 'inert word' can be decisively challenged through dialogic or carnivalesque semiotic practices. The crux of Bakhtin's subversion of traditional modes of literary and linguistic representation is one he shares with many of the practitioners of left *avant-garde* art during the 1920s and 1930s: the demonstration, through various techniques and textual strategies (e.g. the interruption of traditional narrative structure, the use of collage or photomontage, Brechtian 'alienation devices', etc.) of the conventional or socially-constructed character of any artistic or linguistic material. By placing familiar, everyday objects in unfamiliar situations – good examples being Marcel Duchamp's famous urinal-sculpture (ironically entitled 'Fountain') which was a *succès de scandale* in New York in 1917, or the Dadaist predilection for bizarre poetic images and strange phonetic juxtapositions – the fetishization of high culture (Benjamin's 'aura') could be subverted and the formal conventions of language or art thereby exposed, challenged, and created anew. This strategy can be clearly ascertained in the interest displayed by the Cubists, the Dadaists (and their successors, the Surrealists), and the Soviet Constructivists in the production of so-called 'ready-made' art or 'found objects' (echoes of which can be found in the Situationist strategy of *détournement* or the postmodernist penchant for visual puns and parody). 'Ready-made' art involved the recontextualization and rearrangement of existing materials (particularly utilitarian building substances) and everyday objects (everything from bicycle wheels to lampshades) in novel and provocative situations. The intent was to draw attention towards the artifice of cultural production and to its social and technical aspects, and thereby to dismantle the bourgeois myth of pure creativity. The *avant-garde* penchant for 'ready-mades' identifies a crucial feature of modernism, what Eugene Lunn has referred to as 'aesthetic self-consciousness' or 'self-reflexiveness':

Modern artists, writers and composers often draw attention to the media or materials with which they are working, the very processes of creation in their own craft. [. . .] The modernist work often wilfully reveals its own reality as a construction or artifice, which may take the form of an hermetic and aristocratic mystique of creativity (as in much early symbolism); visual or linguistic distortion to convey intense subjective states of mind (strongest in expressionism); or suggestions that the wider social world is built and rebuilt by human beings and not 'given' and unalterable (as in Bauhaus architecture or constructivist theatre). [. . .] At best, such an 'aesthetic of the new' could freshen perceptions and cleanse the senses and language of routine, habitual, and automatic responses, to 'defamiliarize' the expected and ordinary connections between things in favour of new, and deeper ones.

(1982: 34–6)

As it turns out, Bakhtin himself was not particularly enamoured with the left *avant-garde* art which had a strong foothold in both Vitebsk and Petrograd during the 1910s and 20s.[36] Perhaps he found their tendency towards nihilism and rather ambiguous politics disturbing (witness, for example, the enthusiasm for Fascism displayed by many of the Italian Futurists, though not of their Russian namesakes), or found them (like the Formalists) altogether too willing to fetishize form and to dispense with the cognitive and emotive qualities of human communication. Duchamp, for instance, wanted to expunge every aesthetic judgement or sentiment from art, to evoke a mocking sneer vis-à-vis the banalities of bourgeois life through the use of crude puns, often violent absurdities and the nonsense combination of random words and images – not unlike the hollow and malicious laughter envisaged by the likes of Bergson and Schopenhauer, which Bakhtin condemned as a tragic deterioration of true carnivalesque laughter which dialectically embraces both the negative and the positive.[37] Such a self-aggrandizing bohemian flippancy could hardly have been endearing to Bakhtin's populist sympathies and Kantian-derived ethical outlook. It is true that, aside from a few scattered comments, the Bakhtin Circle rarely discusses or even acknowledges the major modernist artists of their day. Nevertheless, Bakhtin's aesthetic conforms to the following four characteristics which Lunn (1982: 34–8) identifies as being central features of the modernist *Weltanschauung*: (i) self-reflexiveness (as discussed above); (ii) simultaneity or spatial montage (the disruption of linear narrative structure in favour of interaction in space); (iii) the cultivation of paradox or ambiguity, particularly through the use of complex images, sounds and authorial points of view; and (iv) the demise or fragmentation of the individual subject. In particular, the movement of modernist art towards linguistic reflexivity or self-referentiality unarguably resembles Bakhtin's notion of multiaccentuality and the reaccentuation of past literary works. For what else is carnival, one could argue, if not the recontextualization of existing words and images, thereby 'making strange' or 'defamiliarizing' them? Carnivalesque mésalliances reveal the arbitrariness of not only established linguistic or literary conventions, but also of a whole range of institutional arrangements and social roles right down to our conceptions of history, of individuality and sexuality, and even of time itself. It demonstrates that other, less rigid and hierarchical social relations are possible and indeed desirable, through the utopian enactment of an integrated, egalitarian community.

In any event, Bakhtin's attack on monologic forms of representation involves the transformation of a musical metaphor into a visual one: just as no single voice can constitute polyphony, no one viewpoint can be adequate to the apprehension and understanding of the object. In order fully to conceptualize the object in its totality, that is to say, a multiplicity of perspectives or vantage-points is required. In developing such a principle of 'perspectivalism', Bakhtin displays strong affinities with the Cubist aesthetic developed by Braque, Picasso and Gris in the first two decades of the 20th century (and eventually introduced to Russian audiences through such 'Cubo-futurists' as the painter Burliuk and the poet Kamensky). It might prove useful to examine this analogy in some detail.[38] Not content with the 19th-century stress on mimesis (the imitation of nature), particularly with the development of photography and the mechanical reproduction of cultural objects (both factors that Walter Benjamin continually alluded to in his studies), the Cubists sought to challenge the apparent solidity of the world and the taken-for-granted nature of perception. Cubist paintings, while still incorporating recognizable objects or figures (full-blown abstraction was still a few years away), fragmented the external object-world into a plurality of intersecting geometric surfaces and multiplanar forms in a manner which ended the privileging of a single, unitary perspective. Moreover, by dispensing with the realist attempt to preserve the illusion of depth (the *trompe-l'oeil*), they drew attention toward the inherent 'flatness' of the painted surface. This served to emphasize the human construction of the art-work in particular and the social world in general (which was further reinforced by their incorporation of everyday mass-produced commodities or fragments of newspaper headlines into their paintings). Finally, and perhaps most importantly, the Cubists aspired to engage the viewer in an active rather than a passive relation to the art-work. They did this through the production of 'unfinished' images and ambiguous pictorial spaces, which shifted the responsibility of making coherent sense of the art object from the creator to the perceiver, in that the onus was now upon the viewer to 'reconstitute' the fractured and fragmented image into a recognizable form. By so problematizing the process of perception and devolving the task of representation onto the spectator, Braque and Picasso encouraged 'the relativistic abandonment of a notion of fixed and absolute truths, or a monolithic objective order seen from a stationary point by an outside observer' (Lunn 1982: 48). Or, as Braque himself put it: 'Art is polymorphic. A picture appears to each onlooker under a different guise'.

THE ISSUE OF CRITIQUE

This analogy is a revealing and apposite one, one that could be extended to include a number of modernist textual strategies (such as Eisenstein's montage) or the degraded carnival of postmodernism, not least because Bakhtin's writings are replete with visual metaphors which he utilizes to describe his philosophy of language. The goal for Bakhtin is to break the stranglehold of the omniscient, authorial viewpoint, to challenge the pretence of any one mode of representation to 'reflect' reality and fully to depict the external world:

> Languages of heteroglossia, like mirrors that face each other, each reflecting in its own way a piece, a tiny corner of the world, force us to guess at and grasp for a world behind their mutually reflecting aspects that is broader, more multi-leveled, containing more and varied horizons than would be available to a single language or a single mirror.
>
> (1981: 414–15)

This epistemological pluralism is more 'adequate' to the object in the sense that the fullness of potential meaning and the natural metaphoricality of language is preserved and strengthened. He attempts to achieve this by directing the reader's 'mind's eye' toward the multiplicity of language-forms that constitute the social world, but also toward the unequal relations of power which hold between them. And – as has been often pointed out – he does this not only through the ideas and theories he discusses, but also through the reflexive and self-deconstructive style of his own prose.[39] Every voice within the 'great dialogue' of the age, he writes, projects a different socio-verbal 'image' of the object. In order to end the ideological hegemony of a 'firm, stable linguistic nucleus', each such voice must be preserved, allowed to be given the autonomous 'power to signify'. Accordingly, another of Bakhtin's aspirations is to 'democratize' the process of inter-pretation by encouraging the 'revolt of the reader', to give this reader or addressee the opportunity and the critical acumen to reaccentuate or recontextualize the authorial word without fear of retribution or coercion, whether symbolic or 'real', to encourage the cultivation of 'human discernment, on mature objectivity and the critical faculty' (1981: 40).

The allusion here to the importance of critical reflection is not accidental. Ken Hirschkop (1989a: 32) has correctly stressed the intimate connection between the ethical ideal of dialogism and the category of self-reflection which has been so pervasive in the history of German idealist philosophy. Through the structural dissonance of polyphony – the interplay of unmerged voices and consciousnesses – Bakhtin argues that we can become more aware of our location in the dense network of discursive and ideological practices. Monologism, in its purest form, blocks or occludes this process. Again, he considers the (linguistically mediated) relation between self and other to be constitutive of individual subjectivity and social identity. This process – of becoming aware of ourselves and others, of acting, thinking and speaking as responsible and culturally-competent members of our society – involves the acquisition and 'selective assimilation' of the alien word. That is, much of our own speech is concerned with the (re-)representation and transmission of the speech of others, which involves assessing these words, judging their felicity or accuracy, and responding to them in kind. Through this continuous process of linguistic-ideological 'becoming', we build up an 'interpretive frame', a kind of living hermeneutics which allows us to hear, contextualize, understand, and respond to the words of the other. The paradox is that, whilst we need the other to be a complete social being, this other also has the capacity to circumscribe our thoughts and words, to exercise power over us (the 'authoritative word'). So while we require a dialogic relation, this must be a voluntary and not a forced or coerced one. It must be motivated by the desire to be mutually understood and respected, to be enriched by the other's point of view. For Bakhtin, then, this process of assimilating or 'objectifying' the alien word is of crucial importance for the development of critical reflection and the enhancement of autonomous thought and action.

As a concluding remark, it is important to stress the historical dimensions of this process. That is, the phenomenological self/other relation discussed above has a socio-historical analogue: just as the individual subject gains an awareness of self and society as a whole through the dialogic relation to a polyphony of competing voices and perspectives, so too does the interaction of different cultures and languages free us from the grip of a 'sacrosanct and unitary linguistic consciousness'. Thus, feels Bakhtin, it is only through perspective of another 'cultural-semantic' viewpoint that the nature of our own culture and languages can be reflected upon and understood. Thus, whereas for Hegel increasing self-consciousness was a matter of the abstract evolution of *Geist* or spirit, and for Marx it resulted from the dialectical development of the productive forces through history, for Bakhtin it can be explained by reference to the increasing pluralism and 'fundamental socio-linguistic heteroglossia and hetero-languagedness', particularly in the intertextual relation between novelistic discourse and everyday speech genres.[40] The temporal shift from monoglossia to polyglossia and finally to the situation of modern heteroglossia requires certain socio-historical conditions – the breakdown of the absolute domination of the Catholic church, the development of a fairly high general level of literacy, changes in the nature of class domination (the Gramscian shift from 'minimal' to 'integral' hegemony), the creation of a public sphere or civil society, and so on (all features, curiously enough, that were conspicuously absent in 19th-and early 20th-century Russian society). In any event, through this process of what Paul Ricoeur has termed 'distanciation', we can adopt a more critical orientation toward our linguistic and ideological determinations, in order to understand how the world is 'seen and felt' through our linguistic and cultural situation and to overcome the 'reality effect' fostered by dominant ideological discourses. It is toward a more extended consideration of the issues of critique and reflection from the standpoint of hermeneutic theory that I concern myself in the following chapter.

Chapter 4

Bakhtin's critical hermeneutics

Not only is utopia not 'realizable', but it could not be realized without destroying itself.

Louis Marin

INTRODUCTION

The brief discussion of Bakhtin's views on language and reflection which closed the preceding chapter raises a crucial (and unavoidable) problem: that of the normative justification of critique, of the standpoint from whence the exercise of critical reason and reflection is to be conducted. For, as J. B. Thompson (1984) has convincingly argued, any viable criticism of ideological phenomena must (i) make a claim to 'truth' or adequacy vis-à-vis other interpretations (and therefore implicitly or explicitly appeal to particular grounds or standards); and (ii), on the basis of this claim, censure existing relations of domination from a conception of alternative forms of social organization which would be better suited to the satisfaction of the legitimate needs, desires and capacities of human beings. These two considerations (that is, the task of interpretation and that of critique) are not, of course, unrelated: the question of the limits and aims of critical reason has always been an extremely contentious one. This issue is itself intimately connected to the 'problem of modernity', to the ideological vacuum which has followed the decline of religious and mythological beliefs from the 17th century onwards. Responses to the modern situation have been, needless to say, exceedingly diverse: to take one extreme example, Frederick Nietzsche argued that any talk about reflective knowledge or even 'reason' was an insidious (and 'feminine') delusion, a pathology of consciousness which had infected humankind ever since the consolidation of the Platonic–Christian world-view. The pursuit of 'truth' in whatever form only concealed or legitimated an ubiquitous 'Will to Power', a primordial desire to colonize the external world regardless of conventional moral constraints in order to realize the ultimate goal of the aesthetic transfiguration of the self: 'each specific body strives to become master over the whole of space, and to spread out its power – its Will-to-Power – repelling whatever resists its expansion' (cited in Danto 1965: 220). One result of this striving was a perpetual conflict or agonism, which he felt was constitutive of both human life and nature, and Nietzsche believed that there could be no Archimedean point above the fray whence to view this struggle in a dispassionate or objective manner. The only viable epistemology could therefore be a radically relativistic or sceptical one: that every view or perspective was an idiosyncratic interpretation, a *post-hoc* justification of this eternal strategy of domination and self-realization. Nietzsche's nominalistic anti-foundationalism was at least in part derived from his belief in a fundamental schism between language and the world, between the mercurial flux of reality and any particular conceptual system. The desire for objectivity was a 'philosophical mythology' that was more symptomatic of the rhetorical force of language than its capacity for felicitous description.[1] As he wrote in *Beyond Good and Evil*:

> Indeed, what forces us at all to suppose that there is an essential opposition of 'true' and 'false'? Is it not sufficient to assume degrees of apparentness and, as it were, lighter and darker shadows and shades of appearance – different 'values' to use the language of painters? Why wouldn't the world *that concerns us* be a fiction? And if somebody asks: 'but to a fiction there surely belongs an author? – couldn't one answer simply: *why*? Doesn't his 'belongs' perhaps belong to the fiction too? By now one is not permitted to be a bit ironic about the subject no less than the predicate and object. Shouldn't the philosopher be permitted to rise above faith in grammar?
>
> (1966: 236)

Nietzsche's privileging of the Dionysian as opposed to the Apollonian side of modernity has been eagerly seized upon by the French poststructuralists, who view his work as a welcome antidote to Marx's rationalistic quest for 'totalizing knowledge' and for his allegedly Cartesian view of the subject and language.[2] Given that Bakhtin's own project undoubtedly resembles Nietzsche's in certain respects, yet still remains in some measure committed to Enlightenment standards of reason and critique and to the German philosophical tradition of reflection, this seeming paradox requires further investigation. It is apparent, for instance, that Bakhtin explicitly rejects the objectivist position that a particular interpretation or description can be value-free or disinterested. He would certainly agree, therefore, with Kenneth Burke's suggestion that '*every* insight contains its own special kind of blindness' (1984: 41). Nor, as discussed earlier, does Bakhtin shy away from swallowing the 'Mannheimian pill': he refuses to deny that his own viewpoint is in some sense 'ideological', or is at the very least conditioned by a background framework of assumptions and prejudices that cannot be entirely eliminated or brought to consciousness. Indeed, Bakhtin seeks to problematize any particular mode of representation or perspective (including his own), to demonstrate the relativity and boundedness of any viewpoint, and to open up the interpretive process to the inherent semantic complexity and ambiguity of both socio-cultural life and our linguistically-mediated understanding of it: 'Thought only knows conditional points; thought erodes all previously established points' (1986: 162). Hence, Bakhtin clearly refuses the Hegelian impulse toward 'total knowledge', and he affirms that all understanding is fallible, limited and practical. Given this, however, how would he react to Nietzsche's argument that nothing lies behind the endless clash of different interpretations, that all is perspective, without the possibility of 'truth' in any sense? Does this mean that Bakhtin's own 'perspectivalism' is a form of radical scepticism, that we must remain, as Medvedev (1985: 84) himself once put it, 'indifferent to cognitive truth, poetic beauty [and] political correctness'? In order to clarify the nature of these issues, however, and to identify more precisely what is at stake, this chapter will pursue two major aims: first, to situate the Bakhtin Circle's critical-interpretive approach with respect to the hermeneutic tradition of Gadamer and Ricoeur as well as Habermas's critical theory; and second, to attempt to elucidate the thorny issue of the justification of ideological critique. A detailed consideration of Bakhtin's theories from the standpoint of hermeneutic theory should prove illuminating with respect to the understanding of these issues of reflection, interpretation and modernity.

BAKHTIN AND THE HERMENEUTIC TRADITION

Hermeneutics has a long and complex history.[3] At its inception during the medieval period, it was a scholastic method of solving philological disputes with respect to the origin and authenticity of biblical and theological texts. By the 18th century, however, the discipline began to move beyond textual exegesis per se to reflect on the general nature of social and historical knowledge. And by the end of the 19th century, as represented by the work of Schleiermacher, Dilthey and Rickert, hermeneutics became linked with Romanticism and emerged as a distinctive methodological approach to what eventually became known as the 'human sciences' or *Geistewissenschaften*. This method primarily involved the interpretive understanding [*Auslegung*] of the 'meaningful' or 'purposeful' qualities of human actions and texts which, it was argued, was made possible through the ubiquity of shared tradition and the technique of empathic self-identification. Modern hermeneutics was therefore part and parcel of the 'revolt against positivism' which blossomed in the later half of the 19th century, a development which rejected positivism's effacement of the intending subject and its emphasis on 'objective explanation' through the application of universal rules and procedures.[4]

My aim in what follows will be to demonstrate Bakhtin's continuity with hermeneutic inquiry and to situate his theories with respect to this tradition with special emphasis on the problem of critique. As a prefatory remark, there can be little doubt that Bakhtin's work is closely identified with the characteristic concerns and procedures of contemporary hermeneutics.[5] In common with all advocates of the hermeneutic approach, he insists that the meaning of what Marx called 'consciousness and its products' is not transparent or self-evident insofar as the symbolic representation of experience is always mediated by pre-existing semiotic and linguistic practices which are in need of creative interpretation (or an 'active dialogic understanding'). Genuine understanding therefore entails the comprehension of meaning through a creative reconstruction of the original 'verbal-semantic context' of textual production in a form which is analogous to a conversation or dialogue. Only then can we grasp the inherent situatedness of symbolic practices and their reception by specific social audiences or reading communities, including that of the interpreter. Moreover, a properly dialogic understanding of a text requires that we make it meaningful to ourselves, to encourage it to 'speak' to our practical concerns as moral and social beings. Understanding is certainly a textual process, but it is also 'inter-contextual', involving the active translation of meaning across different contexts which may be temporally and geographically remote. Given that the relevant contexts of semiotic-linguistic production and reception are embedded in history, the act of understanding itself is radically historical in nature. Bakhtin's position here therefore conforms to the hermeneutic demand for an on-going interpretive dialectic between the text and the relevant contexts or historical circumstances, a continual movement between the part and the whole (the famous 'hermeneutic circle').

Insofar as this process cannot avoid an entanglement with signs, which are constitutively polysemic and unstable, Bakhtin rejects the position that a particular interpretation can be justified by reference to either a positivist-empiricist bedrock of 'certain' concepts or sense-datum or an Hegelian-style metanarrative. If interpretation cannot be so legitimated by resort to an objectivistic, a priori methodology, then it must be grounded in the observer's ontological relation to history and to society. That is, the interpreter must reflexively enter the 'stream of language' as an active participant; she or he must make a Wittgensteinian descent into the relevant language-game (or, more accurately, a conflicting plurality of such language-games) in order to comprehend living speech as it is 'actually and continuously generated'. Only then can the full 'semantic potential' of a text or utterance be revealed and ourselves enriched through a dialogic encounter with other practices and traditions. Understanding so conceived precludes the detached or 'neutral' contemplation of textual materials; rather, Bakhtin insists that the knower and the known are inescapably linked in a meaningful, dialogic relationship, in an almost mystical co-mingling through the medium of the word (what he refers to as an 'interrelation and interaction of "spirits"').[6] Accordingly, 'facts' about the social world are not 'given' but at least partially constructed through the theoretical or conceptual categories the knower brings to bear in the act of interpretation: 'The observer has no position outside the observed world, and his observation enters as a constituent part of the observed object' (1986: 126). Moreover, this dialogic encounter is inherently reflexive. It compels the observer to enter

into both an introspective and 'extrospective' confrontation with
his or her own preconceptions and biases, with the particular
cultural-linguistic 'framework of expectations' into which we are
socialized. As such, the observer no less than the observed is an
inescapable object of study in the human sciences:

> The transcription of thinking in the human sciences is always
> the transcription of a special kind of dialogue: the complex
> interrelations between the *text* (the object of study and
> reflection) and the created, framing *context* (questioning,
> refuting, and so forth) in which the scholar's cognizing and
> evaluating thought takes place. This is the meeting of two texts
> – of the ready-made and reactive text being created – and,
> consequently, the meeting of two subjects and two authors. The
> text is not a thing, and therefore the second consciousness, the
> consciousness of the perceiver, can in no way be eliminated or
> neutralized.

(Bakhtin 1986: 106–7)

Since the human sciences must inevitably confront a
pre-interpreted social world, and because the observer's status as a
knowing agent plays a crucial role in the production of knowledge
about this object-world, these disciplines are qualitatively different
(on both an epistemological and a methodological plane) from
their natural science counterparts. The essence of this distinction
lies in the different 'object-domains' of these two classes of
scientific practice, which for Bakhtin can only be explained by
reference to a specific ontology of relations. He accepts that the
natural world is governed by purely causal connections between
things (object–object relations). A knowledge of this object-world
(the stated goal of the natural sciences) thus involves the passive
contemplation of nature by a subject (a subject–object relation).
Because these natural phenomena cannot respond to dialogue, a
cognizance of such objects can only be monologic: 'Only
mechanical or mathematical, empty tautological abstractions are
possible here. There is not a bit of personification' (1986: 165).
Bakhtin argues that the 'methodological apparatus' of the natural
sciences is therefore 'directed toward mastery over *mute objects,
brute things*, that do not reveal themselves in words, that do not
comment on themselves' (1981: 351). As it stands, of course, this is
hardly a desirable state of affairs. Indeed, Bakhtin's position here
is strongly reminiscent of the Frankfurt School's account of

'instrumental rationality', the domination of both the natural and social worlds through the overwhelming desire to quantify and control. The control over non-human nature has led to a 'denial of nature in man', Adorno and Horkheimer once wrote in their *Dialectic of Enlightenment* (1972). For them, this state of affairs represented a 'cancer-cell for a proliferating mythic irrationality' (cited in Wellmer 1971: 131).

Yet the threat posed by the logic of positivism (in its many forms and guises) to what Bakhtin terms the 'dialogic sphere' is considerably intensified when the methodological procedures of the natural sciences are utilized to explain the dynamics of the social world. Historically, this tendency can be attributed to the hegemony of scientific discourse in European society since the 18th century and the undisputed success of scientific rationality in the prediction and control of nature.[7] Yet Bakhtin feels that this model is entirely unsuitable for the elucidation of a third possible type of relation: that which is *inter vivos*, between living persons. He insists, not surprisingly, that this subject–subject relation must be dialogic and moral-affective. While there are all sorts of 'meta-relations' between the three possible relation-types outlined above (for example, subjects exist in the natural world, and are liable to certain physical and biological constraints), Bakhtin clearly believes that dialogic relations are qualitatively different from natural ones and cannot be grasped in mechanical or causal terms insofar as they are 'not technical but *moral*' (1986: 168). The confusion of these relations, or the reduction of one into the other, can only reify and dehumanize social actors by treating subjects as objects. As Bakhtin was only too aware, the impulse to replicate the methods and procedures of natural sciences with respect to the explanation of socio-cultural processes was not an uncommon one. Rather, it represented a tenacious and wide-spread feature of modern European intellectual culture.[8]

It is worth considering in more detail why Bakhtin unequivocally rejects positivist methods and modes of explanation as inappropriate for an adequate understanding of the life-world. For Bakhtin, all possible forms of human interaction and cultural-linguistic practice (and, *inter alia*, our reflexive comprehension of these processes) are necessarily mediated by our dialogic relation to others. To disregard this dimension of human existence quite simply negates the possibility of a 'deep and actual understanding', because it precludes a satisfactory comprehension of the 'living, ideological power of the word to mean, [of] its truth or falsity, its significance or insignificance, beauty or ugliness'. Positivism seeks to avoid a dialogic encounter with the text, yet even the 'driest positivism' is obliged to 'initiate talk not only about words but in words, in order to penetrate their ideological meaning – which can only be grasped dialogically, and which include evaluation and response' (Bakhtin 1981: 352). Because the human sciences must confront this stratum of pre-interpreted words and meanings, it is the text which constitutes their central focus and *raison d'être*. Humanity for Bakhtin is therefore defined by its ability to produce texts, to express itself and engage in self-reflection through the medium of the text. It is this object-domain which unifies a host of otherwise disparate disciplines: 'Where there is no text, there is no object of study, and no object of thought either' (1986: 103). In common with a number of contemporary interpretive theorists, then, Bakhtin conceives of all human actions and cultural artifacts as modes of symbolic communication – that is, as semiotic practices which display certain textual or quasi-textual properties that can be 'read' and responded to dialogically.[9] This stance also provides the human sciences with the categorical imperative to challenge the reification of human thought and action as practised by positivist forms of knowledge, in order to transform an 'ought' into an 'is'. As Bakhtin asks rhetorically in his essay 'The Problem of the Text':

> Is it possible to find any other approach to him and his life (work, struggle, and so forth) than through the signifying text that he has created or is creating? Is it possible to observe and study him as a phenomenon of nature, as a thing? [. . .] Everywhere the actual or possible text and its understanding. Research becomes inquiry and conversation, that is, dialogue. We do not address inquiries to nature and she does not answer us. We put questions to ourselves and we organize observation or experiment in such a way as to obtain an answer. When studying man, we search for and find signs everywhere and we try to grasp their meaning.
>
> (1986: 113–14)

The human sciences cannot possibly achieve the kind of accuracy or objectivity that Bakhtin apparently believes is possible in the natural sciences – nor should they aim to. This is partially for epistemological reasons: as mentioned above, the study of humanity necessarily involves a dialogic encounter with pre-existing linguistic and semiotic practices.[10] Insofar as any such practice is located within a wider (and potentially endless) 'chain of signification', meaning is notoriously 'slippery' and unstable: 'The interpretation of symbolic structures is forced into an infinity of symbolic contextual meanings and therefore cannot be precise in the way the precise sciences are scientific' (1986: 160). Moreover, as intimated above, Bakhtin feels that there is a definite ethical component to his argument against naturalism. Echoing Theodor Adorno's 'negative dialectics', he argues that whilst the natural sciences aim for precision in the form of 'identity-thinking', accuracy in the human sciences is of a very different sort.[11] It is a matter of 'surmounting the otherness of the other without transforming him into purely one's own (any kind of substitution, modernization, non-recognition of the other, and so forth) (Bakhtin 1986: 169). The 'depth of the insight' is what counts, not the accretion of a body of objective, instrumentalized knowledge. Success in social or cultural inquiry can only be measured by the degree of mutual understanding achieved between subjects engaged in dialogue (whether direct or meta-phorical). The ultimate aim, that is to say, is the enrichment of self without the coercion or impoverishment of the other: 'Under-standing as the transformation of the other's into "one's own/ another's"' (1986: 168). The integrity or 'rights' of both author (or text) and reader are maintained in the dialogic encounter; both equally share in the disclosure of meaning. Structuralism (or any similar theory) which aims to explicate the abstract structure of a language or semiotic practice with the precision of a mathematical science cannot hope to illuminate the 'creative nucleus of the personality' that lies behind the production of any text or utter-ance: 'beginning with any text [. . .] we always arrive in the final analysis, with the human voice, which is to say, we come up against the human being' (Bakhtin 1981: 71). As Bakhtin never tired of repeating, human beings are 'expressive and speaking' entities which are fundamentally spontaneous and unpredictable: 'Such a being never coincides with itself, that is why it is inexhaustible in its meaning and signification' (cited in Todorov 1984: 23–4). Someone like Derrida might well say that Bakhtin's ostensive humanistic orientation merely succumbs to an illusory 'meta-physics of presence', although one could counter that for Bakhtin any such 'voice' is a complex admixture or hybrid of competing voices, intentions, and accents. At any rate, it demonstrates the significant gulf between Bakhtin's 'personalism' and the more detached, rarefied approach of deconstructionism.[12]

GADAMER'S PHILOSOPHICAL HERMENEUTICS

Since the mid-1960s the discipline of hermeneutics has been dominated by the work of Hans-Georg Gadamer, particularly his massive, characteristic work *Wahrheit und Methode* (*Truth and Method*). It is worth noting that Gadamer's 'philosophical hermeneutics' represents something of a departure from previous hermeneutical approaches with respect to the discipline's essential aims and methods. For example, whilst Dilthey argued that *Verstehen* was a systematic method which, through a process of 'reliving' or empathic projection into the meaningful experiences [*Erlebnis*] under scrutiny, generates a privileged understanding of cultural practices, Gadamer asserts that hermeneutics is not a method at all but rather a universal, *a priori* condition of all human intersubjectivity and all possible forms of knowledge. Hermeneutic understanding cannot be gained through a psychologistic 'reliving' of prior deeds and actions, but only through an encounter with 'tradition' as it is mediated by ordinary language communication. Tradition in Gadamer's view corresponds to a 'structure of prejudices' [*Vorurteile*] which is constituted in and through the historical evolution of a given cultural-linguistic community. To understand a text therefore requires that we form a conceptual bridge between the tradition within which the text itself was generated and our own. However, this knowledge is never complete or finished: the historicity of tradition ensures that our understanding is in a constant state of 'becoming'; that is, engaged in an endless dialectic of recapitulation and re-evaluation. In broader terms, Gadamer seeks to investigate the 'structures of understanding' which operate in all possible socio-cultural domains – aesthetics, history, theology, philology, and so on -- by grasping how a shared language and culture constitutes our fundamental mode of being-in-the-world as the latter is embedded in a process of historical becoming.

Unlike Wittgensteinian approaches to cultural interpretation (which seek to conceptualize the life-world through a particular 'language-game'), Gadamer insists that we are constantly shifting back and forth between different linguistic practices and cultural traditions in our lifetime. Each such 'form of life' is therefore open to a multiplicity of external influences and processes, and the result is that we can become aware of our own tradition (within certain limits) and reflexively relate to other such traditions: 'The historical movement of life consists in the fact that it is never utterly bound to one standpoint, and hence can never have a truly closed horizon' (1975: 271). If this were not the case, then language truly would be a prison-house and any type of cross-cultural understanding would be impossible. Moreover, Gadamer strongly argues that such an understanding is not a matter of gaining an 'insider's knowledge' of another tradition, but rather depends on our ability to mediate between at least two pre-existing traditions. As such, Gadamer feels that 'translation' and not 'participation' is the most suitable metaphor for a *Verstehen* approach to the human sciences. We must maintain a respect for the 'foreignness' of other texts while simultaneously rendering them intelligible in relation to our own life-world. The encounter with another text and tradition ideally takes the form of a dialogue or conversation, which is animated by a desire to understand the other's words in an atmosphere of mutual respect and open-mindedness. Hence, a successful interpretation is, in Gadamer's famous words, a 'fusion of horizons'.

As mentioned above, the historicity of tradition ensures that a given interpretation can never be complete or infallible, insofar as tradition is the mode through which our understanding of the world evolves and is expressed. Each succeeding historical epoch embodies new experiences and perspectives; each period interprets past texts in different and novel ways. Thus, meaning is 'open', incomplete, in a continual state of becoming. Moreover, Gadamer suggests that insofar as understanding is not a formal method which produces a systematic knowledge of social actions and events but an 'action-oriented self-understanding' which facilitates enlightened social interaction, hermeneutics contains an irreducibly practical dimension. That is, the historicity of tradition means that the understanding of 'foreign' beliefs and practices requires that we not only become self-aware of our own framework of tradition, we can 'test' our prejudices and subject them to critical scrutiny in order to distinguish between false (or 'blind') and valid prejudices. Thus, because the interpreter belongs (in a very real sense) to the very object-domain under study, such a self-consciousness of our own 'horizon of expectations' promotes a mutual, intersubjective understanding of the life-world: 'The person with understanding does not know and judge as one who stands apart and unaffected; but rather, as one united by a specific bond with the other' (Gadamer 1975: 288). This 'applicative moment' has another pragmatic dimension as well. To understand a given text requires that we deconstruct its symbolic content and reconstruct it in a form which 'speaks' to our own horizon of expectations. Thus we build what could be termed 'conceptual bridges' between the text under scrutiny and our own prejudices: we look for connections, analogies, shared points of reference and so on. The desired outcome of this process is a heightened cultural sensitivity, an appreciation of 'the common perspective of humanity', and an opportunity to expand the boundaries of human self-awareness and freedom. Whether we display a tolerance and respect for this culture, or whether we dismiss it as unintelligible rubbish ultimately depends on the success of hermeneutic inquiry. A failure to understand brings an abrupt end to any potential cultural dialogue, resulting in an intolerance towards the 'other' and a labelling of other traditions and beliefs as 'deviant' or 'primitive'. A successful comprehension of tradition, on the other hand, can play a positive and enabling role vis-à-vis our self-understanding and our moral actions in the social world.

This brings us to Gadamer's confrontation with the Enlightenment tradition of critical reason. He feels that the philosophical legacy of the Enlightenment is seriously flawed, because it insists on an abstract conception of 'reason' as the sole yardstick by which to measure all values and to provide the foundation for legitimate authority. This has led to the domination of a narrow form of technological rationality which represents an 'inner longing in our society to find in science a substitute for lost origins'. Genuinely to regain such 'lost origins' – that is, to realize the Aristotelian ideal of the higher synthesis of technical reason [*techne*] with both theoretical [*episteme*] and practical-ethical knowledge [*phronesis*] – Gadamer asserts that we must re-engage the standards of rationality with the exigencies of lived, shared tradition if we wish to recover 'authentic' existence.[13] Otherwise, reason will remain an impoverished and reified human capacity, lacking any practical relevance for our everyday moral and social conduct. Thus, Gadamer is not suggesting that we abandon reason *en bloc*. Rather, his position is that 'reason' is itself part of the wider ontology of tradition, that it has a concrete, pragmatic role to play in the expansion of our own horizon and the intersubjective relations within which we inevitably find ourselves: 'Reason [is] not its own master, but remains constantly dependent on the given circumstances in which it operates' (1975: 245). Accordingly, Gadamer argues that we must rescue the original meaning of the concept 'prejudice' from its currently negative connotation in order to vitiate the unfounded prejudice of the Enlightenment against prejudice: 'what authority states is not irrational and arbitrary, but can be accepted in principle. This is the essence of the authority claimed by the teacher, the superior, the expert' (1975: 249). Prejudice represents the fundamental historical reality of being – an 'ontological given' of lived experience – that is so much a part of us, of how we think, speak and act, that it is not entirely transparent or open to reflection. As such, hermeneutics cannot provide 'objective' knowledge in the positivist or natural-scientific [*Naturwissenschaften*] sense, and any pretence to 'truth' must be related to authentic tradition from which particular, historically-specific standards of argumentation and explanation are ultimately derived.[14]

BAKHTIN, GADAMER AND THE CRITIQUE OF IDEOLOGY

At this point I wish to compare Bakhtin's interpretive stance with that of Hans-Georg Gadamer with respect to the critique of ideology. In many of his texts (particularly in 'Discourse in the Novel' and throughout the *Speech Genres* book) Bakhtin sounds uncannily like Gadamer, even down to some of his terminological choices (or at least as they have been translated), and it is clear there are significant convergences between these two thinkers which can be summarized as follows:

(i) Arguably, 'dialogism' is virtually a synonym for Gadamer's 'hermeneutic', and therefore both thinkers arguably follow Heidegger's shift from hermeneutics as 'method' to an ontology of understanding which stresses the communicative interaction between subjects in the context of the life-world or *Lebenswelt*.[15] Dialogue is not a 'type' or sub-variant of experience for Bakhtin, but the archetype, the 'master key' of all possible experiences: 'Life is by its very nature dialogical' (1984: 293). Dialogism therefore figures as an essential component of humanity's 'species

being' or philosophical anthropology, which parallels Gadamer's
assertion that hermeneutic experience is 'an attempt to
understand what the human sciences truly are, beyond their
methodological self-consciousness, and what connects them to the
totality of our experience of the world' (1975: xiii).

(ii) For both, the disclosure of meaning is a co-creative
endeavour, involving a dialogic encounter between text and the
interpreter both already located in a particular historical and
cultural environment. Because this background tradition is
transient and mutable, representing only a passing moment in
what Bakhtin refers to as the 'historical chain of human
communication', there can be no final, authoritative revelation of
a single meaning, but only a tentative and provisional one which is
subject to continual re-evaluation and re-appraisal. From Bakhtin's
point of view, succeeding generations can invest the text with an
'infinite diversity of interpretations, images, figurative semantic
combinations, materials and their interpretations' (1986: 140).[16]
For his part, Gadamer stresses the fundamentally historical nature
of understanding and belongingness [*Zugehörigkeit*] and the
open-ended and indeterminate nature of human experience:
'Every such world, as linguistically constituted, is always open, of
itself, to every possible insight and hence for every expansion of its
own word-picture, and accordingly available to others' (Gadamer
1975: 405).

(iii) Both thinkers are exceedingly hostile toward the legacy of
scientific rationalism with respect to the human sciences. That is,
both Gadamer and Bakhtin seek to recover a 'lost' humanistic
tradition from the dead weight of positivist-objectivist methods
which have dominated European intellectual life since the 19th
century. They would agree that the human sciences should not
seek to discover general laws of society or culture, but to divulge
what Gadamer calls the 'unique and historical concreteness' of
understanding and of social being. Or, as Bakhtin writes: 'The
deeper the person, that is the closer we edge to personal boundary,
the less applicable any generalizing method; generalization and
formalization efface the boundary between genius and mediocrity'
(1986: 161). They also agree that it is the scientific and not the
hermeneutic mode of inquiry that is particularistic and not
universal, and that naturalism is both methodologically suspect
and morally unacceptable. As Gadamer puts the matter: 'If
Verstehen is the basic moment of human *In-der-welt-sein* then the

human sciences are nearer to human self-understanding than the natural sciences. The objectivity of the latter is no longer an unequivocal and obligatory ideal of knowledge (1979: 106).

(iv) For Bakhtin, the disclosure of meaning (in terms of what he calls genuine 'evaluative-semantic understanding') is only possible if there is a shared social purview or a common evaluative orientation between the interlocutors in dialogue, for here can be found the 'bonds of brotherhood on a high level'. This echoes Gadamer's claim that shared tradition – likewise conceived of in terms of a given cultural-linguistic community – helps to secure our attachment to others. And, of course, for both this connection is always mediated by pre-existing linguistic structures and categories. Language for both thinkers represents humanity's universal mode of being and the alpha and omega of any possible knowledge. Human communities are first and foremost linguistic communities; language is synonymous with tradition, with social being, and with understanding itself. As Gadamer puts it: 'Being that can be understood is language' (1975: 450).

(v) This shared orientation in terms of the linguisticality of understanding and social being involves another dimension as well: that the ideal hermeneutic encounter between subjects (or between the interpreter and the text) takes the form of a conversation or dialogue, which is jointly regarded as an exemplar of mutual understanding. Both continually underscore the 'open' or unfinalized nature of our experiential relation to the world and to others, and the fact that the logical structure of this openness is best exemplified by the dialectic of question and answer. Through such a dialogic relation to the object of our inquiry, the disclosure of meaning leading to mutual self-understanding is best effected through a free and uncoerced exchange of perspectives and views, what Gadamer terms an 'imperceptible and non-arbitrary transfer of viewpoints' (1975: 348).

(vi) Finally, both assert that reflection and self-understanding are made possible by the distance between the interpreter's 'effective-historical consciousness' and the tradition(s) that are being studied. Gadamer and Bakhtin would agree that our exposure to a plurality of linguistic and cultural practices precludes our passive assimilation into a unitary, all-encompassing language-game or tradition. This again brings us to Gadamer's concept of the 'fusion of horizons' which, as intimated above, is conceived of along dialogic lines. For Gadamer, whilst we can only effect such a 'fusion of horizons' if there is some distance between them in the first place,[17] it is inconceivable that we should wish completely to jettison our own historical horizon in the hermeneutic encounter with another tradition. All claims to understanding are for Gadamer made from a given set of prejudices (what Heidegger called 'fore-structures') which cannot be eliminated, but only corrected or modified. Hence, the famous 'hermeneutic circle' is not a circuitous or vicious one, a lamentable lapse into an idealist *Subjekphilosophie*; rather, it is the only possible route to genuine self-knowledge. Similarly, Bakhtin argues that understanding an alien culture does not mean we should attempt to forget our own situation. Understanding and evaluation 'are simultaneous and constitute a unified integral act', in that the interpreter inevitably brings certain background expectations and frames of meaning (what he calls 'socio-ideological conceptual horizons') to bear in the act of understanding, and these cannot be arbitrarily ignored or conveniently forgotten. But this does not mean that our own perspective is not open to change. Rather, Bakhtin suggests that the confrontation with the other can potentially result in 'mutual change and enrichment' and, as such, understanding is a co-creative endeavour which 'multiplies the artistic wealth of humanity' (1986: 142).

There are certainly other parallels between Gadamer and Bakhtin, affinities which are significant and certainly deserving of more attention than I have allowed myself here. Nevertheless, when these similarities are subjected to critical scrutiny, particularly with respect to the background assumptions and perspectives the two thinkers respectively utilize, significant differences come to light. To begin with, let us inspect Gadamer's suggestion that hermeneutics must be concerned with ontology and not epistemology, and must therefore abandon the Enlightenment conception of 'truth', at least as it has been traditionally formulated. Gadamer's position here has led many of his critics to conclude that his philosophical hermeneutics necessarily succumbs to the pitfalls of subjectivism, nihilism, and so on. This is because, it is alleged, he denies a role for critical reason and abrogates the need for some standard (political, epistemological, etc.) whence to adjudicate the particular validity-claims made by rival interpretations. More balanced assessments of Gadamer, such as the recent works by Susan Hekman (1986) and Georgia Warnke (1987), have effectively demonstrated that this attack is in many respects misguided and unfounded. They counter that Gadamer's stance does not entail a kind of nihilistic relativism, insofar as Gadamer emphasizes the need to separate false from true prejudices and to ground hermeneutic experience in 'authentic' self-reflection (although, of course, he continues to insist that this decision-making process must still be based on one's 'belongingness' to tradition). More specifically, Hekman argues that the only 'privileged vocabulary' Gadamer allows is the one generated by the community (either the community of the interpreter or the interpretand) through the everyday social existence of the participants that comprise it. In the fusion of horizons – i.e., the mediation of traditions through the conversational structure of dialogue – a consensus over meaning can be realized between these interacting traditions which prevents a crisis of faith in communal authority. In Gadamer's opinion, true or legitimate prejudices are those which serve to enhance our awareness of the superiority of tradition by securing our connection to a body of shared meanings which define a particular human linguistic community. False prejudices, on the other hand, in some sense fail to meet this criterion. Accordingly, Hekman suggests that the correctness or acceptability of a given interpretation must lie in its 'conformity to the horizon of meaning from which an interpretation is made and the prejudices which constitute that horizon', and that such a horizon must 'necessarily privilege a vocabulary in each historical period' (1986: 165–6).

For Gadamer, therefore, what incorporates us into a common tradition is our shared membership in a particular linguistic-cultural community. Language for Gadamer unites; it defines our collective humanity, our belongingness to tradition and to history itself. In his long-running debate with Habermas, Gadamer argues that there is no getting 'outside' this dimension of human existence: even non-linguistic economic or political forces, if they are to acquire relevance for a particular tradition's self-understanding, must go through a process of 'symbolization'. This does not, however, preclude the critique of ideology, but only the presupposition that this critique can be undertaken from some arbitrary point beyond our own historical and cultural situation. In the encounter with historical actions and texts, new and unexpected meanings are brought to light which can elucidate the unacknowledged presuppositions of our own beliefs and ideas.[18]

Through this 'reciprocal testing' of prejudices via dialogue, a consensus or agreement over meaning is achieved in a manner which enhances our self-understanding and the supersession of 'blind' prejudice and ideological distortion.[19] Hence, because for Gadamer the achievement of consensus seems to be an inherent aspect of human communication itself, understanding is 'built into' hermeneutic experience and cannot be systematically distorted. However, at least from a Bakhtinian point of view, this position is less than acceptable. The problem here is not the simple acknowledgement of the limits of reason, of the necessarily tentative and cautious nature of our knowledge about the world. Such a position now finds a wide measure of support, and Bakhtin himself would undoubtedly agree with Gadamer on this point. However, Bakhtin would take issue with the suggestion that the cultural-historical situatedness of understanding necessarily precludes a radical questioning of the legitimacy of tradition. As discussed earlier, Gadamer rejects the Enlightenment distinction between rational criticism and the received authority of tradition because there is no justified metaphysical standpoint outside tradition whence to validate this judgement. At some level we must accede to the unquestionable supremacy of tradition as the only viable arbiter of a given community's self-understanding: '[Tradition] lives not from dogmatic power but from dogmatic acceptance. What is this dogmatic acceptance, however, if not that one concedes superiority in knowledge and insight to the authority, and for this reason believes that authority is right?' (Gadamer 1976: 33-4). However, as Warnke astutely observes, such a Socratic admission of our own fallibility with respect to tradition does not mean that this tradition is *ipso facto* superior or legitimate nor closed to critical interrogation.[20]

Bakhtin would therefore concur with Gadamer that the distortion of true dialogue and of the creative co-disclosure of meaning can be largely traced to the domination of Western culture by naturalist and positivist ethos, and that this form of rationalized 'identity thinking' is a primary source of human reification and alienation. But whereas for Gadamer this is a contingent aspect of modern society, for Bakhtin it is in the material interests of specific social elites to encourage the corruption of dialogue by uni-vocalizing the 'verbal-ideological sphere'. In other words, Gadamer's hermeneutics ignores the crucial dimension of power, and of the specifically *ideological* deformation of language-use. Gadamer's social thought therefore succumbs to a metaphysics of the popular, a fetishization of the everyday. Like the later Wittgenstein, Gadamer seems to imply that the realization of authentic community is simply a matter of mutual understanding through dialogue and self-understanding. Yet there are enormous, perhaps even insurmountable practical and political tasks to be completed before the dialogic ideal that Gadamer envisages can provide the foundation for a viable human community. Of course, one could also censure Bakhtin for failing to address this issue in a convincing or coherent manner, a question I intend to return to in the concluding chapter. But at least Bakhtin is aware – even acutely aware – that such a problem exists.

HABERMAS AND THE CRITIQUE OF PHILOSOPHICAL HERMENEUTICS

In a series of wide-ranging debates with Gadamer during the 1960s, Jürgen Habermas attempted to come to grips with the implications of the 'hermeneutic challenge' vis-à-vis critical theory's conception of social inquiry and ideological criticism.[21] There is much that Habermas finds attractive in Gadamer's general approach, such as the latter's insistence on the historicity of knowledge-claims, the importance of reflection, and the practical ramifications of hermeneutic inquiry. Nevertheless, he identifies certain elements of the hermeneutic tradition which must be supplanted if the dialectic of reflection and understanding is to be radicalized for the purposes of ideological critique. Whilst Habermas accepts Gadamer's view that one cannot arbitrarily step outside tradition in the act of understanding, he argues that this does not mean that the 'horizon of expectations' cannot itself be subjected to critical reflection. In other words, Habermas is criticizing what he takes to be a powerful conservative strain in philosophical hermeneutics. This conservativism can be described as a naive or tacit acceptance of the authority of tradition, involving a romanticization of abstract 'community' or *Gemeinschaft*-type social relations. What Gadamer seems not to realize, he asserts, is that any such community is riven with contradictory material interests and exploitative social relations. Received tradition typically manifests elements of blind obedience and domination, not simply mutual understanding and historical self-awareness. Habermas is therefore affirming the necessity of being aware of one's 'structure of prejudices' while simultaneously maintaining a critical distance from it, wherein the 'element of authority that was simply domination can be stripped away and dissolved in the less violent force of insight and rational decision' (1977: 358). More broadly, whilst Habermas accepts Gadamer's position that language is a 'metainstitution' which mediates all forms of social action and understanding, he insists that language is not simply a 'neutral' medium that facilitates intersubjective relations. Rather, language masked as tradition also serves to justify particular relations of domination and thereby curtails the expression of autonomous thought and action. In a crucial passage, Habermas writes:

> It makes good sense to conceive of language as a kind of metainstitution on which all social institutions are dependent; for social action is constituted only in ordinary language communication. But this metainstitution of language as tradition is evidently dependent in turn on social processes that are not reducible to normative relationships. Language is *also* a medium of domination and social power; it serves to legitimate relations of organized force. Insofar as the legitimations do not articulate the power relations whose institutionalization they make possible, insofar as these relations merely manifest themselves in the legitimations, language is *also* ideological. Here it is a question not of deceptions within a language but with language as such.
>
> (1977: 360)

Habermas charges that Gadamer commits Marx's cardinal epistemological blunder, albeit in a transverse fashion. That is, whereas Marx collapsed interaction into labour, Gadamer treats labour as coextensive with symbolic interaction. But labour, interaction and domination are irreducible facets of the life-world. Each such element of the human self-formative process is qualitatively different from the others, and each must be examined according to divergent methods and procedures. The domain of symbolic interaction normally facilitates a self-awareness of human praxis and of the life-world in general. However, the usual functioning of this communicative sphere can be disrupted through a series of 'subjectively produced illusions'. Such a distortion of the reflective capacities of the human subject – which allows us to grasp the conditions of our actions and (at least in principle) alter these conditions – corresponds to the pheno- menon of ideology.[22] Thus, critical theory cannot be satisfied with the explication or disclosure of a pre-interpreted world of meaning. It must be linked to a critique of ideology, and also to some procedure of redeeming counterfactual claims vis-à-vis a just and equal society in which the maximization of individual freedom and autonomy is the ultimate goal. Accordingly, Habermas charges that Gadamer's 'linguistic idealism' hypostatizes language to the point where it cannot account for either the material practice of social life or the oppressive nature of existing social relations.

Habermas argues that because labour and domination do not conform to the ontological conditions of communicative interaction, they must be examined within a theoretical framework which elucidates the causal conditions and unintended consequences of human action. These conditions – which function independently of social agents' own linguistically- mediated beliefs and conceptions about the social world – can contribute to the systematic or structural distortion of communicative interaction. The hermeneutic method can only deal with contingent misunderstandings; it cannot account for the systemic or institutionalized disruption of communicative interaction. This necessitates the incorporation of the methods of the empirical/analytic sciences and hermeneutics into the broader project of critical theory. Certain social scientific approaches – including theories of social evolution and the cybernetic functioning of social systems – utilize bodies of nomological knowledge which are generally unavailable to most lay actors. Such knowledge-forms can be organized into quasi-natural explanations of social forces, which serves to reduce the context-bound nature of the interpretive process. It is because of this 'detour' through scientific explanation that critical theory cannot simply be thought of as a form of hermeneutics per se. Of course, knowledge (even social-scientific knowledge) cannot be restricted to such a nomological form, because social relations would only be grasped as things, as reifications. If this were the case, then the cycle of ideological mystification would be reproduced because it would reduce the symbolic components of human self-activity to 'invariant regularities'. For Habermas, therefore, critical social science must go beyond (yet incorporate) the nomological or 'quasi-transcendental' knowledge, in order to separate 'social facts' from 'ideologically frozen relations of dependence'. Habermas makes the controversial step of utilizing psychoanalysis as a methodological exemplar for critical theory, which for him combines hermeneutic-linguistic analysis and an investigation of causal conditions with an emancipatory interest in critical reflection. More recently, Habermas effectively abandons the model of psychoanalysis and seeks to investigate the universal criteria through which reason operates in the sphere of communicative action, a project which involves such concepts as the 'ideal speech situation' and 'universal pragmatics'.[23] In any event, Habermas's basic position is that through such a synthetic methodology we can come to an awareness of the 'interest orientation' of our thoughts and deeds. This can render the law-like causal conditions of action 'inapplicable' and release the subject from a 'dependence on hypostatized powers' which, in turn, increases the overall likelihood of the collective transformation of constraining structures and asymmetrical power-relations:

> ... [in the] experience of the emancipatory power of reflection [. . .] the subject experiences in itself to the extent that it becomes transparent to itself in the history of its genesis. The experience of reflection articulates itself substantially in the concept of the self-formative process. Methodically it leads to a standpoint from which the identity of reason with the will freely arises. In self-reflection, knowledge for the sake of knowledge comes to coincide with the interest in autonomy and responsibility [*Mündigkeit*]. For the pursuit of reflection knows itself as a movement of emancipation. Reason is at the same time subject to the interest in reason. We can say that it obeys an *emancipatory cognitive interest*, which aims at the pursuit of reflection.
>
> (Habermas 1978: 197–8)

In direct contrast to Gadamer, therefore, Habermas seeks to 'shake the dogmatism of life-praxis', to investigate tradition not simply as a received form of 'cultural heritage' but as the terrain of ideological obfuscation and coercive force in the service of particular social elites. And Bakhtin would certainly side with Habermas on this point. For Bakhtin, linguistic-cultural tradition certainly has the potential to unite, but more typically – or at least in the context of a society fractured by intransigent class divisions – it is both source and medium of a very real socio-ideological conflict. In particular, Bakhtin would want to ask where the 'commonly shared meanings' that Gadamer continually alludes to as being constitutive of tradition are derived from and in whose interests they operate. The notion that modern society already represents a commonality of interests and shared tradition is for Bakhtin a spurious illusion of the most dangerous and pernicious sort. Indeed, he considers the appearance of linguistic and cultural homogeneity to be one of the major bulwarks of ideological hegemony. Certain perspectives are not simply 'different'; they can be ideological if they help to shore up a repressive social system and legitimate or universalize a particular social group's point of view. Hence, Bakhtin's emphasis on the negative or repressive functions of certain forms of ideological discourse, his insistence on the centrality of class conflict in modern society, and his commitment to the necessity of radical critique all demonstrate his convergence with the critical theory of Habermas, at least on these specific points. Both theorists would undoubtedly sympathize with Albrecht Wellmer's stinging rebuke of hermeneutics' political naiveté in his *Critical Theory of Society*:

> ... the Enlightenment knew [what] hermeneutics forgets: that the 'dialogue' which (according to Gadamer) we 'are,' is *also* a relationship of coercion and, for this reason, *no* dialogue at all. [...] Consequently, the universalist claim of the hermeneutic approach can be upheld only if one assumes that, as the location of possible truth and factual comprehension, the context of tradition is at one and the same time the location of factual untruth and permanent coercion.
>
> (1971: 47)

To put it bluntly, both Habermas and Bakhtin would argue that Gadamer uncritically submits to the legitimacy of received tradition. Symptomatic of this conservativism is Gadamer's construal of the 'fusion of horizons' as a form of mediation in which the truth of the text-object is appropriated not through some kind of critical distancing [*Verfremdung*] but through a purely contrastive relation to another tradition. Given that Bakhtin and Habermas feel that 'tradition' should be critically interrogated, the question then becomes what form this distanciation should take and what kind of ideological criticism it makes possible. For

Habermas, it will be recalled, the critique of ideology must involve two distinct phases: (i) a genetic explanation of the underlying causes of social forces, with respect to the domain of labour or instrumental action, incorporating such existing methods as systems theory and psychoanalysis; and (ii) a hermeneutical exploration of intersubjective meanings. All these apparently different methodological strategies are guided by a desire on Habermas's part to transcend the perceived subjectivistic limitations of a purely interpretive social science by recourse to a more objective explanatory framework, thereby explicitly denying the universality of hermeneutics. Yet it is also clear that Habermas's project of rescuing the Enlightenment stress on critical reason, at least in this area, runs into intractable difficulties which cannot be easily surmounted.[24] For instance, Habermas's critical stance is premised upon an ontological distinction between 'labour' and 'interaction', the former understood as 'purposive-rational action' which is guided by systematic technical rules and which can be explained by recourse to general laws, whilst the latter is construed as a symbolically-structured mode of practical intersubjectivity. Yet such a distinction is now almost universally regarded as untenable, even by many of his closest supporters, because it hypostatizes 'labour' as something which lacks an ideological or symbolic dimension, and because it reduces social relations to symbolic interaction. It is also dubious because Habermas, as Ricoeur (1981: 83–5) points out, has generally failed to provide a plausible account of how the methodological procedures of such 'meta-hermeneutical' practices as psycho-analysis or systems-theory could actually be adapted for the critique of ideological phenomena. Finally, and perhaps most importantly, Habermas's stance reproduces the traditional opposition between 'understanding' [*Verständis*] and 'explanation' [*Erklärung*] that Gadamer and others have been so concerned to overcome. Habermas's assertion that the 'nomological' sciences are valid within their sphere of knowledge-constitutive interests implies an uncritical acceptance of the positivist model of science which manages to ignore the crucial developments in the post-Kuhnian philosophy of science and the sociology of science. It is now broadly accepted that science does not and cannot restrict ontology to the realm of observable entities or events, as if causation in the external world could be appropriated objectively by the sensory apparatuses of a neutral observer (or even a community of such observers). Rather, the process of cognitively appropriating the external world with respect to any object of knowledge is always mediated by a pre-existing normative framework of linguistic and theoretical categories, and therefore knowledge cannot be objective or 'value-free' in the positivist sense. Accordingly, the natural no less than the human sciences necessarily involve an interpretive dimension.[25] Such an admission seriously damages Habermas's claim that hermeneutics must be restricted to the sphere of communicative interaction, and it simultaneously lends credence to Gadamer's insistence on the universality of hermeneutics as an *a priori* of all possible experience and understanding.

Bakhtin (like Habermas) feels that the deformation of dialogue in class society is not a matter of simple misunderstanding, but is rather ideological both in that it is systematic or structurally-induced and because it is congruent with the material interests of particular social classes. He would also concur with Habermas that ideological criticism should be guided by some ideal of unconstrained communication, which departs significantly from Gadamer's stated goal of encouraging an intersubjective awareness of our ontological constitution vis-à-vis a particular linguistic-cultural tradition. Yet whilst Bakhtin would agree with Habermas's stress on the significance of ideological domination in modern society and the necessity for its critical interrogation, it is doubtful he would acknowledge the latter's solution: of adopting the explanatory procedures of a generalizing social science in order to justify or validate the critique of a particular set of social arrangements.

THE CRITICAL HERMENEUTICS OF PAUL RICOEUR

At this point it is worth pursuing an examination of the similarities between Bakhtin's dialogic critique of ideology and the recent work of the French hermeneuticist, Paul Ricoeur.[26] Ricoeur seeks to preserve both Habermas's stress on epistemology (the critique of ideology) with Gadamer's hermeneutical ontology (the non-separateness of being and tradition). Ricoeur agrees with Habermas that 'critique' is also an important part of tradition, arguing that 'nothing is more deceptive than the alleged antimony between an ontology of false understanding and an eschatology of freedom' (1981: 100). Yet he simultaneously rejects Habermas's turn to a nomological or objectivizing social science to explain the extra-communicative aspects of social systems. This is because Ricoeur unequivocally denies that the structure of human action ('instrumental' or otherwise) can be separated from its symbolic or ideological component, insofar as symbolism 'is not a secondary effect of social life; it constitutes real life as socially meaningful' (1978: 51). Because scientific-rationalist methods cannot adequately comprehend this dimension of human life, they cannot play a significant role in the understanding of the symbolic organization of the social world. Yet Ricoeur also argues, against Habermas, that hermeneutics can foster a critical stance through what he terms a 'depth semantics' or a 'hermeneutics of suspicion'. This critical strategy is not grounded in structures of formal rationality but, he asserts, in an Aristotelian conception of practical reason. The inevitable (and indeed desirable) conflicts of interpretation which result from the utilization of different conceptual or theoretical systems to understand the world cannot be resolved through an appeal to some postulated realm of 'objective facts' which cannot be contested. Such conflicts can only be arbitrated through the socially- and culturally-grounded procedures of rational argumentation and warranted assertion, which means that 'objectivity' in this context is relative to concrete political and ethical concerns.

To clarify what Ricoeur has in mind here, we need carefully to unpack his conception of 'ideology' and ideological critique in more detail. To begin with, he strongly censures Marxism for assuming that ideology is a purely negative phenomenon – that it is defined solely in terms of the legitimating or obfuscating function it performs for the ruling class. He feels that by making such a presupposition, the equally important issue of social integration is ignored or undervalued. Drawing on Max Weber's account of the legitimation of traditional authority, Ricoeur suggests that ideology is linked to 'the necessity for a social group to give itself an image of itself, to represent and to realize itself, in the theatrical sense of the word' (1981: 225). Thus, ideology is a form of 'social memory', a symbolic projection of a primordial and mythologized past through which groups creatively construct a symbolic representation of their past origins. This self-representation constitutes a shared interpretive framework by which contemporary actions, events and texts are categorized and understood. Insofar as it constitutes an inescapable medium of social interaction, it has a dynamic or 'generative' character which constitutes the fundamental basis for social motivation and praxis. Thus, argues Ricoeur, whilst Marx was correct to insist that ideology justifies the existing system of class domination, this insight must be balanced with a concomitant stress on the more general role that ideology plays in the symbolic constitution of social bonds.[27]

Yet although Ricoeur seeks to remove the concept of ideology from a purely pejorative connotation, he does not succumb to a Gadamerian lionization of received tradition. This is because he concurs with the Marxist tradition that ideology also has a darker, more negative side which justifies the need for critique. In particular, Ricoeur suggests that ideology functions as a simplifying and schematic code or grid which provides an explanatory framework for understanding social existence and human history, and which sacrifices intellectual rigour and coherence in the interests of social efficacy. This schematization – which Ricoeur refers to as the *doxic* character of ideology – facilitates its legitimizing function, and it allows a group's self-image to be idealized and manipulated in the service of political domination. This helps to explain why ideological discourse tends to be expressed in pat slogans and ritualized formulae, in the various 'isms' of the modern world. Ideology is therefore intimately connected with the art of rhetoric – the ability to persuade through emotive phrases or force of conviction rather than rational argumentation: 'an ideology is operative and not thematic. It operates behind our backs, rather than appearing as a theme before our eyes. We think from it rather than about it' (Ricoeur 1981: 227). This indicates yet another function of ideology which must be combated: the distortion or inversion of social reality, which presupposes and incorporates the twin functions of integration and domination mentioned above. *Contra* Habermas, then, Ricoeur is emphatic that ideology is not fully accessible to critical reflection, insofar as 'social reality always has a symbolic constitution and incorporates an interpretation, in images and representations, of the social bond itself' (1981: 231). Such a realization casts doubt upon the Marxist position that the interpreter can pass judgement on an ideology yet escape its effects through an appeal to 'science' or some privileged insight into the *telos* of history *à la* Lukács. For Ricoeur, the fundamental *aporia* in this conception of critique is that it illegitimately presumes the possibility of 'total reflection', of a systematic and non-distorted understanding of social reality which is only 'scientific' by methodological fiat. This wrongly suppresses the inevitable question of the historical constitution of being, of the ontological features of human existence which involve ideology as much as 'tradition' or 'history' or even 'critique'.

None the less, Ricoeur feels that such criteria as 'truth' and 'objectivity' are still relevant with respect to the analysis of ideology, but only if we reformulate some of the more questionable ontological and epistemological theses of the hermeneutic tradition as it currently stands and adopt a more dialectical view of the relation between ideological and non-ideological knowledge. In short, he defends the position that hermeneutics can foster a critical stance – indeed, Ricoeur argues, the hermeneutic tradition cannot remain dispassionate, given the current pervasiveness of social antagonisms and the abject moral bankruptcy of most present-day political and social systems. He suggests that the issue of critique has never been convincingly addressed in the history of hermeneutics because, from Heidegger onwards, it has been preoccupied with a return to ontological foundations. This has displaced strictly epistemological questions relevant to critique in favour of an emphasis on the ontological structure of understanding. According to Ricoeur, the 'return trip' to epistemology is not possible within the confines of existing interpretations of hermeneutics – not simply because of the legacy of Heideggerian foundationalism, but because of the Gadamerian claim to universality which effectively denies *Verfremdung* or distancing upon which the possibility of objectifying knowledge is based.

However, Ricoeur feels that such an emphasis on the possibility (and desirability) of an alienating *Verfremdung* should not preclude a realization of the hermeneutical character of all understanding. This entails the acknowledgement of a partial, not total reflection; and degrees of, not absolute knowledge. In fact, he argues that hermeneutic interpretation merely represents a more self-conscious and explicit version of the kind of ontological understanding we constantly engage in during everyday social life. Thus, any 'objectifying knowledge' we may acquire of social reality is balanced off by a 'relation of belonging' to our tradition, our history and culture. We therefore unwittingly participate in all functions of ideology, including dissimulation and distortion.

Nevertheless, if a relation of belonging always 'precedes' the possibility of objectifying knowledge, the latter can still retain a degree of relative autonomy from the negative effects of ideology. The critical moment is made possible by the preservation of a measure of critical distance in the movement back towards the structure of pre-understanding which constitutes us. Thus, we must retain a distinction between prejudice – which reinforces distortion and deception – and pre-understanding – a legitimate 'belonging' which links a group to a shared history and culture.

But how is *Verfremdung* itself possible, in Ricoeur's view? The crux of his interpretive theory is premised on a distinction (initially advanced by the linguist Emile Benveniste) between language as 'system' and as 'discourse'. The former is an articulated totality, a system of differences between constituent units (phonemes, morphemes, etc.) which make up a particular language which can be conceptualized using established semiotic or structuralist methods. However, such an analysis can tell us nothing about semantics, because meaning resides at the level of the sentence, not the sign. While it is composed of signs, the sentence manifests certain 'synthetic' characteristics (referentiality, contextuality, etc.) which cannot be reduced to its constituent sign elements. Hence, the sentence is the basic building block of discourse, a phenomenon which is qualitatively different from language-as-system. This movement from system to discourse marks a number of important changes: diachrony replaces synchrony; semantics supplants the sign; and function or process attains prominence over structure. Ricoeur suggests that the endless creativity of language is premised on the inherent polysemy of words, which is best exemplified by the welter of metaphors, puns, synonyms and so on which permeate concrete language-use. The polysemic character of language implies at least two things: first, that discourse is always characterized by a 'surplus of meaning', which requires an interpretive phase in order to grasp its meaning and referentiality. Second, such an act of interpretation can only take place within a dialogic exchange between two or more acting subjects, which in turn facilitates the process of intersubjective communication.

Yet for Ricoeur the real focus of hermeneutics is not the sign or the sentence but the text. He conceives of the text as an extended sequence of units of written discourse, a 'structured totality' which cannot be reduced to the level of a sentence. It is also a work, a product of creative intellectual labour which evinces a particular genre (an underlying system of codes) and style (a certain configuration of rhetorical devices and characteristic narrative strategies which marks the work as singular and unique). In this context, Ricoeur is mainly referring to literary texts, but he also feels that ideology – being a meaningful symbol-system – can be incorporated into the model of the text he proposes. In any event, it is at this point where the issue of distanciation attains particular relevance, mainly because he argues that *Verfremdung* is made possible by the very nature of the text itself. A text for Ricoeur is 'any discourse fixed by writing'. This act of 'fixation' or inscription imparts to the text a certain degree of autonomy which makes it qualitatively different from spoken discourse. The upshot is that the text (unlike the speech-act) is no longer dependent on the immediate dialogic situation for its meaning. Accordingly, the text is 'decontextualized' and thereby attains a high degree of independence from the socio-historical conditions of its production, from the intentions of the author, and from audience expectations. But more importantly for the critique of ideology, the text is freed from the constraints of 'ostensive reference'. Since it is unable to manifest a direct or ostensive reference, the written text opens up a second-order, non-ostensive form of reference: it projects a 'mode of being', a 'proposed world' which is uncovered in front of the text. The text transgresses closure because the world it projects outward can be 'appropriated' or recontextualized in a number of different ways concomitant with the socio-historical context of its reading-reception. Ricoeur considers such an 'emancipation of the text' to be of the utmost importance for a critical distancing in the act of interpretation. More specifically, he feels that it is possible to respond productively to the autonomy of the text by a complex interpretive process which can potentially overcome the pervasive dichotomy between explanation and understanding. This 'dialectic of interpretation' involves several stages. The first phase is a quasi-structuralist analysis of the immanent relations of the text. Yet although this 'objectification' of the text is necessary, Ricoeur feels that it is not sufficient. For in order fully to grasp the non-ostensive references mentioned above, a hermeneutic reading must be re-introduced in order to restore the text to 'living communication'. Although mediated by the formal arrangements of the text, this phase goes beyond 'explanation' and aims at a reconstructive understanding of the world it projects. Only then is a 'depth semantics' of the text possible, which seeks to close the gap between a Gadamerian duality of 'truth' and 'method':

> . . . writing tears itself away free of the limits of face-to-face dialogue and becomes the condition for discourse itself *becoming text.* It is to hermeneutics that falls the task of exploring the implications of this becoming-text for the work for interpretation. [. . .] The most important consequence of all this is that an end is put to the Cartesian and Fichtean – and to an extent Husserlian – ideal of the subject's transparency to itself. To understand oneself is to understand oneself as one confronts the text and to receive from it the conditions for a self other than that which first undertakes the reading. Neither of the two subjectivities, neither that of the author nor that of the reader, is thus primary in the sense of an original presence of the self to itself.

> (Ricoeur 1983: 193)

This has several crucial implications for the nature of ideological critique.[28] Because the text opens up an imaginative dimension which may contradict 'given' reality, it holds up the possibility of a critique of the real: 'A hermeneutics of the power-to-be thus turns itself towards a critique of ideology, of which it constitutes the most fundamental possibility' (Ricoeur 1981: 94). Moreover, he argues, if it is correct to assert that the task of hermeneutics is not to discover a hidden meaning behind the text, but rather to unfold a world in front of it, then one does not appropriate the 'intentions' of the author but the meaning of the text itself. The subject is enriched and self-awareness enhanced through this encounter with the proposed worlds which are unfolded by the interpretive process. If such a critique of ideology can partially distance itself from its prior embeddedness in pre-understanding, it can thereby effect the passage from illusion to knowledge. Again, however, Ricoeur stresses that this knowledge must be understood as remaining partial and fragmentary. Its very non-completeness is a necessary result of its hermeneutical grounding in a relation of belonging, from which a critical distanciation can only be relatively successful. Hence, the critique of ideology is a never-ending process. Although critical knowledge aims to transcend the grip of ideology, the latter remains a necessary reference point from which to conduct the search for understanding: 'nothing is more necessary today than to renounce the arrogance of critique and to carry on with patience the endless work of distancing and renewing our historical substance' (Ricoeur 1981: 246).

Perhaps more importantly, however, the critique of ideology not only cannot completely remove itself from the influence of ideology: it must acknowledge a utopian dimension as well.[29] This is one of the most interesting (and most often overlooked) aspects of Ricoeur's critical hermeneutics and, as I shall demonstrate later on, it can be fruitfully applied to Bakhtin's social philosophy. Ricoeur seeks to conceptualize ideology and utopia not as irreconcilably opposed concepts, but as complementary elements of a more inclusive system of social action. If we delve beneath the surface content of particular (mainly literary) utopias, he suggests that it is possible to discover an underlying 'utopian mode', a rich and complex grammar of 'cultural imagination'. Utopia represents a peculiarly well-suited vantage-point whence to view our own social arrangements, because these are suddenly illuminated in a new and very different light. Without such an imaginative leap 'outside' our own socio-historical situation, the critique of ideology would lack force and conviction. If an important element of the functioning of ideology is social integration, argues Ricoeur, utopia operates as 'social subversion'. That is, whilst ideology operates to produce a hidden 'surplus value' of belief vis-à-vis the legitimacy of authority, in order to secure the normative adherence of the majority of the population, utopia exposes this surplus to public view and poses awkward questions about the moral and political validity of the system itself:

> This development of new, alternative perspectives defines utopia's most basic function. May we not say that imagination itself – through its utopian function – has a *constitutive* role in helping us *rethink* the nature of our social life? Is not utopia – this leap outside – the way in which we radically rethink what is family, what is consumption, what is authority, what is religion, and so on? Does not the fantasy of an alternative society and its exteriorization 'nowhere' work as one of the most formidable contestations of what is?
>
> (Ricoeur 1986: 16)

At the same time, however, Ricoeur suggests that the 'pathology' of ideology has a counterpart in the sphere of utopia: utopia's very 'nowhereness', which gives it its rhetorical potency and critical force, also results in a kind of escapism, a headlong retreat from the possible into the manifestly impossible. At its best, then, utopia is a formidable weapon in the struggle against the negative effects of ideology and the structure of illegitimate authority and domination; yet at its worst, it represents a kind of doleful nostalgia for an unrealizable 'paradise lost' that is perhaps no less debilitating or distorting than ideology itself: 'Escapism is the eclipse of praxis, the denial of the logic of action. [This] eclipse of praxis may be referred to as the flight into writing and the affinity of the utopian mode for a specific literary genre, to the extent that writing becomes a substitute for acting' (1976a: 26). Yet ideology and utopia are none the less intimately intertwined; both are inescapable elements of what Castoriadis has termed *l'imaginaire social*.[30] Each is inconceivable without the other. Ideology mirrors the social order, whilst simultaneously occluding an understanding of its social constitution; utopia, on the other hand, aims at the dissolution of this order through projecting a vision of an alternative existence. The dialectical tension between these two phenomena results in a permanent oscillation between fantasy and praxis, and between escape and return:

> We only take possession of the creative power of imagination through a relation to such figures of false consciousness as ideology and utopia. It is as though we have to call on the 'healthy' function of ideology to cure the madness of utopia and as though the critique of ideologies can only be carried out by a conscience capable of regarding itself from the point of view of 'nowhere'.
>
> (Ricoeur 1976a: 28)

Of all the thinkers examined in this chapter, Ricoeur's 'critical hermeneutics' is arguably closest to that of Bakhtin's dialogism. Indeed, there are often startling similarities:

(i) Interpretation for both should aim at the preservation of the inherent metaphorical richness of the text, its polyvalent 'surplus of meaning', in order to avoid the arbitrary reduction of polysemic meaning to a monolithic, all-embracing ideological perspective. As Ricoeur writes: 'hermeneutics aims at demystifying a symbolism by unmasking the unavowed forces that are concealing within it, it aims at a re-collection of meaning in its richest, its most elevated, most spiritual diversity' (1983: 192–3). Or, as Bakhtin says:

'Complete maximum rectification would inevitably lead to the disappearance of the infinitude and bottomlessness of meaning' (1986: 162). Thus, the inevitable conflicts over meaning which result from the profusion of interpretive approaches is not to be decried as some kind of epistemological fall from grace; rather, such a multiplicity of perspectives makes possible a more nuanced and well-rounded understanding of the object.

(ii) The outcome of the interpretive or hermeneutic process is for Ricoeur no less than Bakhtin (and here they would agree with Gadamer) practical, leading to the enhancement of self-understanding through the encounter with other cultures and texts. Through a solidaristic recognition of the integrity of 'otherness', one can 'burst into the circle of life, to become one among other people', as Bakhtin puts it. As such, both thinkers would agree that any 'emancipatory interest' which animates the critique of ideology must be connected to the creative reinterpretation of cultural heritage and to the practical-moral concerns of particular social groups. It cannot be grounded in an abstract, rationalist construction, such as Habermas's conception of the 'ideal speech situation'. This explains their shared position that ideological criticism can have no epistemological guarantees. Yet, at the same time, neither theorist is blind to the realities of systemic, institutionalized domination, and they equally maintain that the ingrained features of tradition must be brought to consciousness and contested. As such, our inherited structure of prejudices or ideological horizon is not (*pace* Gadamer) more or less fixed and immutable, but potentially open to critical scrutiny and re-evaluation, if not on an arbitrary or wholesale basis.[31]

(iii) Both stress the intrinsically dialogical nature of this process, and they equally affirm the centrality of reflection and self-knowledge vis-à-vis their respective philosophical anthropologies. As Ricoeur puts it, interpretation 'represents a process by which, in the interplay of question and answer, the interlocutors collectively determine the contextual values which structure their conversation' (1981: 107). Moreover, both regard the hermeneutic study of culture not as a social scientific 'method' in the strict sense (although Ricoeur feels that it is necessary to incorporate a more properly methodological phase in the form of structuralist analysis), but as a self-conscious 'working up' of the kind of reflexive social interaction each of us engages in on a day-to-day basis. Bakhtin, therefore, would doubtless concur with Ricoeur's following statement:

> A reflexive philosophy considers the most radical philosophical problems to be those which concern the possibility of *self-understanding* as the subject of the operation of knowing, willing, evaluating, etc. Reflexion is the act of turning back upon itself by which a subject grasps in a moment of intellectual clarity and moral responsibility, the unifying principle of the operations among which it is dispersed and forgets itself as a subject.
>
> (1983: 188)

(iv) Both agree on the inescapably lingual dimension of human existence and cognition and the central role played by symbolic practice in the constitution of social life – and again, here they would agree with Gadamer that Habermas's separation of instrumental and communicative action represents a reductive materialism. Yet, at the same time, both would acknowledge that Habermas is correct in identifying the sphere of communicative interaction as the *locus classicus* of ideological domination. Thus, all three would unequivocally reject Gadamer's position that tradition is a consensus which is 'given' in being, that genuine understanding is somehow 'built in' to our ontological connection with tradition. By contrast, they would assert that any truly critical hermeneutic approach must address the issue of the disruption of human communication in the service of political or cultural domination.

(v) Finally, what makes a (non-subjectivistic or non-relativistic) interpretation itself possible is not only a shared connection with the text or practice being studied – i.e., a common ontology of tradition – but also a factor of critical distancing which is just as much an aspect of *Dasein* as 'belongingness'. Bakhtin, for instance, emphasizes that the self–other relation is a form of 'outsideness' which should be 'taken advantage of' in the act of understanding an alien text or culture. Both therefore make the crucial transition from the incipient idealism of Husserlian phenomenology, which places an *epoché* on the constitutive influences of the life-world, to a more 'worldly' hermeneutics which makes the practical understanding of social life a guiding concern.

Not surprisingly, however, important differences remain between the two theorists. From a Bakhtinian point of view, Ricoeur is overly concerned with the 'objective' meaning of a text. Despite his rejection of Habermas's turn to nomothetic knowledge to 'solve' the problem of subjectivism, Ricoeur makes much of the claim that distanciation and the method of depth hermeneutics he advocates are an important guarantee of objectivity, because they take their cue from the text *an sich* rather than the subjective intentions of the author (or actor, in the case of social practice).[32] This approach is in fact not dissimilar to that of Habermas, despite Ricoeur's assertions to the contrary, because it appeals to an explanatory phase within a more general process of understanding which is designed to limit interpretive bias. The major difference is that Ricoeur claims that linguistics as an exemplary model is indigenous to the human sciences, and that he is therefore not advocating a version of methodological naturalism. But this begs the question: is this strategy substantially different from Habermas's invocation of a nomothetic social science? Or, to put it a another way, does Ricoeur really transcend the pervasive dichotomy between *Erklärung* and *Verstehen*, as he claims to, or does he in fact reinforce it?[33] Bakhtin would put little stock in such a criterion of objectivity, at least as Ricoeur seems to understand it, because he would agree with Gadamer that such a desire is symptomatic of an unfortunate reifying or monologizing tendency on the part of modern thought.

It is therefore doubtful whether Bakhtin would fully subscribe to Ricoeur's strategy of placing a Husserlian *epoché* on the text in order to consider it from the vantage-point of 'pure interiority', even if this is construed as a temporary phase within a wider interpretive dialectic. That is, whilst he agrees with Ricoeur that interpretive inquiry cannot aim at a reconstruction of the author's intentionality, this does not mean we can completely disregard the ostensive references of the text. It is true that Bakhtin does occasionally acknowledge the preliminary importance of formal analysis. For instance, Bakhtin maintains that there are different 'phases' in the process of understanding, which incorporate a stage of formal analysis as an initial (but necessary) step in the path to what he calls 'creative thinking'. This comprehension of the formal structure of the text must, however, be supplemented by an 'evaluative-semantic' understanding of the text or 'work'. Bakhtin (1986: 110) also suggests that although all communication is a form of externalization, writing is a much more permanent form of objectification than its spoken counterpart. Accordingly, the possibilities for reflection and critique are much enhanced in the former case: the fixation of writing in discourse means that it can be cognized at a 'distance', insofar as the interpreter is at some remove from the original context of discursive production.[34] None the less, Bakhtin is much less sanguine than Ricoeur about the capacity for structuralist-inspired approaches to vouchsafe a distanciated or objective reading of a given text. Texts for Bakhtin are neither purely 'internal' or 'external'; they are constituted through practical human action, through an ongoing 'linguistic praxis' which is itself located within wider social and historical relations. Signification in any form always contains a referential dimension – one cannot legitimately posit a moment of pure immanence, even if only for analytical purposes. There is no 'ideal text' for Bakhtin, no pristine or 'virgin' meaning which is beyond dispute or further argumentation; to suppose so is for him one of the defining features of monologic thought. Moreover, Bakhtin strongly argues that all texts are constructed with a particular audience in mind (even if an 'ideal' one), which he feels radically alters the nature of the communicative process itself. This is true not only of verbal dialogue, where the addressee's role vis-à-vis the utterer's total 'speech plan' is admittedly at its most apparent; it is also an important feature of even the most complex and internally stratified written genres (scientific treatises, novels, etc.): 'the work, like the rejoinder in dialogue, is oriented toward the response of the other (others), toward his active dialogic understanding' (1986: 75).[35] This, of course, is the crux of his (and the Circle's) critique of structuralist and formalist approaches, which should require no elaboration here. Thus, as Robert Ulin adroitly emphasizes, Ricoeur's reliance on the semiotic analysis of immanent textual relations is at odds with the Bakhtinian conception because it invariably reifies what he terms the 'living contradictions' of social life, contradictions which can only work themselves out on the terrain of history and not the 'text' as such:

> Because critique becomes identified for Ricoeur with the self-referential, logical coherence of a text, constructed solely on the basis of its internal structure, then the movement to comprehension, or the restoration of the text's reference on a

new level, merely reproduces its immediacy – the very limitation
for which he has criticized naive consciousness.

(Ulin 1984: 121)

THE POLITICS OF INTERPRETATION

Thus, in many ways, Bakhtin is a more 'sociological' (and certainly
a more historical) thinker than Ricoeur. He is adamant that one
cannot arbitrarily ignore the illocutionary or rhetorical force of an
utterance; accordingly, language must be conceptualized as a
specific form of social practice which is always embedded in
particular social and historical contexts. Despite this, however,
Bakhtin does share with Ricoeur a recognition of the importance
of the recontextualization of past works in the hermeneutic
encounter, in which the process of interpretation encourages the
text to 'speak' to our most immediate and pressing concerns
regardless of this text's cultural-historical distance from our own
situation. That is, Bakhtin would agree with Ricoeur that the
'world of the text' is a world which can play a vital role vis-à-vis our
self-awareness and our moral and political choices in the here and
now. Interpretation is therefore an eminently practical affair, and
it carries with it an inherently political element. Bakhtin, for his
part, is as much concerned with the context of textual reception as
production, which is why such an ostensibly innocuous and
esoteric study of a 16th-century French novelist can be also read as
both a devastating attack on the configuration of political and
cultural power in Stalinist Russia and a heartfelt paean to
intellectual freedom. This, in turn, identifies Bakhtin's 'politics of
interpretation' – that is, the specific criteria by which he articulates
and justifies a particular critical strategy. As outlined earlier, this
justification is not primarily epistemological, but rather
ethico-political. Bakhtin's construal of particular readings or texts
as 'monological' or as 'dialogical' is based on a hermeneutically-
informed assessment of the potential threat a particular signifying
practice holds for the dialogic integrity of the social world. For
Bakhtin, not all discourses are 'equal', or equally valid, because
such discourses have real effects in society, and because they are
connected to linguistic, cultural and social phenomena which are
simply too powerful to ignore. Some discursive practices are implicated in the hegemonic organization and unification of the life-
world in a manner which benefits the ruling groups in society;

other languages, 'voices', texts and so on actively resist these centralizing processes, and therefore must be understood and encouraged. This stance is in turn based on a particular philosophical anthropology – that is, on a conception of the needs, capacities and desires of human beings, and also upon an alternative vision of human community which is non-alienated, egalitarian, and most certainly non-capitalistic (or at least non-bureaucratic). Therefore, Bakhtin's critical strategy is one of 'rescuing' a given text from the dead weight of sedimented dominant meanings, and to challenge this ideological closure by 'opening up' the text to a plethora of different readings or 'reaccentuations' which 'strive to expose and develop all the semantic possibilities embedded within a given point of view' (1986: 69). It is possible ideologically to reinflect or transform the significance of a text (given the appropriate symbolic and cultural resources) because, as stressed above, the text for Bakhtin contains no absolute, fixed meaning. And the touchstone of the textual strategy is in Bakhtin's view represented by the carnivalesque, which rides roughshod over the self-validating truisms of bourgeois reason. The culture of folk laughter explodes inherited meaning from within through a violent confrontation with the libidinal energy of the collective body and the unpredictable mésalliances of an inverted carnival logic in order to celebrate the 'joyful relativity of all structure and order'.[36]

This is not to suggest that Bakhtin believes a consensus over meaning to be impossible. Whilst he does tend to stress the conflictual or antagonistic aspects of language, Bakhtin also notes that 'agreement' is a very important aspect of the dialogic, and at one point he sounds very Habermasian when he describes truth as a form of 'model utterance'. This preoccupation receives its most sustained attention in his study of Dostoevsky, where he discusses at some length how the dialogic tradition in Western society (at least since the time of Socrates) provides an exemplar of an unstructured approach to the 'testing' of the validity of ideas and viewpoints through the auspices of free and open debate.[37] As a kind of Kantian categorical imperative, dialogue must be considered as an end in itself, not as a means to impose one's will upon another. This Socratic or dialogic tradition provides in Bakhtin's eyes a vital counterweight to the Enlightenment or rationalist version of truth, which negates the possibility of difference and subsumes all dialogue under a 'single impersonal truth'. Dogmatism, then, makes dialogue impossible; but Bakhtin equally rejects relativism, because it assumes *a priori* the incommensurability of views and thereby renders authentic dialogue unnecessary. By contrast, Bakhtin argues that there is no good *prima facie* reason why a 'unified truth' cannot be expressed through a plurality of perspectives, wherein agreement is premised upon an uncoerced exchange of views but which simultaneously recognizes the integrity of the interlocutors concerned: 'Truth is not born nor is it to be found inside the head of an individual person, it is born *between* people collectively searching for truth, in the process of their dialogic interaction' (1984: 110).

This is not to imply that Bakhtin subscribes to a kind of supra-individual version of consensus – the right to refuse agreement, to withdraw from dialogue without fear of retribution, is also a right that Bakhtin defends: 'Truth is unjust when it concerns the depths of *someone* else's personality' (1984: 60). To enter into dialogue must be an act of voluntary 'confession', for only then can we avoid the crushing weight of 'externalizing second-hand definitions' and allow a glimmer of the 'unfinalizable something in man' to stand revealed.[38] Bakhtin remains relatively optimistic that a 'carnival sense of the world' can break down the hierarchical social and cultural barriers that divide people and the inherited structures of monologic thought which shackle consciousness and inhibit genuine understanding. The 'liberation and de-reification of the human being' which carnival makes possible encourages a kind of sensuous familiarity with the world and with other individuals, in a manner which sensitizes us to the true ambivalence and complexity of things and human experience itself.

THE UTOPIAN MODE

Bakhtin therefore embraces a distinctive utopian vision in order both to criticize the monologic tendencies within contemporary society and project an image of an alternative set of social arrangements. In this, he goes against the grain of much of the Marxist tradition – except, of course, that 'warm stream' within Western Marxism which has been more favourably disposed toward the value of utopian theorizing and ethical humanism as represented by the work of Ernst Bloch, and to a lesser extent Walter Benjamin and Theodor Adorno.[39] It also indicates the perspicacity of Ricoeur's schematic dialectic connecting utopia and ideology. Bakhtin, that is, utilizes an image of the carnivalesque (and a related constellation of phenomena – folk laughter, 'grotesque realism', etc.) in order to 'defamiliarize' the present state of affairs, to historicize that which is generally taken to be immutable and eternal, and to relativize abstract claims to truth through a 'gay parody of official reason':

> [Carnival] discloses the potentiality of an entirely different world, of another order, another way of life. It leads men out of the confines of the apparent (false) unity, of the indisputable and stable. Born of folk humor, it always represents in one form or another, through these or other means, the return of Saturn's golden age to earth – the living possibility of its return. [The] utopian element, the 'golden age,' was disclosed in the pre-Romantic period not for the sake of abstract thought or of inner experience; it is lived by the whole man, in thought and body. [. . .] The principle of laughter and the carnival spirit on which grotesque is based destroys this limited seriousness and all pretense of an extratemporal meaning and unconditional value of necessity. It frees human consciousness, thought, and imagination for new potentialities.
>
> (1968: 48–9)

It is ironic to note that in one of their many exchanges, Gadamer criticizes Habermas for justifying his critique of ideology on the basis of an implicit appeal to some kind of 'anarchistic utopia'. Gadamer, in common with a number of prominent Marxist thinkers, clearly regards this as unacceptable; yet Bakhtin would undoubtedly embrace this perspective wholeheartedly. However, the utopia that Bakhtin has in mind is not the model of organic order and harmony that has been the stock in trade of literary utopias at least since Plato's *Republic*. It is rather a ceaselessly dynamic one, always remaining confrontational, unpredictable, and self-mocking – a perpetual Ovidian metamorphosis on a grand scale. Thus, whilst carnival does represent a 'tradition' of sorts, as a genre or 'cultural template' it incorporates a Benjaminian 'narrative of the dispossessed' and not a narrative of the kind of homogeneous, abstract community that Gadamer seems to envisage. Carnival is for Bakhtin the 'antibody' living within a pathological social body, always threatening to rupture the latter from within. In other words, carnival is simultaneously continuous with the contemporary social world and desperately at odds with it.[40] It is not therefore a species of 'bad utopianism', for Bakhtin clearly believes that a carnivalistic culture of the people actually existed in the not-too-distant past, and that it continues to be a potent (albeit rarely appreciated or understood) force in the present.[41] Whether Bakhtin is historically correct in this regard has been the subject of intense debate – certainly, Bakhtin does gloss over the negative aspects of carnival, and romanticizes certain aspects of what Brecht liked to call the 'bad old days'. Some of these issues will be addressed in the concluding chapter. Nevertheless, this realization should not obscure the fecundity and originality of Bakhtin's vision; nor should it blind us to the necessity of retaining a utopian moment in the critique of ideology, as Ricoeur and others have convincingly argued.[42] I conclude with Dominick LaCapra's cogent thoughts on this subject:

> For a variety of reasons, the Marxist heritage has shared with those it criticizes a dearth of creative institutional thinking addressed to the problem of alternative social contexts. In Marx this lack of alternatives may be explained by a combination of factors: the suspicion of utopianism, the commitment to immanent critique, and a faith in the proletariat as the revolutionary subject of history. More recently, the realization that faith in the proletariat is problematic at best, and the recognition that even immanent critiques require alternative goals, have often led either to an admission that modern conditions do not permit a bond between theory and practice or the turn toward utopianism of a completely wishful and contentless sort. The great refusal and pure messianic desire are themselves less genuine alternatives than desperate complements.
>
> (1983: 324)

Chapter 5

Bakhtin, ideology and neo-structuralism

The word, the word is a great thing.
Fyodor Dostoevsky

INTRODUCTION

In the preceding chapters, I have characterized Bakhtin's approach to the theory and critique of ideology in a primarily analytical vein, stressing his affinities with the Western Marxian project of *Ideologiekritik* and with the humanist and interpretive preoccupations of hermeneutical theory. For this penultimate chapter, by contrast, I wish to pursue a different line of inquiry. I argued in chapter three that Bakhtin's development of a non-epistemological, non-reductionistic account of ideology, which he conjoins with a sophisticated philosophy of language, represents a valuable corrective to many of the shortcomings to be found within the received view of ideology. Moreover, I suggested that Bakhtin's writings anticipated (and even participated in, albeit obliquely, through the early writings of Julia Kristeva) the emergence of a not dissimilar problematic in the 1960s and 70s which followed the dissolution of the orthodox theory of ideology. This realignment was most strongly demonstrated in French intellectual circles, with the work of Roland Barthes, Louis Althusser and Michel Foucault (including their various disciples and fellow-travellers). Yet given this partial convergence between Bakhtin and the structuralist and poststructuralist traditions, we would seem to be faced with something of a dilemma. The task that confronts us at this point is to trace the genealogy of this theoretical development and, in so doing, to differentiate between the Bakhtinian and the neo-structuralist approaches not only with respect to the conceptualization of 'ideology' as a theoretical object but also to the critical practices bound up with its interpretation and critique. For various reasons, I have chosen to concentrate on the representative writings of Roland Barthes and Michel Foucault. An equally important concern will be to vindicate Bakhtin's superiority in certain crucial areas vis-à-vis a politically-engaged cultural-ideological criticism, particularly with respect to what I term the 'problem of resistance' in contemporary social theory.

IDEOLOGY AND THE 'LINGUISTIC TURN'

Despite the theoretical alterations and innovations which were developed in the first half of the 20th century with respect to the theory and critique of ideology, virtually all the figures concerned (Lenin, Lukács, Gramsci, etc.) claimed direct inspiration from Marx's own writings and affirmed their fidelity to the (often ill-defined) principles of historical materialism. By the 1960s dissatisfaction with the Marxian problematic was rife. It was widely alleged, for example, that the construal of ideology as a form of consciousness ('false' or otherwise) succumbed to a form of individualistic psychologism – that is, to the bourgeois myth of 'man' as an integrated, self-defining subject. Alternatively, the characterization of ideology as the 'belief system' or 'world-view' of a particular class or social group was held to be overly vague (not to mention 'essentialist'), and ill-equipped to illuminate how ideology was actually connected to particular social practices and how it functioned to reinforce existing relations of power and authority. Yet possibly the major objection was that there had been little attempt within classical Marxism to explore the range of articulations between ideology and language; little had changed since V. N. Voloshinov himself wrote in 1929 that language was a phenomenon that was 'untouched or only perfunctorily touched upon by the hands of Marxism's founders'.[1] The most extended commentary of Marx's on the subject of language occurs in *The German Ideology*, where he strongly affirms its inherently social and historical nature,[2] and also in the *Grundrisse* (1973: 163), where he suggests that human thought and cognition can only be expressed through language. But aside from these scattered (if tantalizing) remarks, Marx himself did not give the subject much attention, and given the positivistic and scientistic emphasis of most post-Engelsian Marxism, the question of the status of linguistic phenomena (no less than the issue of ideology) languished for decades.[3]

STRUCTURALISM AND SEMIOLOGY: IDEOLOGY AS MYTH

In the absence of a viable Marxist approach to language and linguistic questions, the inspiration for a theory synthesizing ideology and language primarily came from Ferdinand de Saussure and the related work of the Prague School (today referred to as structural linguistics). Voloshinov noted that at the time he was writing the majority of Russian and European linguists were 'under the determinative influence of Saussure and his disciples'. Yet he could not possibly have foreseen the enormous impact that Saussure's pronouncements on language were to have on the human sciences in the latter half of the 20th century, and that the 'structural allegory' was to revolutionize such disparate disciplines as anthropology, literary criticism, and psychoanalysis.[4] The model of structuralist linguistics is of crucial relevance to the (post-Marxian) theory of ideology, since it was structuralism that virtually monopolized the attempt to forge a theoretical connection between language and ideology – or until, that is, the (re)discovery of the writings of Bakhtin, Voloshinov and Medvedev. As Callinicos (1982) has astutely pointed out, Saussure's theories neatly encapsulated and foreshadowed most of the themes eventually formulated by the discipline of structuralism. Saussure himself actually devoted very little attention to 'semiology' proper, although he did coin the original term from the Greek word *semeion*, meaning 'sign'. However, he did hint at the possibility that language (if properly understood) could constitute the foundation for a general 'science of signs' encompassing all areas of human life – customs, rituals, 'forms of etiquette', and so on. Accordingly, it was left to thinkers as diverse as Roland Barthes, Jacques Lacan and Claude Lévi-Strauss to extend Saussure's ideas into previously uncharted areas of social life. As György Márkus has written, structuralism was distinctive insofar as it grafted a rejection of the Cartesian model of the human subject onto a preoccupation with the formal properties of language. Although these developments were (at least originally) independent from each other, by the late 1950s they

... became interlocked into one characteristic, broad structure
of thought that can be defined through the fact that in it
language and linguistic communication became considered as
the *universal paradigm* of all forms of human intercourse and
human objectification. Language, accordingly, is treated, not
simply as the central or even the sole remaining subject matter
of philosophical enquiry (as in early logical positivism and
analytical philosophy), but as the starting point to recapture
and re-embrace in a meaningful way the metaphysical, anthro-
pological, and social concerns of traditional philosophy.

(Márkus 1984: 105)

Lévi-Strauss was probably the crucial interlocutor in this process,
in that he first mapped out the methodological connection
between structural linguistics and cultural analysis. Accordingly,
his work proved to be a crucial reference point in the later writings
of Barthes, Greimas and even Althusser.[5] Drawing on the phono-
logical research of Trubetzkoy and Jakobson, Lévi-Strauss argued
that structural linguistics could serve as a heuristic model for the
scientific analysis of culture. But rather than concentrate on the
empirical manifestations of language or symbolic systems, he
argued that the proper object of analysis was the 'unconscious
infrastructure' or 'deep structure' which generated these surface
phenomena. Of particular interest to Lévi-Strauss was the predominance of mythical systems in tribal societies. He argued that
the significance of a myth could not be grasped by examining an
isolated feature (the 'mytheme'); rather, one had to reconstruct
the underlying rules of transformation which made possible the
production of any mythical narrative. Such myths were for Lévi-
Strauss 'structuring structures' – they represented only one
example of the universal human impulse to categorize and classify
'reality' into cognitively manageable units. Perhaps most contro-
versially, Lévi-Strauss insisted that mythical thought was not
confined to pre-industrial societies. On the contrary: modern
political ideologies had become the site of mythological thought
par excellence. The reinterpretation of epochal historical events
(such as the French Revolution) approximated the structure of
myth, because these events were projected as 'timeless' or
ahistorical and because they produced narratives which could be
mobilized to legitimate existing forms of social organization.[6]

Until recently, when he has now come to view Marxism as a

dogmatic ideology of modernization, Lévi-Strauss has claimed fidelity to the precepts of historical materialism. This identification with the Marxist tradition did not, however, extend to the examination of the possible connections between myth and power or ideology, and nor did his scattered comments on the possible 'mythological' aspects of contemporary political ideologies add up to anything like a coherent theory of ideology-as-myth. Nevertheless, Lévi-Strauss's writings did have a demonstrable impact on an author whose work has a more direct bearing on the critique of ideology: Roland Barthes. Through an eclectic synthesis of semiology, Marxism, literary criticism and structural linguistics – best represented by his important work *Mythologies* (1973) – Barthes sought to develop a 'double theoretical framework', encompassing a semiotic analysis of how the language of mass culture operated as well as a politicized critique of this ideological language. For Barthes, ideology in modern society is primarily manifested in the form of myths. Myths are 'second-order' signifying systems which are utilized by the capitalist class to enforce a particular network of connotations or signifying associations which both express and reinforce the dominant view of reality. The very omnipresence of such mythical representations means that bourgeois culture is inserted into a wide range of socio-cultural practices – advertising, family life, public ceremonies, religion and so on. Whilst he suggests that 'myth in fact belongs to the province of a general science, coextensive with linguistics, which is semiology' (1973: 111), Barthes in fact advances an important distinction between the linguistic sign and the mythical sign. The latter incorporates and is parasitic upon the former, insofar as the linguistic sign constitutes the signifier in the metalinguistic system of myth. Linguistic signs, being denotative, are transparent and unambiguous. The generation of meaning here is manifest: because it exists on the surface, there is no need for a complex decoding process. Connotative or mythical signs, by contrast, are latent or hidden. Most individuals do not delve below the surface content of such myths to uncover the ideological structures embedded within them.[7] In Barthes's view, myth 'gets hold' of the language-object of the existing linguistic system and transforms it into 'empty, parasitical form' which impoverishes meaning: '*myth hides nothing*: its goal is to distort, not to make disappear' (1973: 121).

Thus, myth-as-ideology functions by naturalization, by transforming history and culture into nature. Myth functions by transforming historical intention into naturalized justification, contingency into eternal necessity. Praxis and agency are unceremoniously deleted from the mythical landscape. Myth is a form of depoliticized speech: it does not deny the existence of things, but it sanitizes them, simplifies them, robs them of all ambiguity and equivocality. It thereby imparts to them a natural and eternal legitimization. Such euphemisms obscure the reality of struggles and contradiction in the womb of bourgeois society. Myth replaces an awareness of these contradictions with a 'blissful clarity', in which meaning is conceived of as self-evident because it is restricted to surface appearances. The decoding and demystification of myth is therefore the responsibility of the critical intellectual who, by judicious application of the semiotic method, can lay bare the underlying processes which organize mythical representations. This 'semiological guerrilla warfare', as Umberto Eco (1987) once called it, makes possible a 'cynical' reading of myth, one that challenges a moribund and sclerotic bourgeois culture. Only through the semiological reading of texts, objects and various cultural practices, Barthes maintains, can their arbitrary and culturally-constructed character be exposed, and the ontological distinction between history and nature be re-established. Towards the end of 'Myth Today', Barthes provides an eloquent indictment of the dead, motionless world created by myth, and he raises a stirring clarion call to resist its effects:

> [Every] day and everywhere, man is stopped by myths, referred by them to this motionless prototype which lives in his place, stifles him in the manner of a huge internal parasite and assigns to his activity the narrow limits within which he is allowed to suffer without upsetting the world: bourgeois pseudo-physis is in the fullest sense a prohibition for man against inventing himself. Myths are nothing but this ceaseless, untiring solicitation, this insidious and inflexible demand that all men recognize themselves in this image, eternal yet bearing a date, which was built of them one day as for all time. For the Nature, in which they are locked up under the pretext of being eternalized, is nothing but an Usage. And it is this Usage, however lofty, that they must take into hand and transform.
>
> (1973: 157–8)

STRUCTURALISM AND IDEOLOGY: ELEMENTS OF A BAKHTINIAN CRITIQUE

The structuralist problematic has been enormously influential over the years, and Barthes's particular brand of semiology is certainly no exception. Following Callinicos (1982: 30–1), we can summarize the guiding themes of 'classical' structuralist or semiotic thought which are of relevance to the critical analysis of language and ideology as follows: (i) the thesis that Saussure's version of structural linguistics (or some variation of it) provides the paradigmatic reference-point for social theory and philosophy; (ii) the decentring of the subject, and hence a pronounced hostility toward phenomenological and existentialist philosophies; (iii) that language is a relational totality in which the signifier attains predominance over the signified, and a concomitant reluctance to address the referential status of (spoken or written) utterances; and (iv), that a wide range of cultural and discursive phenomena can be 'decoded' in a manner analogous to the reading of a text. In bringing these themes into the mainstream of cultural and ideological analysis, structuralism has radically challenged the naive empiricism of the social sciences on a number of fronts. Significant amongst these is the assertion that there is no 'natural' level of human existence which is 'prior to' or 'outside' the signifying matrix provided by the linguistic and cultural system in question. Consequently, the standard positivist assertion that access to the 'truth' is possible via the systematic recording of sense-data is decisively rejected, in that such a position ignores the fact that observation itself can only take place within a pre-existent dimension of representation. Any viable analysis of ideology must therefore proceed from the analysis of the formal properties of linguistic and cultural-mythological systems, and not from the individual's (necessarily limited and distorted) experiential understanding of these systems. One must grasp the underlying codes, the unconscious 'cultural grammar' which organizes social life and makes it intelligible. Given that such codes naturalize and reinforce a particular view of reality, they are a potent site of the reproduction of bourgeois ideology. As Vernon has cogently summarized this point:

If ideologies are structures [...] then they are not 'images' nor 'concepts' (we can say, they are not contents) but are sets of rules which determine an organization and the functioning of images and concepts. [. . .] Ideology is a system of coding reality and not a determined set of coded messages. [In] this way, ideology becomes autonomous in relation to the consciousness or intention of its agents: these may be conscious of their point of view about social forms but not of the semantic conditions (rules and categories or codification) which make possible these points of view. [. . .] From this point of view, then, an 'ideology' may be defined as a system of semantic rules to generate messages. [I]t is one of the many levels of organization of messages, from the viewpoint of their semantic properties.

(1971: 68)

Such an approach is certainly valuable, if only because it draws our attention to the underlying and often unconscious principles which serve to codify and organize cultural texts. It is therefore important to reaffirm the structuralist premise that we never experience social life in a direct or unmediated fashion. We only relate to social and natural reality through the prior mediation of a culturally-constructed system of codes and signs. This system of representations makes the social world meaningful and intelligible; it imparts to us a definite cultural competence which enables us to act and interact in the social world. It is Barthes's specific intention, however, to sensitize us to the fact that these signifying practices are not neutral vehicles of pure, unsullied communication. Insofar as these codes are 'arbitrary', the result of culture and not nature, they can be manipulated in ways that project a particular range of connotations as universal and inevitable. Indeed, Barthes's recognition of the specifically political implications of the 'power to signify' is probably the crucial insight that structuralism has brought to a critical theory of ideology.[8]

That said, however, the overall viability of a structuralist-based theory of ideology is, at least from a Bakhtinian perspective, somewhat problematic. To begin with, Barthes's argument that the mode of domination is induced by the enforcement of various mythical representations would seem to be a textbook example of what Abercrombie *et al.* (1980) have termed the 'dominant ideology thesis', which I discussed at some length in chapter three. Barthes, that is to say, appears to advocate a crudely conspiratorial view of class domination. Myth, a signifying system which imparts an extremely powerful 'reality effect' on the social world, is directly imposed on the 'masses'. These masses then respond to the naturalization of social relations projected by the 'fragments of ideology' expressed through myth by a passive deference to the status quo. Suffice it to say that there is little evidence that subordinate social actors actually adhere to or internalize the dominant value system, at least in such a straightforward or mechanistic fashion. In fact, a wide-spread value dissensus seems to be the norm in modern industrial society, involving a complex mixture of fear, resignation, pragmatic acceptance and overt hostility.[9] As J. B. Thompson (1984) persuasively argues, it is far more plausible that the dominant ideology promotes social division and fragmentation rather than integration, thereby short-circuiting the emergence of coherent counter-ideologies and preventing the dominated classes from posing a unified threat to the established order. Bakhtin, it will be recalled, makes no such assumptions vis-à-vis the ideological coherence of modern society; for him, social languages and the ideological systems that correspond to them are always fractured along antagonistic social lines (including class, gender, race and so on).

But the problem is more deep-seated than this. In bracketing off questions of discursive content and performative context, Barthes's analysis of myth remains divorced from the actual social conditions of ideological production and 'consumption'. Although more recognizably 'sociological' than most of his structuralist contemporaries, Barthes himself makes no apologies about the fact that he is exclusively concerned with the analysis of the internal organization of cultural texts. As such, the premise of semiology is that there is no need to refer to socio-historical context to comprehend myth, insofar as what is of crucial importance is not so much what texts mean as how they mean.[10] For Barthes, texts are codified in a particular manner which encourages (or even enforces) a particular 'reading' which is most in concert with the interests of the dominant class. But this implies that the text is, as Lawrence Grossberg (1984: 394) has put it, merely a 'conduit which determines the necessary modes of its own consumption'. Not unlike the Frankfurt School's disparaging view of 'mass culture', therefore, Barthes tends simply to deduce ideological effects from origins. Symbolic systems are treated as hypostatized, autonomous entities with no theorized connection to existing socio-cultural practices and, as such, the 'practico-social' force of ideology is neglected in favour of an analysis of its formal structure. How myth is inscribed in language and behaviour at the level of everyday social existence, and in what ways it actually helps to organize hegemonic domination (or, conversely, allows for resistance to this domination) are issues that are cursorily hinted at in Barthes's writings but never adequately examined. In its denial or elision of the diachronic and contextual features of signifying systems, structuralism and semiology have encouraged a reduction of the social world into the sign, and have failed convincingly to examine the articulation of discursive systems with non-discursive social practices.[11]

These are by now well-known objections. Suffice it to say that, following Bakhtin, it has to be emphasized that the production, distribution and appropriation of ideological texts or discourses cannot be adequately conceptualized in terms of a such a simple or linear relation, but only as a series of complex 'moments', each with its own relative autonomy, and each mediating the other in important ways. Cultural texts must be disseminated through particular media forms (print, verbal utterances, televisual images, etc.), which significantly modify the text in question and influence the nature of its reception. But more importantly, in his desire to decentre the subject from analysis, Barthes ends up portraying the individual as a passive and uncritical consumer of pre-digested ideological texts. Semiology therefore largely omits the reflexive understanding of subjects – i.e., how they actively interpret the world through the creative appropriation and utilization of shared sets of meaning. Thus, it is important to note that concrete subjects are always located in a complex of historically-situated social and cultural practices, and that the text or symbolic system per se represents only a subset of this wider constellation of institutions, practices and structures. As Stuart Hall convincingly argues in his brief but seminal essay 'Encoding/Decoding' (1980), the twin processes of textual encoding and reception do not have to be symmetrical; that is, there is no guarantee that the 'preferred reading' embedded in the text will be automatically internalized by the subject in an unaltered or unmediated fashion (although, of course, hierarchies of class, race, gender and so on will structure access to symbolic and cultural resources in important ways, as Pierre Bourdieu has pointed out). The 'moment' of decoding necessarily involves the insertion of the text into the existing structure of social practices and institutions within which the subject is located. Thus, the possibility exists that a range of 'negotiated' or even straightforwardly oppositional codes will be brought to bear in the appropriation and interpretation of the text, which implies that the dominant ideology inscribed in this text may be at least partially deflected or inverted. For Barthes, by contrast, there are only two possible decodings of the text: either the naive reader 'lives' the myth, in which case passivity and deference to the status quo are the inexorable result; or one deciphers the myth semiotically and exposes its interest-laden, ideological character. Yet this is a form of intellectual elitism very much akin to the Althusserian suggestion that only Marxist philosophers armed with the science of Marxism-Leninism can escape the 'ideology-effect', a position that has recently been subjected to some rather devastating criticism.[12]

The conclusion one can draw from the preceding discussion is that ideological meaning is radically contextual in nature. Hence, the power of ideology is not simply a matter of the formal structure of ideological discourses: it is crucially a matter of what is said, which involves the performative context of a given utterance's production and the actual 'reading formations' brought to bear in the interpretation of particular texts. *Contra* Barthes, then, the contextual significance of texts must be on the agenda of a critical theory of ideology as much as the mechanisms of signification as such.[13] This 'thesis of contextualism' constitutes a powerful prophylactic against the structuralist insistence on the absolute autonomy of discourse, and upon the supposition that 'ideology' is a certain kind or 'level' of signification (in Barthes's case, the 'mythological'). What is 'ideological' about a textual practice is a matter of how symbolic systems are articulated within the wider social fields of power and hegemonic struggle. Hence, ideology in Bakhtinian terms refers to the primary symbolic-linguistic medium through which individuals gain an awareness of their socio-historical situation and engage in struggle over scarce cultural, political and economic resources. I conclude this discussion with a quotation from one of Bakhtin's last essays, which aptly summarizes his critical attitude toward structuralism (and, by extension, semiology):

. . . I am against enclosure in a text. Mechanical categories: 'opposition,' 'change of codes'. [. . .] Sequential formalization and depersonalization: all relations are logical (in the broad sense of the word). But I hear *voices* in everything and the dialogic relations among them. [. . .] Structuralism has only one subject – the subject of the researcher himself. Things are transformed into *concepts* (a different degree of abstraction); the subject can never become a concept (he himself speaks and responds). Contextual meaning is personalistic; it always includes a question, an address, and the anticipation of a response, it always includes two (as a dialogic minimum). This personalism is not psychological, but semantic.

(1986: 169–70)

FOUCAULT'S POWER/KNOWLEDGE

It is generally asserted in the literature that poststructuralism is either a 'neo-structuralism' – that is, essentially a continuation of the methods and precepts of 'classical' structuralism – or else an 'anti-structuralism' – a conscious repudiation of those same precepts. However, I would agree with J. G. Merquior (1986a) that the truth lies somewhere between these two extremes. Poststructuralism does represent a political rejection of the perceived duplicity on the part of the major structuralist thinkers (Althusser included) with the forces of reaction in the wake of the 'Paris spring' of 1968.[14] One effect of these events on the French intelligentsia was a profound disillusionment with not only the PCF (the French Communist Party) but with orthodox Marxist theory itself, which came under intense suspicion for its perceived economic reductionism and its inability to theorize adequately about power relations (and, indeed, to reflect on its own power-effects). Yet on the other hand, poststructuralism implicitly acknowledged much of the structuralist legacy – the goal of decentring the subject, the arbitrary or culturally-constructed nature of the sign, and so on. Thus, it is perhaps more correct to say that poststructuralism did not so much engage in intellectual patricide as to extend many of the central structuralist tenets to their extreme limits. Hence, whilst most structuralists emphasized the rigid and predictable nature of sign-systems, Derrida and others asserted that the process of signification was essentially anarchic and random, and the severance of the signifier from the signified became absolute. Hence, being opposed to the construction of systematic philosophies per se, poststructuralism emphasized the importance of discontinuity, plurality and diachrony.[15] And being highly critical of what they held to be rationalist and empiricist residues in classical Marxism, most post-structuralists preferred to embrace a kind of Nietzschean scepticism rather than put their faith into more traditional forms of class-based or party politics. Amongst other things, this turn entailed a more pronounced sensitivity than that of their erstwhile structuralist colleagues towards the interrelationship between knowledge and power, and also to the role of the intellectual within this power/knowledge matrix. These differences have led Merquior (1986a: 196) to characterize poststructuralism (not without considerable justification) as the 'combination of a formalism with a Nietzschean standpoint'.

In what follows, I shall concentrate on the work of Michel Foucault – not because he can be considered as 'paradigmatic' of poststructuralism as a whole, but because he is more concerned with the historical analysis of social practices and with the nature of power than with the formal properties of sign-systems. In other words, he is a practitioner of what Edward Said (1984) has termed a 'worldly poststructuralism', a worldliness which can be contrasted with the more abstract, textualist bent of Derrida and his followers. As such, the relevance of his writings vis-à-vis a comparison with Bakhtin's 'dialogism' is much more pronounced. Before examining Foucault's approach, however, some prefatory remarks are in order. Firstly, although it is clear that Foucault's writings are in some important sense politically engaged, his specific stance defies any simple categorization. His attitude to Marxism and to the project of *Ideologiekritik* is complex and ambivalent. Yet it is nevertheless clear that his account of 'power/ knowledge' is an important and influential approach to the analysis of the relationship between language or discourse and power, one that merits sustained attention.

As a prefatory remark, it is important to note that Foucault's work is punctuated by a number of significant theoretical shifts and discontinuities. Given the preoccupation of this study with issues of ideology, discourse and power, I shall concentrate on Foucault's 'genealogical' rather than his 'archaeological' phase, wherein the din of 'war and battle' takes precedence over the 'great model of language and signs' (1980: 114). This phase is exemplified by his essay 'Nietzsche, Genealogy and History' (1984), where he suggests that traditional forms of history-writing (including Marxism) have displayed a pronounced tendency to integrate disparate historical events into rigid *a priori* theoretical schemas. This has had the effect of projecting onto heterogeneous occurrences a particular coherence and linearity which was designed to legitimize a particular ideological viewpoint. Insofar as such a claim to a privileged knowledge of history invariably has undesirable political effects, Foucault seeks to privilege Nietzsche over Marx and advance an alternative method of historical and social inquiry which rejects such a 'will to truth' and which replaces the value-laden fiction of continuity with the problematic of discontinuity. Genealogy (or at least as Foucault understands it) is therefore concerned to preserve the uniqueness and singularity of historical events by rejecting the search for ultimate causes. Moreover, it goes beyond standard historical narratives of kings and proletarians alike in order to unearth hitherto ignored or misunderstood episodes, phenomena, and individual case histories. Genealogy, therefore, seeks to de-legitimize the present state of affairs by radically historicizing social and cultural practices (the body, morality, sexuality, mental illness) that are generally taken for granted as enduring and timeless. This entails an examination of the emergence of particular power regimes, and how they shape and 'naturalize' given patterns of social practice. Moreover, genealogy aims to unearth and 'rehabilitate' local and suppressed forms of knowledge which have been subordinated to 'global' theoretical systems, through the rediscovery of lost practices and discourses. This latter position explains Foucault's hostility toward the claims of cognitive superiority on the part of scientific discourses – not simply because of the 'validity' of their truth-claims (he generally 'brackets off' such epistemological considerations), but because of the intimate relation between instrumental rationalization as such and the elaboration and extension of existing forms of social domination. As Foucault says:

> What [genealogy] really does is entertain the claims to attention of local discontinuous, disqualified, illegitimate knowledges against the claims of a unitary body of theory which would filter, hierarchize and order them in the name of some true knowledge and some arbitrary idea of what constitutes a science and its objects. Genealogies are therefore not positivistic returns to a more careful or exact form of science. They are precisely anti-sciences. Not that they vindicate a lyrical right to ignorance or non-knowledge. [. . .] We are concerned, rather, with the

insurrection of knowledges that are opposed primarily to the contents of a science, but to the effects of the centralizing power which are linked to the institution and functioning of an organized scientific discourse within a society such as ours.

(1980: 83–4)

Foucault is obviously critical of Marxism on a number of fronts (both politically and theoretically), and he is concerned to distance his genealogical method from historical materialism in no uncertain terms.[16] In terms of the theory of ideology per se, he outlines his objections in the interview 'Truth and Power' (1980) as follows:

(i) In an obvious reference to Althusser, Foucault chides the Marxist attempt to maintain a binary division between science and ideology. All discourses, 'scientific' or otherwise, are necessarily partial and one-sided. Foucault's point here is that Marxism's claim to provide a critique of ideology on the basis of its own scientificity tells us more about the processes of discursive self-legitimation than about its alleged epistemological credentials.

(ii) Consistent with his desire to keep the subject firmly in the philosophical grave, Foucault feels that the concept of ideology as it has been traditionally used implies that the ideas expressed in various discourses are the products of individual consciousness, 'false' or otherwise. Foucault maintains that the intelligibility of discourses cannot be located in the subject, and that language is not an 'expressive tool' which allows for the conversion of the individual's thoughts into words. Rather, like all structuralists and poststructuralists, he insists that language is a 'decentred totality', and that production of meaning is derived not from the speaking (or writing) subject but from the relations between signifiers in the given linguistic system.

(iii) Foucault objects to the notion that ideologies can be reduced to an underlying economic structure. He insists that such discourses are so closely intertwined with material practices that there is no methodological justification for reducing them to something 'more' material. Therefore, genealogy should not be exclusively concerned with the formal and relatively systematic ideologies of elites, but should instead concentrate on the more prosaic and mundane discourses of the various 'technologies of power' and how they operate at the level of everyday social existence.

In line with what he takes to be the intractable shortcomings of the Marxist theory of ideology and historiography, Foucault therefore privileges a genealogical account of the historical discontinuities in power/knowledge relations. Central to his approach is the postulation of a qualitative shift in the nature of power with the emergence of modern industrial society. In earlier historical periods, such as during the *ancien régime* of pre-modern Europe, individuals who transgressed the authority of the king were not categorized as 'criminals' in the contemporary sense but rather defined as threats to the stability of a complexly stratified cosmic order. Punishment was not designed to rehabilitate the individual in question, or to compensate the victims of wrongful acts, but to re-establish this cosmic balance through spectacular and (to our eyes) brutal public displays of torture and execution. Yet, Foucault argues, the exercise of power via spectacular displays of violence simply became too unwieldy and costly for effective social control, and unsuited to the demands of an increasingly complex socio-economic system and the demographic pressures of a rapidly expanding population. Consequently, power is increasingly organized and administered by a massive, impersonal bureaucracy which commands both the resources and the 'knowledges' capable of observing the masses, and of developing the necessary corrective procedures to be able to control and manipulate individual behaviour. The ultimate goal is the production of subjects who internalize power, thereby becoming 'regimented, isolated, and self-policing'. This is accomplished via the application of a standardized set of techniques, practices, and discourses which were gradually extended to envelope all major sectors of society (education, medicine, industrial production, and so on). Foucault argues that such a process of 'normalization' with respect to both individuals and populations has historically been associated with the emergence of the so-called 'human sciences' – demographics, psychology, criminology – which create unitary 'knowledges' about the measurement and classification of the 'modern individuals' who are now defined as 'objects' of study. The result is a modern form of domination described by Foucault by a number of ominous neologisms: the 'disciplinary society', the 'age of bio-power' and the 'carceral archipelago'.

This account of the emergence of the 'disciplinary society' reflects a quintessentially Foucauldian theme: that power is not essentially repressive but productive. Foucault regards the notion of 'power-as-repression' – such as Reich's theory that power suppresses the individual's natural creative and biological urges – as *prima facie* wrong, for two major reasons: firstly, because it tends to characterize power as a thing or commodity which can be held or transferred at will; and secondly, because it fixes the locus of power in readily-identifiable institutions, particularly the state apparatus. By contrast, Foucault wants to advance a specifically relational concept of power, in which power is viewed as a strategy, the effect of the play of opposing forces and actions. Thus, power forms a de-centralized network, which continuously flows throughout the entire social field in a 'capillary' fashion, and which is not external to but constitutive of social relations themselves. Therefore, Foucault (in a distinctly Kafkaesque vein) suggests that the dominated and the dominators alike are inescapably caught up within this web of power:

. . . [power] is produced at every moment, at every point, or rather in every relation between points. Power is everywhere; not because it englobes everything, but because it comes from everywhere. And 'power', in so far as it is repetitive, inert, self-reproducing, is merely the general effect which is outlined on the basis of all these mobilities, the concatenation which is based on each of them and which seeks in turn to fix them.

(1981: 93)

However, it is important to note that Foucault does not conceive of power as a unilateral, omnipotent force, because resistance is intrinsic in the operation of power as a necessary compliment. That is to say, freedom is not the absence of power; rather, they are two sides of the same coin. They are both bound up within a perpetual and reciprocal struggle (or 'agonism') for supremacy. And this contest, it would appear, has no winners or losers, but a permanent state of provocation and opposition.[17] In Foucault's opinion, to equate power per se with its more obvious juridical-sovereign forms actually conceals the more important exercise of power at the 'micro' level. Therefore, the analysis of power should seek to grasp the operations and techniques of power at the level of profane social existence and how these form the elemental 'building blocks' of wider power-relations. Because power lacks a centre, and because it is coextensive with the social whole, it is not something that is consciously held or directed by any given class or individual. Moreover, Foucault asserts that power cannot be coercive or repressive because there is no stratum of human existence – even the body or sexuality – which lies outside the existing matrix of power/knowledge relations. Power does not repress because there is literally nothing to repress – for Foucault, the body is a pliable object which is circumscribed and moulded into a politically docile yet productive force via these disciplinary techniques: 'Power relations have an immediate hold upon [the body], they invest it, mask it, train it, torture it, force it to carry out tasks, to perform ceremonies, to emit signs' (1980: 119). Thus, Foucault suggests that because the exercise of power is not designed to suppress or contain the liberatory impulses of individuals or social classes, but rather to create both individuals ('anatomo-politics') and populations ('bio-politics') as 'useful' entities, it is a 'positive' and productive force.

FOUCAULT AND THE PROBLEM OF 'RESISTANCE'

It is clear that Foucault's genealogical method and account of power/knowledge provides a formidable challenge to Marxian and critical social theory. Given the often enigmatic and obscure qualities of Foucault's texts, it is not surprising that his work has provoked a number of very different reactions on the part of Marxist and Marxian-influenced intellectuals – not unlike, of course, the reception accorded to Bakhtin himself.[18] It is clear that Foucault's brand of poststructuralism has some interesting affinities with Bakhtin – quite apart from the general similarities between the Bakhtinian and the poststructuralist philosophies of language, which I have touched upon elsewhere – and also with other thinkers who have identified with the Marxist tradition, but not in a wholly uncritical fashion (such as Antonio Gramsci).[19] For example, both Foucault and Bakhtin share a non-reductionistic view of the social formation – that is, both conceive of society not as a fixed structure but as a constellation or dispersed field of opposed forces and strategies. Accordingly, both reject the metaphysical dualism (i.e., the tendency to assign ontological priority to 'matter' and to treat ideas as secondary and dependent) inherent in positivist and empiricist versions of Marxism. Both criticize the notion that discursive structures are 'ideological representations' of underlying class interests, and they assert that discourses are inextricably intertwined with wider relations of power and social practices which are not explicable by reference to the intentions and desires of individual social actors. In short, Bakhtin no less than Foucault deconstructs the epistemological category of the bourgeois subject. This leads Foucault to insist that disciplinary discourses do not 'work' by concealment or falsity but by shaping and organizing the body which, of course, finds a parallel in Bakhtin's conceptualization of the body as the primary site of ideological discourses. Moreover, neither theorist has any faith in the legitimization of critique by reference to a rigid science/ideology division, and both accept the conclusion that their own discourses are at least partially ideological or motivated by a 'will to knowledge'. Finally, both reject the pervasive Marxian tendency to attribute an overarching teleology to history – both Foucault and Bakhtin are intensely suspicious of grand historical narratives of whatever ideological coloration. In a conceptual move which is indicative of their shared anti-systematic and anti-totalizing orientation, both eschew the Enlightenment pursuit of absolute knowledge and the concerns of official historiography. Instead, they seek to 'rehabilitate' lost or suppressed knowledges and practices, to enable the subaltern to speak. They attempt to encourage this Benjaminian 'return of the repressed' by probing the gaps, silences and discontinuities in the text of history, thereby undermining the abstract claims to truth made by official histori-ography. For Bakhtin, this subversive interest is represented by his preoccupation with the 'thousand-year-old development of popular culture', particularly as manifested within great world (but especially European) literature; for Foucault, it involves the analysis of various documents and records (courtroom proceedings, medical reports, diaries, etc.) concerning the mar-ginalized social groups of early modern Europe.

Yet, less surprisingly, it is also clear that there are many deep-rooted incongruities between Bakhtin and Foucault. In what follows, I will consider Foucault's account of power and his (closely intertwined) theory of the subject from a roughly Bakhtinian perspective. One could begin with the observation that Foucault's analysis of discursive power relations is certainly valuable, mainly because it enables us to theorize about the functioning of power at all levels of the social system, and because it teaches us not to conflate power with juridical or coercive institutions or restrict its operation to the simple reproduction of economic relations. Nevertheless, it is far from unproblematic. As Charles Taylor (1986) rightly points out, Foucault's notion that power 'lacks a centre' and is therefore not consciously 'possessed' or exercised by specific individuals or groups is, in the final analysis, incoherent. That is, it is perfectly reasonable to suggest that power relations are not the result of deliberate implementation, that they have logic without design – take, for example, Bakhtin's construal of speech genres as metalinguistic systems which unconsciously 'define the deep structural aspects' of particular types of utterance. This is precisely what Anthony Giddens (1979) has referred to as the unintended consequences of action, which may (under certain conditions) converge in a systematic and patterned fashion but which is not 'willed' a priori. Insofar as Foucault conceives of power as a (rather mysterious) force or substance that permeates the entire social field and which functions autonomously from the exigencies of human action, he cannot explain how power operates 'strategically' or how it produces the particular effects of domination that it does. What Foucault seems to leave us with is, as Taylor (1986: 88) nicely puts it, a 'strange kind of Schopenhauerian will, ungrounded in human action'. Foucault's post-Heideggerian desire to dispense with the subject prevents him from occupying the middle ground between the subjectivistic Cartesian position that patterns emerge from history because of conscious human will and the Schopenhauerian one that history has a pattern but is unwilled. Taking the position that structure has priority over element is irrelevant, because structures of action or language must be reproduced and sustained by the concrete actions and speech-acts of social agents – a process that Giddens refers to as the 'duality of structure' or what Roy Bhaskar (1979) calls the 'transformational model of the society/person connection'. As discussed in chapter three above, Bakhtin also occupies this 'centre position' which rejects the solipsistic precepts of bourgeois idealism (i.e., the subject as a 'self-certain foundation') but which does not entirely regard the categories of 'agency', 'reflection' or 'experience' as obsolete anachronisms.[20]

Similar problems emerge because Foucault insists that power is not essentially repressive or coercive but productive. Foucault, of course, wants to assert that people are not self-directed, autonomous agents but are in some important sense constituted by the matrix of power/knowledge relations within which they inextricably find themselves. Indeed, he seems to imply that the body is an endlessly malleable object with no intrinsic capabilities or drives whatsoever. And precisely because Foucault rejects a psychoanalytic theory of drives (such as Reich's theory of sexual repression), it is difficult to grasp what power operates against, given that he explicitly states that power is always constituted in opposition to something else. Consequently, Foucault's concept of power tends to degenerate into an all-embracing synonym which encapsulates all social relations and which encompasses every point in the social field. Needless to say, its use as a heuristic to guide research becomes somewhat questionable, if for no other reason than that Foucault is unable to specify how a situation would be different if the effects of power were cancelled – what in philosophical parlance is commonly referred to as a counter-factual. Thus, as Peter Dews asserts, a theory of power which restricts itself to its positive or productive side cannot really generate a critical theory of power, nor can it distinguish between the functioning of power relations and the ordinary functioning of the social system in question. As he writes:

> ... if the concept of power is to have any critical political import, there must be some principle, force or entity which power 'crushes' or 'subdues', and whose release from this repression is considered desirable. A purely positive account of power would no longer be an account of power at all, but simply of the constitutive operation of social systems. [Foucault's] work must therefore contain, if only implicitly, an account of modern power, and hence of the self-reflexive subject formed by such power.
>
> (1984: 87)

The preceding discussion leads us naturally to what is perhaps the most serious theoretical impasse in Foucault's work: his inability to conceptualize adequately the resistance of subjects to the effects of power/knowledge. Foucault asserts that resistance is inherent in the operation of power. Yet insofar that he feels that subjects are constituted by the prevailing configurations of discourses and disciplines that have accompanied the emergence of the carceral society, it is difficult to conceive of how social actors could possibly engage in alternative forms of action or formulate 'counter-epistemes'.[21] This characteristic elision between subjectification and subjugation is an inherent problem in all versions of structuralism and poststructuralism. That power inscribes all social relations, at every conceivable level and in every possible form of society, is as pessimistic as Althusser's (1971) suggestion that ideology (the imaginary relation of the subject to society) is necessary for the functioning of any social formation. Any attempt to transcend the existing power system would, according to Foucault's logic, only result in the establishment of a (possibly worse) one. Why, then, would anyone be motivated to struggle against domination? Because – unlike Bakhtin – he provides no normative arguments for engaging in specific forms of political action, apart from a vague suggestion that spontaneous, individual acts of rebellion are inherently desirable as a kind of Nietzschean heroism, it is not clear how Foucault escapes the charge of nihilism. What Foucault seems to be saying is that any form of resistance that becomes more than a 'revolt of subjugated knowledges' at the local level no longer holds out the prospect of subverting the present power-regime and succumbs to the dialectic of totalitarianism. Ostensibly echoing Bakhtin's notion of the 'carnivalesque', Foucault suggests in the interview 'Powers and Strategies' that the most desirable type of resistance is embodied by the various uprisings and riots of the 'plebs' that have punctuated European history:

> The plebs is no doubt not a real sociological entity. But there is indeed always something in the social body, in classes, groups and individuals themselves which in some sense escapes relations of power, something which is by no means a more or less docile or reactive primal matter, but rather a centrifugal movement, an inverse energy, a discharge. There is certainly no such thing as 'the' plebs; rather there is, as it were, a certain plebeian quality or aspect. There is plebs in bodies, in souls, in individuals, in the proletariat, in the bourgeoisie, but everywhere in a diversity of forms and extensions, of energies and irreducibilities. The measure of plebs is not so much what stands outside relations of power as their limit, their underside, their counter-stroke, that which responds to every advance of power by a movement of disengagement.
>
> (1980: 137–8)

But what is this 'something', this 'inverse energy' or 'discharge' that makes resistance possible? And if Foucault is really interested in resurrecting 'minor knowledges' and encouraging 'local resistance', wouldn't a 'genealogy of resistance' be more important than all of the analyses of disciplinary technologies put together? The problem largely arises because of the over-hasty structuralist desire to rule out the role of the subject (particularly as expressed through particular, historically-contingent forms of human agency) *tout court*, combined with a pronounced tendency to reify the notion of 'discourse'. That is, for all of the structuralist talk about respecting the 'autonomy' of discourse, the notion that discourse (or power/knowledge) more or less automatically 'positions' and 'constitutes' subjects seems to reproduce the worst errors of a crude economic determinism, albeit in a transverse fashion. Human agency, as Giddens (1987) has convincingly argued, is not mechanistically determined by sign-systems or power/knowledge relations, insofar as human beings have the intrinsic capacity to monitor their actions reflexively, a phenomenon that primarily occurs in the non-discursive realm of 'practical consciousness'. Insofar as this process occurs through the medium of social interaction, individuals come to develop and share a 'mutual knowledge' which serves to contextualize these forms of action. This shared matrix of symbols and practices – a culture or tradition, if you like – forms an essential resource which is brought to bear in the appropriation and interpretation of external texts and discourses. And precisely because of this framework of inter-textual referencing, the (arbitrary) meanings contained in dominant discourses are not abstractly 'beamed downwards' and passively internalized but are subject to various forms of prosaic social deconstruction and reinterpretation.[22] Foucault's rejection of subjectivity entails the *de facto* acknowledgement that the enforcement of a dominant system of norms and 'disciplines' can never be resisted by an intersubjective, reflexive consciousness that could (at least potentially) be directed against that system. In order to avoid this overly pessimistic conclusion, the old structuralist bugbear – the realm of experience, as manifested within dialogical forms of social interaction – must be retained as an essential element in social analysis (without, of course, blithely assuming that as a theoretical concept it is entirely problem-free).

(RE)THEORIZING RESISTANCE

The recent assault on the 'dominant ideology thesis' as chronicled in chapter three above has prompted the abandonment of various questionable assumptions advanced by the more traditional theories of ideology – in particular, the supposition that the integration of modern society must be premised upon the normative integration of subordinate groups into the status quo. Again, this questioning has also paralleled a 'linguistic turn' in thinking about ideology – i.e., the proposition that an adequate understanding of the effects and functioning of 'ideology' must involve a conceptualization of its interconnection with forms of oral or written discourse, as opposed to a debilitating preoccupation with the epistemological status of ideological phenomena ('false consciousness', 'cognitive distortion', and so on).[23] The crux of this realignment is the assertion that language does not simply express or reflect extant social relations; it actually helps generate such relations in the first place. As Michael Shapiro (1988: 11) puts it, one result of this theoretical shift is that we now tend to 'view statements not on the basis of their truth value but on the basis of their capacity for value creation in human relations'. Given this, however, relatively little work has been carried out on the problem of how the legitimating or obfuscating effects of ideology can be subverted or 'deconstructed' (in short, resisted) by marginalized groups in society through the mobilization (or generation) of particular symbolic, cultural or material resources. 'All systems leak', Edward Sapir once wrote. Ideological 'systems' are certainly no exception, but a more important question is how they leak.[24] The inability of much contemporary social theory to respond adequately to the problem of resistance has been compounded by the fact that the currently-fashionable avatars of poststructuralist and postmodernist thought (Lyotard, Baudrillard, *et al.*) have typically deferred rather than directly addressed it. Bakhtin and the Circle provide a more considered, plausible, and certainly more optimistic response to this issue, but one that does not lapse into poststructuralism's nemesis, a banal humanism.

Briefly to recapitulate some earlier points, for Bakhtin the primary ideological or monological function of official discourses and genres is the projection of one language as the only one possible, in a manner that encourages an immediate (self-evident, commonsensical) identification of this language with one's experience of external reality and the hierarchical subordination or emasculation of other, potentially oppositional sociolects. The 'official genres', that is to say, constantly efface their own socially-constructed and inherently dialogic nature.[25] This effect facilitates the misrecognition that our own perceptions and experiences are self-directed, but which are in fact ideologically skewed in a number of (often unconscious) ways. Bakhtin's critical strategy is not just to demonstrate the conventional architectonics of discourse. He also wants to show that texts can be re-constructed or discursively re-ordered, be made to produce very different meanings through recontextualization, the juxtaposition of different narratives or texts, and so on.[26] Carnival exemplifies Bakhtin's ethico-political aesthetic: it represents one such 'reading formation' which can significantly 're-author' dominant ideological discourses in politically subversive ways.[27] The populist rebellion he describes at length in *Rabelais and His World* is not a form of knowledge produced by an autonomous moral agent, which of course epitomized the Enlightenment practice of critical reason. Rather, it is grounded in the collectivity, in the 'body' of the subaltern mass which retains a distinctive relationship to society and to history. 'The people' as Bakhtin understands it is an aggregate body with a characteristic cultural tradition (the carnivalesque), which constitutes a kind of unconscious Jungian archetype 'behind the backs' of those involved. Unlike the numbered 'units' of Zamyatin's famous dystopian novel *We*, however, this is not an amorphous, faceless mass, an abstract and artificial collective 'I'. Rather, it is unpredictable, open and heterodox in nature, and the tradition that it represents is reflexive, self-critical and dialogical.[28] Accordingly, Bakhtin conceives of the subversion of monologic discourse as taking the form of a peculiar kind of deconstructive tradition which is enacted by the people, one that (to use Marx's apocalyptic wording) breaks the fetters of the old world.[29]

What this implies, as discussed at length in previous chapters, is that the 'self' for Bakhtin is not constituted through a unified, monadic relation to the external world; rather, the phenomenon of 'self-ness' is constituted through the operation of a dense and conflicting network of discourses, cultural and social practices and institutional structures, which are themselves bound up with the intricate phenomenology of the self–other relation. And since this process is fundamentally historical and not a singular 'event', it is continuous and 'mobile' – which is why the subject in Bakhtin's eyes is unfinalized (and, yes, 'decentred'), in a perpetual state of 'becoming'. Unlike those intellectual trends which take their cue from the Saussurean tradition, language for Bakhtin is therefore not entirely coextensive with 'experience'. That is, human experience is not simply the outcome of a singular, primal 'interpellation' vis-à-vis a unitary discourse or language-system, or even a multiplicity of such interpellations. The alternative in Bakhtin's view is to conceptualize human beings as neither entirely autonomous, self-directed entities nor as surface effects of a deep epistemic structure, but rather as reflexive agents embodying a range of socially-determined practical capacities, a repertoire of collective skills and resources. The early Bakhtin referred to this process as 'architectonics' (a term he originally borrowed from Kant), which roughly denotes the dynamic construction of relations between diverse entities through the medium of reflexive human action.[30] Not unlike Bourdieu's *habitus*, Bakhtin feels that subjects can draw on this ensemble of embedded practices and techniques in the pursuit of particular strategies and goals, although pre-eminently he was concerned with what could be called 'linguistic praxis'.[31] Such localized and embodied practices are in turn bound up with historical forms of social organization, or with what Voloshinov has termed 'behavioural genres'. Subjects therefore do not have a general relation to reality, but only a 'regional' or localized one – which is why Bakhtin always refers to speech and behavioural genres in the plural.

To conclude this chapter, Bakhtin believes that subordinate groups can generate a differentiated, incomplete set of 'knowledges' which are embedded in traditions and practices which are (at least partially) resistant to dominant discourses and ideologies – more or less what the French social theorist Michel de Certeau (1984) has termed the 'oppositional practices of everyday life'. It could be noted that Bakhtin and the Circle neglect to analyse in sufficient detail the various institutional sites (class, gender, race, and so on) through which access to symbolic-cultural resources is constituted and regulated, an issue I will return to in the final chapter. Nevertheless, it is to Bakhtin's credit that he did not neglect this feature of social praxis which is, it must be said, generally overlooked by those intellectual traditions which continue to labour under the aegis of the Saussurean problematic. And, moreover, it helps to vindicate the relevance of Bakhtin's ideas for the aims and methods of radical cultural-ideological critique, insofar as it carves out a 'conceptual space' whence to theorize about the possibility of resistance. Bakhtin's dialogism, therefore, manages to avoid what Perry Anderson (1983: 45) has termed a 'megalomania of the signifier', a reduction of the social world into the sign.

Chapter 6

Towards a dialogical ideological criticism

The first stones of the new world, however coarse or unpolished they may be, are more beautiful than the sunset of a world in agony, and its swan songs.

Antonio Gramsci

INTRODUCTION

In this final chapter I seek to explore a series of more general reflections with respect to the legacy of Bakhtin and the Bakhtin Circle. Hopefully, such a strategy will avoid the banalities of a 'balance-sheet' type of appraisal, with a simple two-columned account of theoretical 'credits' and 'debits'. Nevertheless, an evaluative survey of Bakhtin's *oeuvre* can lead to a better comprehension of the Circle's theoretical activities as a whole and also encourage a more informed and judicious assessment of Bakhtin's potential contributions to a critical theory of ideology and culture. It is also necessary if one is to avoid hagiography, however sincere or heartfelt – which, it must be said, seems to be an occupational hazard of much Bakhtinian scholarship. I begin this chapter by examining his writings in relation to the traditions of modernism and romanticism, and consider the more negative aspects of his unfettered utopianism. I will then discuss the implications of his cultural politics and his characterization of 'folk-festive culture' in more detail, with particular reference to Gramsci's theory of hegemony. Finally, I conclude with a brief discussion of Bakhtin's strengths and with how some of his insights may be appropriated by a radical cultural and social theory.

BAKHTIN, ROMANTICISM AND MODERNITY

It might prove useful to begin this section by briefly juxtaposing Bakhtin's attitude toward reason and the dilemmas of modernity with that of Michel Foucault. As will be recalled from the previous chapter, Foucault's self-appointed role as a 'master of suspicion' leads him to argue that progress (moral or otherwise) is not immanent within human history, and that the appeals to 'truth' and 'science' are not neutral epistemological standards but distinct rhetorical strategies which have been utilized to justify the exercise of domination. So far, so Nietzschean. But Foucault goes much further than this: he also asserts that the exercise of reason per se has inevitably repressive effects. Rationality, in his view, can be implicated in the construction of a carceral or 'disciplinary' society which is the hallmark of modernity. There is no possibility of providing some standpoint (normative, epistemological, etc.) whence to adjudge which *epistemes* produce domination as an 'effect' from those which are (even potentially) 'positive' or 'liberating'.[1] These latter considerations are anathema to Foucault. He is uninterested in delineating any basis or grounds which would facilitate the conduct of ideological-cultural critique – at least with respect to any form of recognizably collectivistic politics based on the principle of solidarity or even shared interests. Foucault insists that such a politics, despite the most noble or laudable intentions, would inevitably degenerate into its antithesis. Foucault's 'solution' lies in a kind of Nietzschean or Baudelairean conception of self-actualization which is conceived along strictly aesthetic and individualistic lines. Evoking Baudelaire's notion of the cultivation of 'heroism' in the modern world (epitomized by the *flanêur*, the cultivated but disinterested explorer of urban space), Foucault writes:

> The critical ontology of ourselves has to be considered not, certainly, as a theory, a doctrine, nor even as a permanent body of knowledge that is accumulating; it has to be conceived as an attitude, an ethos, a philosophical life in which the critique of what we are is at one and the same time the historical analysis of the limits that are imposed upon us and an experiment with the possibility of going beyond them.
>
> (1984: 50)

Bakhtin would be in broad agreement with the initial premises of

Foucault's attack on modernity. It is no accident, for instance, that Bakhtin's nemesis – monologism – is for him epitomized by the 'grey, monotonous seriousness' fomented by the various examples of scientific rationalism, utilitarianism and positivism which have played a dominant role in European thought since the Enlightenment. Indeed, he implies that there is a strong elective affinity between the impulse to suppress dialogism and the dogmatic and abstract cast of the scientific mind. These knowledge-forms aspire to treat human relations (which are constitutively unpredictable and open-ended) as analogous to natural processes, and therefore as fully knowable and quantifiable. For Bakhtin, this is a form of domination masquerading as a 'value-neutral' methodology which must be decisively rejected for its reifying and dehumanizing proclivities: 'The consciousness of people cannot be perceived, analyzed, defined as objects or things – one can only *relate to them dialogically*' (1984: 68).[2] The positivist desire to formulate general, objective laws of social or individual behaviour on the basis of empirical observation and logical deduction was widespread in 19th-century social thought – in the sociology of Spencer or Comte, for example, or the literary school of Naturalism. If by the early 20th century positivism no longer held the predominant position it had formerly enjoyed, it none the less remained extremely influential – indeed, one unifying feature of the various modernist currents that emerged in the first quarter of the 20th century was their shared antipathy to the legacy of positivism.[3] In sounding such a heartfelt warning against the promotion of a 'cult of unified and exclusive reason', Bakhtin therefore finds much in common with the romanticist-influenced 'revolt against positivism' which began in the 1870s with the writings of Nietzsche, Bergson and Baudelaire, and which finds its contemporary expression in the poststructuralist tradition. A similar temperament can also be detected (albeit in a more overtly Marxist form) in Adorno and Horkheimer's influential treatise *Dialectic of Enlightenment* (1972). Although not quite so willing to dispense with the notion of autonomous subjectivity, this text belies a similar despondency in the face of the perceived spiritual and cultural degradation of the modern world.[4]

Bakhtin's pronounced affinity with the themes and concerns of 18th- and 19th-century German philosophy (particularly that of Kant and Goethe) certainly helps to explain his desire to preserve some measure of 'value' in language and in interpersonal relations, to 'cleanse the word of all of life's automatism and object-ness', and to stress change and process rather than the rigid, abstract *a priori* conceptual categories of the rationalists.[5] It also signals his links to the Symbolist poets, although Bakhtin viewed their cultivated decadence with some distaste. Finally, in line with the general collapse of faith in the secular optimism of liberalism that accompanied the severe economic crises of the late 19th century and the Great War of 1914–18 – that is, the belief in the incremental but irreversible progress of humanity through the advance of science, technology and reason (culminating in either a classless society or the perfect self-regulating mechanism of the *laissez-faire* market, depending on one's political preferences) – Bakhtin steadfastly refused to attribute any overarching *telos* to historical development. Such a tendency would have been anathema to his proto-existentialist philosophical anthropology and his pronounced suspicion of Hegelianism in particular and grand philosophical systems in general.

There is another aspect of Bakhtin's thought which is congruent with the romantic tradition, which also connects up with Kant's suspicion of the more extravagant, aggrandizing claims of rationalism. Since he clearly feels that dialogue is the most important medium through which the self is realized and expressed, Bakhtin continually emphasizes the presence of what Barthes once called the 'grain of the voice', the trace of the flesh-and-blood personality that lies behind every utterance, however removed it may be from its original spatial-temporal location of production. His acute sense of the dense particularity of 'lived' experience, of the thing-in-itself, leads him to decry the reification of language and the attendant hypostatization of concrete human actions and utterances effected by formalist-rationalist approaches. Bakhtin's on-going phenomenological concern with the categories of 'value' and 'intention' (which can be traced to his earliest writings) explains why some of his sharpest critical barbs were reserved for the arid abstractions of philosophical idealism, as exemplified by the 'agelasts' and humourless scholars who are so often the butt of Rabelais's comic jests. Similarly, this concern illustrates his position that a viable metalinguistics must come to grips with the ambivalent, sensuous materiality of human existence, and also with the pragmatic moral demands that 'lived life' continually makes upon us.[6] In short, Bakhtin's 'dialogism' could be termed a dialogics of the concrete.

An important element (perhaps even a categorical imperative) of this dialogism is that the fetishization or reification of social relations in modern society (either capitalist or a bureaucratized socialism) be challenged not only through critical intellectual practice but also in the carnivalesque enactment of utopian community, which helps create a transgressive or 'liminal' social space of freedom and authenticity.

In this regard, the metaphorical resonance of 'dialogism' perhaps suggests a reassuring immediacy and directness which he feels is 'truer to the object' than reifying modes of abstract rationalism. Of course, Bakhtin often stresses that the concept of 'dialogue' is not to be taken literally, as implying a form of direct, face-to-face oral interaction in a question and answer mode, but rather as a wider phenomenon that encompasses much more complex forms of what he terms 'inner dialogism' (hybrids, indirect speech, 'words with a loophole', and so on) and even biological and physical processes. On the other hand, the choice of the concept of 'dialogism' is certainly not a whimsical one – the 'dialogic ideal' is ultimately rooted (and Bakhtin is quite clear about this) in early Platonic or Socratic dialogue and, moreover, many of the empirical examples of discourse he discusses at length take the form of conversations between fictional characters (or the inner dialogue of a particular character), the paradigmatic case being the polyphonic nature of dialogue in Dostoevsky's novels. Perhaps this represents the main streak of romanticism in Bakhtin's thought, a yearning for the immediacy and close personal contact characteristic of a pre-capitalist, primarily oral culture, where hearing is the primary sense and where timbre, intonation and so on are the most important elements of human communication – roughly, in short, what Jacques Derrida has termed 'phonocentrism'.[7] It is indeed strange that Bakhtin, although living in a period of accelerated technological and industrial development (that was, of course, even more pronounced in the Russian context, which helps explain why Russia was such a hot-bed of *avant-garde* modernist experimentation in the arts, architecture, design and so on)[8] never attempts to assess the nature or importance of other forms of media (film, photography, radio) and their possible impact on the prevailing structures of human communication and consciousness. This is congruent with his seeming lack of interest in modernist literature, and his habitual utilization of pre-bourgeois writers as exemplars of a literary dialogism (Cervantes, Rabelais, classical Greek and Roman authors) or, in the case of Dostoevsky, on the periphery of capitalism. Parenthetically, it could be remarked that the loss of 'immediacy' in speech and writing was inevitable with the consolidation of typographic culture after the mid-19th century.[9] This can certainly be 'dehumanizing' in a certain sense, but in another (*pace* Benjamin's account of the demise of 'aura' in the modern world as developed in his seminal essay 'The Work of Art in the Age of Mechanical Reproduction'),[10] typographic culture is at least potentially more democratic and emancipatory than previous modes of communication and information storage (chirographic, oral, and so on).

In most other respects, however, Bakhtin cannot be legitimately characterized as a 'romantic anti-capitalist' – at least in the sense that this epithet fits the work of the early Lukács (particularly his *History and Class Consciousness* and his pre-Marxist writings) or as can be found in certain elements of Adorno and Horkheimer's *Dialectic of Enlightenment*.[11] That is, for Bakhtin modernity is a complex and contradictory historical development, but one that is not wholly lacking in positive ramifications. To compare Bakhtin and Foucault again, it could be said that whilst the latter maintains a distinctly monolithic view of the interconnecting processes of modernity and modernization (in spite of his stated desire to expose the discontinuities and transformations in history),[12] Bakhtin echoes Benjamin's sentiment that there 'is no document of civilization which is not at the same time a document of barbarism' insofar as he affirms that modernity paradoxically carries with it the promise of both liberation and domination.[13] He ultimately rejects the romanticism and deep Weberian pessimism which characterize the baroque *Kulturkritik* of much of Western Marxism no less than the anarchistic negativism of Foucault.[14] At least in broad terms, Bakhtin can be said to embrace the (relatively) optimistic but not uncritical assessment of the modern age which also can be ascertained in the writings of Trotsky and Brecht, Benjamin and Gramsci.[15] Like Marx himself, it could be argued, Bakhtin combines an awareness of the deleterious effects of modernity – reification, exploitation, and alienation – with an appreciation of its potential to further the cause of human emancipation. He writes, for example, that a 'reified model of the world is now being replaced by a dialogic model' (1984: 293), and he continually underscores the liberatory and egalitarian promise of

modern vernacular speech, which he feels displays a healthy suspicion of the 'cultured' veneer of authoritative discourse.[16] With
the demise of monolithic mythological and religious systems, the
'sacred word' has lost its mystique and its power to fuse language
and reality into an indissoluble whole. The 'proclamatory genres'
– the languages of priests, politicians, and self-appointed prophets
– have been by and large delegitimized. Language has now been
thoroughly secularized: it is 'sober', democratic and open: 'our era
is characterized by an extraordinary complexity and a deepening
in our perception of the world; there is an unusual growth in
demands on human discernment, on mature objectivity and the
critical faculty' (Bakhtin 1981: 40). The modern vernacular
springs not from the pulpit or the palace, but from the street, the
marketplace and the public square.[17] Concurring with the famous
observation that irony is the defining characteristic of the modern
Zeitgeist, Bakhtin also writes that: 'Irony is everywhere – from the
minimal and imperceptible, to the loud, which borders on
laughter' (1986: 132). For Bakhtin, the 'dialogic sphere' is certainly
a fragile domain, and it remains in constant peril, threatened by
the forces of linguistic-ideological closure and centralization.
None the less, he continued to believe throughout his life that the
'carnivalesque tone' was deeply embedded in human history and
culture and managed to maintain a foothold, however tenuous, in
contemporary life. Monologism is always infected by its opposite,
the 'parodic antibodies' of a transgressive dialogism which
promise to rupture this 'grey, monotonous seriousness' from
within – or, to put it more prosaically, semiotic contestation is
immanent within linguistic and cultural practices themselves.

Yet is Bakhtin's ostensive optimism about the liberatory possibilities of the modern world (at least from the standpoint of the
late 20th century) overly credulous, and audacious chiefly in its
naiveté? Consider, for instance, the following passage chosen from
his essay 'From the Prehistory of Novelistic Discourse': 'We live,
write and speak today in a world of free and democratized language; the complex and multi-levelled hierarchy of discourses,
forms, images, styles that used to permeate the entire system of
official languages and linguistic consciousness was swept away by
the linguistic revolutions of the Renaissance' (1981: 71). It is worth
pointing out that the essay in question was written in 1940 and
delivered as a lecture to the House of Literati in Moscow in 1941.
This was after Bakhtin's harrowing exile to Kazakhstan and

Mordovia, long after Stalin had consolidated his grip on power, following the adoption of the state-sponsored aesthetic of 'socialist realism' and the forced curtailment of cultural and social experimentation by the vast machinery of state repression after an initial period of efflorescence in the early 1920s, and after the infamous purges and Moscow show trials of the late 1930s. In short, it was one of the bleakest and most oppressive eras in the history of the Soviet Union. The obvious question to ask is: if the increasing linguistic-ideological differentiation characteristic of the modern world (as effected through the processes of heteroglossia) is accompanied by an enhancement of the possibilities for critical self-reflection and socio-cultural pluralism, then (as some commentators on Bakhtin have already noted) it would seem that we have already been liberated by the anonymous forces bound up with the evolution of language and consciousness itself. In other words, Bakhtin's conception of heteroglossia almost seems to be a kind of superstructural analogue to economistic forms of Marxism, in that both uphold the notion that oppressive social orders will be superseded without the intervention of concerted political action. Yet as Ken Hirschkop (1989a: 2) legitimately argues, insofar as this ideal of dialogism cannot be said (even remotely) to approximate the actual distribution of economic, political and cultural power in contemporary society, how should we respond to Bakhtin's apparent sanguinity given the existence of a social and political system which so blatantly contradicted his cherished ideal of 'free and familiar' dialogue and the recognition of difference and 'otherness', a system to which he himself fell victim? Perhaps it is indicative of a stoic Benjaminian faith in the 'return of the repressed' which, in Bakhtin's case, is represented by a belief in an irrepressible and ultimately triumphant folk-carnival culture of 'the people'. Or maybe it represents a 'pessimism of the intellect', an ironic, Aesopian commentary on the nature of totalitarianism in the USSR.

THE NOVEL AS POLITICS

Before attempting to answer this question directly, it should prove worthwhile to examine in more depth the fundaments of Bakhtin's belief in the subversive potential of popular culture and its intrinsically progressive or socialistic nature. It should be recalled from chapter two that, for Bakhtin, the positive pole of the 'carnivalesque' had be filtered through the medium of the novel form and syncretically fused with elements of 'high' or literate culture before it could operate as a socially or culturally efficacious force to promote the ideal of dialogism. In other words, the most significant repository of the 'dialogic imagination' and the revered quality of 'novelness' is (not surprisingly) the genre of the novel. Why, then, is the novel so vitally important in Bakhtin's eyes? A partial answer might include the following points: (i) It deconstructs the authorial pretence to omniscience by making this author an equal (and not a privileged) participant in dialogue, and also by empowering the reader with respect to the 'active understanding' of the text. (ii) It juxtaposes different historically-significant sociolects, thereby making us more aware of the plethora of social languages and ideological points of view that surround us. Hence, by incorporating multiple points of view on reality into its structural logic, the novel challenges the legitimacy of a unitary representational perspective, thereby relativizing abstract claims to absolute truth. (iii) The novel incorporates humour, irony, and parody into the very tissue of the novelistic text, and thereby eliminates 'all one-sidedness, dogmatic serious-ness (both in life and thought) and all one-sided pathos'. (iv) It ruptures the absolute distance of epic time. In so doing, it challenges the authority of received tradition and seeks to replace it with a mode of frank and familiar contact with the world, a relation which encourages free observation and invention and the unfettered search for truth through dialogic intercourse. Accordingly, the novel can 'test' characters as ideologues in the context of a fictionalized social situation, thereby providing an ideal space for something like a Habermasian 'ideal speech situation'.[18] Because it is intrinsically future-oriented, and because (contra Lukács) it refuses to submit to canonization and the hegemony of a moribund, epic past, the novel preserves a utopian moment which is 'open and free', a world where 'everything is still ahead, and always will be'. (v) The novel is the most significant genre in Bakhtin's view which maintains a reflexive orientation to itself. For instance, the novel form is not above self-parodization; indeed, it positively revels in a free, innovative play with its own formal elements, it 'novelizes' other, less dialogic genres, and so on. (vi) The novel is the primary genre which maintains an inti-mate connection to the vibrant well-spring of a carnival culture, however truncated this might be in the modern era. Folk-festive culture is the novel's ultimate source of vitality and energetic self-transformation, which helps immunize consciousness against the monologic petrification of thought. And it is within this popular culture, suggests Bakhtin, that 'a fundamental new attitude toward language, toward the word, can be seen taking form'. Accordingly, the quality of 'novelness' (best exemplified, of course, by the literary form of the novel) has played an important, perhaps even a pivotal role in the shaping of modern consciousness and our 'entire artistic and ideological perception'.

One could go on at length, but the main point should be clear enough: for Bakhtin, the novel is a repository of critical social knowledge which most closely approximates his cherished ideal of dialogism and which positively accentuates this ideal, whilst most other bodies of systematic knowledge (literary, theoretical, etc.) serve to attenuate it. And it is the novel, in concert with the explosive centrifugal forces of popular culture and social heteroglossia which will eventually burst asunder the reigning social order. With the progressive emasculation of 'true' carnival from the 17th century onwards, Bakhtin believes that the 'carnival tone' is increasingly found in what Marcuse called the 'aesthetic dimension', in the domain of art and literature. Of course, his idealization of the subversive potential of art and culture has had a long history in Western philosophy, at least as far back as Plato (although his response was very different than Bakhtin's: he wanted to ban poetry from his ideal Republic because he felt that art was an iconoclastic and destabilizing force). More specifically, it is a position that Bakhtin shares with the Western Marxists, who became increasingly preoccupied with aesthetic and cultural questions after the wide-spread failure of the workers' movements in the late 1910s, and also with the left *avant-garde* in the inter-war period. In any event, this point serves to identify what is perhaps the central shortcoming in Bakhtin's critical strategy, at least from the standpoint of a politically-engaged social and cultural theory: that he seriously overestimates the capacity of dialogic literature and popular culture to effect the liberation of human consciousness from the grip of monologism. The corollary is that he fails adequately to grasp the social and institutional realities of power and domination – indeed, at times Bakhtin seems to equate the whole machinery of class rule with the suppression of unhindered dialogic communication. This is a serious charge, one that is generally admitted even by Bakhtin's staunchest supporters, and it is not without some justification. It thereby behoves us to investigate this issue in more detail.

To begin with, although Bakhtin is certainly cognizant of the political nature of discourse, which is most apparent in the struggle between an 'official' language and the popular forces of heteroglossia, nowhere does he examine in detail how the sign can actually be mobilized for the purposes of class domination outside the auspices of literary or theoretical texts. This would necessarily involve an investigation of a myriad of educational, media, cultural and political practices through which the dominant class attempts to arrest the inherent semantic flux of discourse and to impose a rigid code of equivalences between 'language' and reality. Thus, although the early Bakhtin railed against such linguists as Saussure for ignoring the embeddedness of discourse in concrete social practices, his analyses often (though not always) remain at a curiously rarefied level, as if linguistic communication essentially consisted in the interaction between disembodied individual 'consciousnesses' without the mediation of existing institutional structures.[19] Although in *Rabelais and His World* Bakhtin materializes discourses or ideologies by 'embodying' them in the collective mass of 'the people', he still neglects to take into account the institutional context of feudalism and the hegemonic role played by the Catholic Church, at least in any great depth. This problem harkens back to Bakhtin's rather vague conception of ideology. By suggesting that ideology is co-terminous with the process of signification itself (and by not developing a more precise conception of ideological processes in the negative sense), it is difficult for Bakhtin to maintain an image of ideology as a particular type of signifying practice which is intimately connected with the maintenance of class domination. As such, the 'struggle over the sign' seems to be more of an expression of an abstract battle between the forces of monologism and dialogism than the attempt by the dominant class to secure hegemonic domination over state and civil society through the mobilization of meaning and the acquisition of more tangible forms of economic and political power. In this, Bakhtin owes more to the metaphysics of Heraclitus (and to Nietzsche's duality of the Apollonian and Dionysian) than to Marx's historical materialism. What are the institutional parameters of the linguistic-ideological sphere? What are its historical configurations, its linkages to other social-cultural practices, to politics and the economy? Bakhtin does not really ask, much less attempt to answer, these questions. Perhaps belying the influence of Nietzsche, Bakhtin often seems to imply that power is desired by elites for its own sake, rather than as a strategy which aims at the accumulation of forms of economic, political and cultural capital *à la* Bourdieu. Accordingly, Bakhtin's dialogism precludes a social-historiographic analysis of the roots and dynamics of 'monologism'.

The corollary of this is that Bakhtin does not conceive of the opposition to monologism in specifically political terms. As with Jürgen Habermas, the problem of class struggle and the institutionalization of asymmetrical power relations is supplanted by the hermeneutic problem of misrecognition and recognition – which, like Bakhtin's, is a 'dialogical' relation. That is, Habermas can be criticized for transforming critique into a purely intellectual process of self-reflection and discursive argumentation.[20] He rarely refers to the material social conditions which engender ideology (which for him only affects the realm of communicative interaction), nor does he identify a viable agent of social transformation outside of a vague populism akin to Marcuse's 'great refusal'. This position, of course, explicitly contravenes Marx's famous injunction that 'ideology cannot be dissolved by mental criticism'. Bakhtin's intention is certainly not to provide ammunition for counter-hegemonic action (in spite of his remark on 'justified revolutionary violence'), but to facilitate the mutual recognition of 'I' and 'Thou' through dialogue and moral persuasion in a manner which enhances the self-understanding of both the individual and the social grouping to which he or she belongs. This involves, not an interrogation but, in Ricoeur's words, a conversation. The point is not that the hermeneutic problematic of 'misrecognition' is invalid or unimportant, but that in Bakhtin's (and Habermas's) case it precludes a viable understanding of the socio-historical dynamics of class and other forms of domination and the effective means of resisting them.

GRAMSCI, BAKHTIN AND POPULAR CULTURE

In this section, I wish to examine in more detail some of the problematic aspects of Bakhtin's positive valuation of 'folk-festival' or popular culture. Certainly, Bakhtin's interest in carnival, in the 'festival of the oppressed', is not a purely textual or academic one, nor is it derived from strictly literary sources. Bakhtin, after all, lived in a time of great political, social and cultural tumult. During a relatively brief period in the 1920s, utopia was definitely on the agenda, despite the occasionally ambivalent (but usually hostile) attitude of the Bolshevik leadership. As Richard Stites (1989 and 1990) has recently chronicled, the early years of the newly-born Soviet state were awash in revolutionary iconoclasm and daring social experimentation. One of the greatest tragedies of the bureaucratization of the Russian Revolution is that these utopian experiments were cut short after a short period of effervescence, sometimes through official neglect and indifference, but more often by force, mainly because they were viewed as being incompatible with the principal Communist goal of rapid modernization within the framework of a centralized command economy. In Petrograd itself, for instance, the first two anniversaries commemorating the October Revolution (which were encouraged by the Soviet commissar for culture Anatoly Lunacharsky,[21] who took an active interest in their proceedings) were marked by massive street festivals and popular celebrations, and buildings were festooned with banners and art-works created by simple craftsmen, amateurs and *avant-garde* artists alike. These floats, murals and so forth drew extensively upon the rich store of folk motifs and rituals to be found in Russian popular culture, and the festivities included mass theatrical events which sometimes involved tens of thousands of ordinary people – a clearly carnivalesque erasure of the traditional barrier between performers and observers.[22] Petrograd (later Leningrad) was, of course, the epicentre of the Russian modernist *avant-garde*, ranging from Symbolism to Cubo-Futurism and Constructivism, and it was here that Bakhtin spent his formative years completing a degree in classical philology.[23] Yet even Vitebsk, ostensibly a small provincial town where Bakhtin spent the period 1920–4, was the favoured destination of many artists and intellectuals fleeing the ravages of revolution and civil war. It was home to many now-famous exponents of the so-called 'left art': El Lissitzky, Malevich, and Chagall, to name but a few. Bakhtin was not particularly enamoured of much left art (as discussed earlier), and therefore it is perhaps unwise to portray him as an uncritical avatar of modernism. None the less, he could not have been altogether uninfluenced by his close proximity to the far-reaching socio-cultural upheavals occurring in Russia in the late 1910s and early 1920s, and to the undeniably carnivalesque profanation of the hated emblems of Tsarism and the church and the millennial hopes and ecstatic, apocalyptic visions generated by the 'world turned upside down'.

Clearly, then, Bakhtin is not content to advance a dispassionate, scholarly analysis of folk culture and trace its influence upon the literary techniques of such Renaissance novelists as François Rabelais. Much of *Rabelais and His World* is given over to a lyrical, almost chiliastic celebration of the liberating potential of carnival laughter and the utopian promise of popular culture that at times seems embarrassingly fulsome and naive. Hence, far from being merely a contribution to the aesthetics of laughter and 'nothing more', as Bakhtin himself says in the opening pages of *Rabelais*, it is in fact his most politically-engaged and passionate piece of writing. There is always the possibility that Bakhtin's rather exaggerated grandiloquence is intended ironically. Certainly, his texts are often so dense and multi-levelled – in a word, dialogic – that one should be wary of taking them at face value. This is the interpretive route that Clarke and Holquist (1984a) take in their by now well-known intellectual biography of Bakhtin. Here, they claim (reasonably enough) that *Rabelais and His World* must be placed within the cultural and political context of late 1930s Soviet society. By this time, Stalin's grip on the party and the state was virtually complete. It was a period of extreme repression, accompanied by innumerable purges and show trials and the strict enforcement of orthodoxy in the arts, humanities and sciences. Soviet society was progressively polarized into two major strata: the masses, who were to be used as human material for the modernization of Soviet Russia, and the party leaders – self-styled visionaries who believed they were uniquely qualified to engineer the project of socialism. The ideology of Stalinism – encompassing an unquestioning acceptance of party authority, puritanism, and asceticism – must have struck Bakhtin as having numerous parallels with the 'monolithic seriousness' of official medieval society. Hence, Bakhtin's laudatory attitude toward the freedom and licence of carnival can be read, or so claim Clarke and Holquist, as a kind of palimpsest, as a cryptic, allegorical attack on the mentality of 'barracks-communism' and rule by bureaucratic fiat that characterized Stalin's statocracy.

But the situation is more complicated than this. For, paradoxically, Stalin himself employed recognizably 'carnivalesque' techniques of inversion and mockery to denounce stubborn opponents and consolidate his own power – examples being the famous 'Stakhanovite' movement, or the use of gigantic parades and festivals to glorify his rule – in a manner which was diametrically opposed to Lunacharsky's (and certainly Bakhtin's) conception of popular celebration. Moreover, the officially-sanctioned aesthetic of 'socialist realism' encouraged artists and writers to abandon 'petit-bourgeois' concerns and adopt the traditions of Russian folk literature and oral traditions. Even musicians such as Shostakovich were censured and charged with 'formalism' for failing to incorporate folk melodies and themes into their symphonic works.[24] However, this appeal to popular values and styles promoted a prettified, sanitized image of the 'people' as paragons of noble virtue. Soviet propaganda art of the 1930s, for instance, utilized a manifestly anti-grotesque and almost neo-classical conception of the body in their paeans to the virtues of the common people (which, it may be noted, had uncomfortable similarities with Nazi art of the same period). In combating the utilization of an emasculated image of the common people for the purpose of legitimizing an increasingly totalitarian state, Bakhtin emphasized the inherently anarchic and subversive (in a word, Rabelaisian) qualities of popular-festive culture which cheerfully defied the strictures of officialdom. To quote Clarke and Holquist:

> . . . in a time of increasing regimentation, Bakhtin wrote of freedom. In a time of authoritarianism, dogmatism, and official heroes, he wrote of the masses as ebullient, variegated, and irreverent. At a time when all literature was composed of mandated canons, he wrote of smashing all norms and canons and ridiculed the pundits who upheld them. At a time when everyone was told to look 'higher' and to deny the body and its dictates, he extolled the virtues of the everyday and advocated revelling in the basic functions of what he called the 'lower bodily stratum'.
>
> (1984a: 312)

This reading of Bakhtin is certainly interesting, and it brings a number of important issues to the fore. Yet even if one acknowledges that Bakhtin's texts are intended in a partially ironic or parodistic sense, he still projects an almost entirely positive – indeed, utopian – image of carnival and related folk-festive practices. Bakhtin firmly believed that these features of carnival culture were inimicably opposed to all forms of class domination and political centralization, whether ostensibly in the interests of the masses (as with Stalin's impoverished conception of barracks communism) or not. Moreover, this is true not only of his study of Rabelais; it is a sentiment which can be found in all of his later work and even in his private notes and essays which were never intended for public (or at least the censor's) scrutiny. If this is the case, then two important questions arise: firstly, how accurately has Bakhtin characterized these carnivalesque genres from an historical point of view? And secondly, is he justified in maintaining such an apparently ardent faith in the utopian potential of popular culture and other expressions of 'novelness'? It must be said that a common enough criticism of Bakhtin is that his understanding of carnival is overly idealized and ahistorical, and that his conception of 'the people' is vague and virtually bereft of any real sociological content.[25] It is pointed out (rightly enough) that carnival in the Middle Ages and early modern Europe was not only a time of equality and freedom; it was also an opportunity to use various marginalized groups (but particularly Jews) as scapegoats for various social ills and do retributive violence to them.[26] More often than Bakhtin seems to recognize, carnivalesque rituals and misrule were tolerated by the authorities largely because they provided a relatively efficient method of social control at the community level – a variation of the familiar 'bread and circuses' argument.[27] And yet, at the same time it is important to stress that carnival did occasionally make the transition from ritualistic theatre (which was easily co-opted or manipulated by the ruling groups) to actual revolutionary upsurges, whatever their ultimate outcome.[28] Hence, it is reasonable to conclude that carnival can either support or undermine the prevailing social order, depending on the constellation of socio-historical forces at play at any given juncture and the particular socio-cultural practices with which these rituals and symbols are intertwined.[29]

Following Graham Pechey (1989: 52), it should be stressed that Bakhtin's understanding of ideological domination is primarily based on his experiences of Stalinism and Tsarism and his mainly literary knowledge of medieval feudalism. Accordingly, Bakhtin's account of monologism can tell us little about the realities of power in the more advanced bourgeois-liberal societies. It would undoubtedly prove useful at this point to consider Bakhtin's ideas in relation to another thinker who theorized the connections between ideology, culture and power at length: the Italian Marxist Antonio Gramsci. In the *Prison Notebooks*, Gramsci argued that in unstable and backward countries (such as Tsarist and Stalinist Russia), 'the state was everything, [while] civil society was primordial and gelatinous' (1971: 238). In this situation (what he termed 'minimal' hegemony), the 'statocracy' ruled almost exclusively through the exercise of naked political power (the police, army, judiciary, etc.). Popular legitimacy was generally nominal and cultural and political integration tended to be low. By contrast, in the nations of Western Europe, there was a 'proper' relation between state and civil society, in that the dominant class governed mainly (though not exclusively) through the 'sturdy structure of civil society'. In such a condition of 'integral hegemony', the ruling class succeeded in exercising 'intellectual and moral leadership' and managed to garner a fairly high degree of consent (whether active or passive) for its rule. For Gramsci is not simply referring to the more visible manifestations of political and economic class power, as in the Leninist model, but an intricate interlocking of coercion and consent embodied in a wide range of social, political and cultural forces which are necessary for the continued dominance of the bourgeoisie and the reproduction of the capitalist social formation as a whole. Accordingly, hegemony does not simply correspond to a formal and coherent 'ideological system', because it submits largely unconscious and taken-for-granted meanings, values and practices – that is, culture itself – to asymmetrical relations of power. Elements of the world-view of the dominant class, however abstract and philosophical, eventually became 'sedimented' in what Gramsci termed the 'common sense' of the subaltern classes:

> Every social stratum has its own 'common sense' and its own 'good sense', which are basically the most widespread conception of life and of man. Every philosophical current leaves behind a sedimentation of 'common sense': this is the document of its historical effectiveness. [. . .] 'Common sense' is the folklore of philosophy, and is always half-way between folklore properly speaking and the philosophy, science, and economics of the specialists. Common sense creates the folklore of the future, that is as a relatively rigid phase of popular knowledge at a given place and time.
>
> (1971: 326)

Because class domination was not exercised exclusively through the state apparatus but mainly through the partially autonomous sphere of civil society, Gramsci felt that the dominant culture and ideology were not totally monolithic and all-pervasive. No matter how successful hegemony was at securing the 'historical bloc', he believed that the maintenance of consent necessitated a certain amount of freedom with respect to the internal elaboration of popular forms of thought and culture: '[hegemony] limits the original thought of the popular masses in a negative direction, without having the positive effect of a vital transformation of what the masses think in an embryonic and chaotic form about the world and life' (1971: 420). Thus, common sense was not simply the sedimented deposits of dominant philosophies and world-views; to an important extent it also consisted of experiences and ideas generated by the everyday experience of class solidarity. According to Gramsci, the consciousness of subordinate classes was profoundly contradictory, in that aspects of the passive acceptance of the dominant world-view coexisted in an uneasy relationship with elements of apathy, equivocal consent, resent-ment and even overt hostility to the status quo. This embryonic critical consciousness was rooted in the everyday practical experience of work, leisure and the family, as well as the daily struggle against the demands of capital. He also asserted that regional dialects, local customs, songs, proverbs – the folk culture of the subordinate classes – represented a force which contested the absolute domination of a hegemonic culture and ideology.

Yet Gramsci equally realized that this common sense conscious-ness was a mode of thought which by its very nature was limited in horizon and scope: it was generally anti-theoretical, relying on personal experience and 'immediate empirical perception' rather than sustained critical reflection of a philosophical sort.[30] So although common sense (as embodied in the practices, rituals and symbols of popular culture) remained an important aspect of class solidarity and expressed a healthy suspicion of officialdom, it could not provide the political or cultural basis for an effective counter-hegemony in and of itself. Generally, under 'normal' cir-cumstances, the culture and ideology of the subordinate classes remained 'corporate' – that is, restricted to immediate and self-interested concerns.

If Gramsci is correct in making such distinctions between different manifestations of hegemony, and if hegemonic domi-nation takes such a pervasive and multivalent form, then the administration of ideological hegemony in the context of Western liberal-bourgeois societies is much more complex and nuanced than Bakhtin seems to acknowledge. For Gramsci, any viable opposition to an entrenched hegemony must revolve around the transformation of the limited 'common sense' consciousness of the subordinate classes into a critical and reflexive world-view. This is in turn premised upon the development of a genuinely counter-hegemonic culture, which requires the participation of what he termed 'organic intellectuals' aligned with the working classes and peasantry. If the maturation of such an oppositional culture in fact occurred, Gramsci was fairly confident that the agencies of civil society could be conquered by degrees (the famous 'war of position'), thereby precipitating a revolutionary crisis and creating a situation of dual power. But Gramsci was under no illusions that this would be a simple or uncomplicated process; nor was he blind to the very real limitations of popular cultural forms vis-à-vis an effective resistance to political oppression and economic exploitation. It required the nurturing and consolidation of a cultural-political movement that was revolutionary not only in rhetoric but in deed, something that he felt would take years and decades, perhaps even longer – which explains his adoption of Romain Rolland's famous maxim 'pessimism of the intellect, optimism of the will'.

There are certainly a number of affinities between the respective approaches of Gramsci and Bakhtin which could be stressed at this point. For instance, the nature of linguistic phenomena and their role in social and cultural life was one of Gramsci's central concerns.[31] He studied linguistics at the University of Turin with M. Bartoli, at a time when Croce's view of language as an expression of inner will tended to predominate. Arguing against this conception, Gramsci suggested that language was fundamentally a collective and historical phenomenon: not a system of 'words grammatically devoid of content', but a 'totality of determined notions and concepts' which contained a distinct conception of the world. As such, language could not be analysed apart from its social and political function insofar as the semantic meaning of words and utterances was the result of ideological accentuation. This led Gramsci to distinguish between the form of a language (the organization of signs into a coherent system) and its content, and he speculated that whereas the former retained a certain degree of autonomy from the operation of both base and superstructure, the latter was properly 'superstructural' in that it was open to the influence of wider ideological and political forces.

For Gramsci, the political character of language was most apparent in the attempt by the dominant class to create a common cultural 'climate' and to 'transform the popular mentality' through the imposition of a national language.[32] Therefore, he felt that linguistic hegemony involved the articulation of signs and symbols which tended to codify and reinforce the dominant viewpoint. Thus, Gramsci argued that there existed a close relationship between linguistic stratification and social hierarchization, in that the various dialects and accents found within a given society are always rank-ordered as to their perceived legitimacy, appropriateness, and so on. Accordingly, concrete language usage reflects underlying, asymmetrical power relations, and it registers profound changes which occur in the cultural, moral, and political worlds. Such changes were primarily expressed through what Gramsci termed 'normative grammar'; roughly, the system of norms whereby particular utterances could be evaluated and mutually understood (which, parenthetically, seems very close to Bakhtin's notion of the 'evaluative accentuation'), which was an important aspect of the state's attempt to establish linguistic conformity. Gramsci also felt that the maintenance of regional dialects helped peasants and workers partially to resist the forces of political and cultural hegemony, which explains his interest in the folk culture of his native Sardinia and southern Italy and with the wider connection between folklore, common sense, and hegemony. And, finally, Gramsci suggested that an integral feature of language was its metaphoricality, and that the attempt to eliminate this feature of language-use could in his view only have repressive political consequences. This accords with Bakhtin's stress on the multiaccentual character of the sign and of the threat of monologism to a healthy heteroglossia.

Of course, the work of Bakhtin and Gramsci has much more in common than their respective views on language and ideology. Both stressed the active side of human will and consciousness, and they abhorred the reductionism and naive empiricism of existing positivistic varieties of Marxism. And, most importantly, both strongly believed that within popular forms of culture and language were barely understood forces which, if properly encouraged and directed, had the potential to undermine the ossified traditions and institutions of bourgeois society. Yet from the perspective of Gramsci's materialist theory of ideological hegemony it is possible to detect a certain degree of idealism in

Bakhtin's critical project, in that Bakhtin tended to undertheorize the relation between the 'verbal-ideological' sphere on the one hand and wider social and institutional processes on the other. Unlike Gramsci, Bakhtin seems more or less to equate the common sense of the 'people' with 'good sense' – that is, he generally fails to see the degree to which popular culture is permeated or at least circumscribed by elements of the dominant culture and ideology. Occasionally, Bakhtin does recognize the limitations of any folk-festive subversion of officialdom in strikingly Gramscian terms.[33] Yet he equally argued that the inchoate nature of carnival culture did not detract from its importance, nor from its ability to cast serious doubt on official dogmas and create some 'social space' for an alternative, egalitarian popular culture. Accordingly, his conception of cultural politics seems to involve a somewhat questionable belief in the capacity of the 'people' for self-liberation, insofar as he felt that the imposition of an official language and culture could be effectively countered by the spontaneous heteroglossic forces contained within popular culture and novelistic discourse without being translated into forms of specifically political organization and struggle. In short, Bakhtin is keenly aware of the subjective dynamics of deconstruction as a transgressive social practice, but he tends to overlook the objective factors (particularly the possible mode or agency of social and cultural transformation) which are of equal importance.[34] In Bakhtin's (largely implicit) cultural politics, repression is portrayed as relatively conspicuous and straightforward (primarily a matter of the obfuscation of the dialogic character of language), and counter-hegemony thereby becomes a straightforward exposure or subversion of monologism through the irrepressible antics of a perpetually laughing festival culture.[35] It is in this sense that Bakhtin can be identified with the French utopian socialists who raised the ire of Marx and Engels. He manifestly fails to develop a convincing critique of the institutional organization and historical dynamics of political or ideological power; nor does he suggest a plausible means of assailing this power structure with the ultimate goal of realizing an egalitarian, radically democratic *communitas.*

It is worth stressing that Bakhtin's situation in this respect has parallels not only with the dissident Soviet intelligentsia in general but with many of the prominent thinkers of the Western Marxist tradition. As Perry Anderson has chronicled in his *Considerations on*

Western Marxism (1976), the Western Marxists (with the partial exception of Gramsci, although he also wrote extensively on cultural matters) tended to forgo questions of economic history or practical politics which had preoccupied their immediate predecessors (Lenin, Luxembourg, the Austro-Marxists, and so on). Instead, they concentrated their increasingly convoluted analyses in the sphere of culture and ideology, with a pronounced concern for alienation or reification of social relations under capitalism. Anderson convincingly suggests that the isolation of these theorists from the day-to-day struggles and points of resistance of the subaltern classes led not only to a failure to understand such struggles, but also an abstract theoreticism which had little relevance for the understanding of concrete political and economic developments. Moreover, it encouraged many of the Western Marxists (especially the central members of the Frankfurt School) to overestimate the stability of capitalism and the degree of manipulation 'from above', and led them to suppose that an all-pervasive power structure had effectively neutralized all opposition and critical thought. Increasingly, the sphere of art came to be regarded as the last form of human endeavour which contained some moments of a 'negation' of the existing social order, however incomplete or fleeting. As Adorno wrote in his *Aesthetic Theory*:

> . . . art is more than praxis because, turning its back even on praxis, art equally denounces the limitations and falsity of the practical world. Praxis can perhaps have no direct cognisance of that fact as long as the practical rearrangement of the world has not yet succeeded.

(cited in Slater 1977: 135)

In many respects, Bakhtin's rather more optimistic brand of dialogical criticism is considerably different from the cultural observations of Adorno and Horkheimer, insofar as the latter's views are irrevocably tinged with a nostalgia for a mythical era wherein the individual was autonomous and non-alienated and where art and culture were untainted by utilitarian commercial values. In this sense there exists a clear line of thought extending from such conservative mass culture critics as de Tocqueville, T. S. Eliot and Ortega y Gasset to the work of Adorno and Horkheimer. What they share is a pre-bourgeois contempt (or at least misunderstanding) of the masses and the levelling effects of the 'age of the common man', combined with the teleological notion that society is inevitably evolving toward a collectivist, totalitarian state dominated by a universal but vulgar and standardized mass culture. Because they tended to equate culture per se with so-called 'high culture', and because they neglected the historical analysis of the evolution of different cultural forms and styles, the Frankfurt School (*sans* Benjamin, and perhaps the later Marcuse) generally failed to recognize the importance or even the existence of subaltern cultural forms and oppositional practices.[36] For Adorno and company, all culture in late capitalism was subverted and dominated by the culture industry and reified thought. As a result, they vastly underestimated the heterogeneity and variety of contemporary culture, and how these cultural forms absorbed and reflected many different elements and influences in ways that simply could not be reduced to standardization and political or ideological domination. Adorno's characterization of 20th-century music, for example, does not allow for the possibility of the expression of dissident elements in rock or folk or the musical/cultural products of ethnic minorities. Unlike Ernst Bloch and the later Marcuse, who identified moments of protest embedded in some expressions of popular culture and such musical forms as jazz, blues or rock – and of course Bakhtin himself, who developed a sophisticated social and cultural theory revolving around the deconstructive proclivities of popular cultural forms – Adorno had little if any respect for popular art and culture. The latter's hatred and complete misunderstanding of jazz is a case in point, one that belies a rather curious brand of Eurocentric cultural elitism. Whilst some of the observations of the Frankfurt School regarding the harmful effects of the commercialization of art and culture are incisive and revealing, they are on rather more shaky ground when they insist that all popular artistic or cultural forms have been irrevocably degraded or commodified. In short, what primarily divides Bakhtin from Adorno *et al.* is an elitist versus a populist view of artistic and cultural practice. Having said this, however, it must also be acknowledged that Bakhtin was very much a 'traditional intellectual' who remained aloof from direct political struggle, and he does share with this stream of Western Marxism a theoretical failure to come to grips with the extra-superstructural features of the social world, and a concomitant hyper-inflation of the critical potentialities of art and aesthetics. In Bakhtin's case, this was exacerbated by a manifest lack of a developed political culture in the USSR, and the long tradition of displaced intellectual dissent or 'Aesopianism' in Russian society.[37] As J. G. Merquior has cogently written: 'what sets Western Marxism apart, beyond a mere shift from economics to culture, is the near absence of infra-structural weight in the explanation of cultural and ideological phenomena' (1986b: 4).

CONCLUSION: THE DIALOGICS OF CRITIQUE

Much of this final chapter has dwelt on the shortcomings of Bakhtin's social and cultural theory. In what follows, by contrast, I will briefly attempt to summarize what I feel are some of Bakhtin's main contributions to the project of *Ideologiekritik*. In general terms, Bakhtin's approach is valuable because of his remarkable ability to think through many of the sterile dichotomies (e.g. subject/object, form/content, individual/society) which have plagued existing philosophical and sociological pronouncements on language, the self, and society, and to transcend these limitations via a whole series of innovative syntheses. His (or rather Voloshinov's) critique of Saussure's 'objectivistic' linguistics, for example – which remains as relevant today as it ever was – does not lead him to fall into the trap of subjectivism. By insisting on a constitutive dialectic between individuals engaged in continuous social interaction and ideological forms, which prefigured more recent theories of the 'duality of structure', Bakhtin is therefore able to reconcile the systematicity of language with its obvious historicity and dynamism. Likewise, in his rejection of the psycho-biological theories of Freud and the hermeneutic idealism of Dilthey, Bakhtin avoids the pitfalls of a psychological reductionism (the *bête noire* of structuralism and poststructuralism). Thus, he is able to retain an almost Gramscian appreciation of the efficacy of human consciousness and agency – of the acting subject – without having to dispense with an account of the social and intersubjective character of language or succumbing to the powerful objections levelled at the Cartesian conception of the subject by the poststructuralist tradition. His version of the semiotic and ideological nature of the sign – which forms the central raw material for any possible form of human cognition and social interaction – combines structuralist insights on the formal process of signification with an appreciation of the interpretive moment which necessarily accompanies the production and reception of all discourses.

In common with other hermeneutic thinkers, Bakhtin stresses that because all discourse is always-already an interpretation, a meaningful construct which is continually monitored and apprehended by 'lay actors' in the course of everyday social intercourse, ideological and cultural analysis must take into account what J. B. Thompson (1984: 133) has called the 'creative character of the interpretive process'. As such, Bakhtin's work directly addresses a number of theoretical weaknesses characteristic of structuralist-inspired approaches. These include the latter's manifest inability to account for the reflexive qualities of the subject and the active side of human understanding, and the conceptualization of the extra-verbal social and cultural contexts within which discursive interaction occurs. Hence, any attempt to comprehend fully the ideological ramifications of written or verbal texts must seek to grasp reflexively both the intertextual and contextual connections which organize our utterances into particular generic forms, and how these utterances are generated, disseminated, and appropriated by conscious and culturally-competent social agents. Similarly, Bakhtin's 'translinguistics' also highlights the pronounced tendency on the part of structuralism to hypostatize the process of signification itself via the abstraction of formal language systems, and the simultaneous reification or elision of the concrete socio-historical basis through which the sign is expressed and embodied. The latter is most clearly demonstrated in the incapacity of structuralism to deal adequately with the question of the semantic content of the word or the historical dynamics of given sign-systems. This explains why Saussure in particular (and structuralism in general) treated language as monologic and static rather than dialogic and interactive, and why it constantly privileged empty form over symbolic meaning or 'value'. From a Bakhtinian point of view, therefore, language is best understood as praxis, as a continual performance or 'lived event'.

However, as discussed in chapter four above, Bakhtin's *Hermeneutik* is of a distinctive character. Whilst he acknowledges the embeddedness of 'Being' or *Dasein* in tradition and in history, he does not shy away from the Marxian conclusion that modern society is riven with antagonistic material interests and that, accordingly, language can be seen as a medium of dissimulation and domination as much as a conduit of interpersonal communication and self-understanding. In drawing such a conclusion, Bakhtin sides with Habermas against Gadamer on this issue; yet, with certain provisos, he refuses the former's recourse to a nomothetic or generalizing social science to justify the conduct of critique. In this, he subscribes to Goethe's famous dictum that 'theory is grey, but life is green'. To justify his particular interpretive stance, Bakhtin appeals to distinct ethical or moral standards which owe much to the tradition of German idealism (especially Kant) and, as Clarke and Holquist point out, to certain theological/religious idioms (such as Russian Orthodoxy and the Jewish dialogical tradition of Buber, Levinas and others).

In terms of Marxian theory, Bakhtin's assertion that language is irreducibly material (in that it is a form of practical consciousness grounded in everyday social practice) avoids the economistic tendency to posit language as a 'reflection' of production relations. His view that society forms a complex totality, in which each sphere interacts with all others, anticipated Althusser's attempt to develop a theory of the 'relative autonomy' of the superstructure. However, Bakhtin's postulation of the active role played by human agency and consciousness provides a powerful corrective to Althusser's determinism and functionalism. If such a 'relative autonomy' approach does not fully solve all of the problems associated with the architectural metaphor itself, it does have the advantage of side-stepping the twin errors of economism and reductionism that have long disabled Marxism. A *propos* the theory of ideology itself, Bakhtin manages to conjoin an account of ideological processes with a sophisticated philosophy of language in a manner which allows us to conceptualize both the 'positive' (ideology as the central medium in the symbolic constitution of social relations) and the 'negative' (ideology as monologism, as an 'authorial voice' which suppresses difference and restricts free dialogic intercourse) functions of ideology in an eminently dialectical (or Ricoeurian) fashion. And because ideology as a symbolic medium of social interaction is inherently dialogic, this allows for the possibility of actively responding to or even resisting dominant discourses. Hence, Bakhtin's notion that signifying practices are always constituted in and through conflicting social forces – the so-called 'struggle over the sign' – helps to open up a vast and relatively unexplored area of social inquiry which could be termed the 'politics of signification'. It is to Bakhtin's credit that he first recognized – whilst writing in the mid-1920s, it must be remembered – the profound political and theoretical implications of the polysematicity of the word. The amenability of the sign to diverse forms of ideological accentuation (which is present in all literary, cultural and media texts, and not just everyday speech) implies that the mobilization of meaning plays a central role in the maintenance and the (potential) subversion of asymmetrical and exploitative power relations. Bakhtin successfully demonstrated that the interrogation of this process – of the point of articulation between ideology and particular discursive practices – can and indeed should be an integral feature of a critical theory of ideology.

In many respects, M. M. Bakhtin can be characterized as what the Soviet writer Kagarlitsky (1988) has termed an 'Aesopian' thinker. That is, he utilized the transgressive and disruptive elements of popular genres and folk-festive culture in order to criticize and de-legitimize the authoritarian tendencies of the society he lived in, but he did this in a largely allegorical, even oblique fashion. It is undoubtedly true that this was a necessary strategy he was forced to adopt in order to circumvent state censure. Of course, Bakhtin did not escape this repression unscathed. But if he was thinking in terms of what he liked to call 'great time', whilst his writings failed to make much of an impact during his lifetime, they now constitute not simply a critique of Stalinism (there are many of these), but a powerful and extensive body of radical-democratic thought which is grounded in a distinctive metatheory of language and an unapologetically humanistic philosophical anthropology. This stance is, in turn, ultimately premised upon a utopian vision of a de-alienated, egalitarian community which, as a repository of transcendent 'carnivalesque' desire, still manages to animate and energize a myriad of textual and cultural practices in the here and now. In this study, I have concentrated on a particular aspect of this legacy; namely, his attack on monologism in thought and deed and his attempt to formulate a utopian-deconstructive strategy to contest it. But a full appreciation of the ethical, theoretical and philosophical depths of this inheritance has only barely begun.[38] One important ethical component of his dialogism is one he shares with most Western Marxists: that is, Bakhtin envisages the prospect of redemption, of the re-integration of the fractured and fragmented consciousness of the modern individual into a non-estranged whole. In his

Problems of Dostoevsky's Poetics, for example, he makes much of the fact that Dostoevsky's fictional characters constantly strive for authenticity and wholeness despite their degraded and marginalized existence.[39] Hence, Bakhtin considers the cessation of an alienating and reifying monologism and the blossoming of an unconstrained dialogism to be a necessary corollary of both an enlightened self-understanding and a fully democratized and genuine human community.

Charles Taylor has convincingly written that the successful prosecution of the human sciences 'requires a high degree of self-knowledge, a freedom from illusion, in the sense of error which is rooted in one's way of life; for our incapacity to understand is rooted in our own self-definitions, hence in what we are' (1985: 57). This is a sentiment which would meet with Bakhtin's full approval. However, for Bakhtin the fulfilment of the Socratic injunction to 'know thyself' cannot take place outside the dialogic alterity of self and other, and it also requires at least one additional premise: a critical penetration into the logic of dominant ideological discourses and a reflexive appropriation of this practice. Like Walter Benjamin, perhaps the Western Marxist he has the most affinity with, Bakhtin therefore exhorts us to probe the gaps and silences, the fractures and fault-lines that expose the operation of a monologism which seeks to effect an ideological closure in order to 'blast a specific era out of the homogeneous course of history'. Only then can the meaning of a suppressed history have its own 'homecoming festival'; that is, be allowed to speak to us, and we in turn have the linguistic capacity and the cultural resources to answer it in a 'free and familiar' manner, without fear of censure or retribution. But Bakhtin provides no elaborate epistemological or eschatological justification for this stance, he makes no dogmatic appeal to 'science', 'truth', or 'the historical mission of the proletariat'. In short, his is a critical hermeneutics without guarantees. The Bakhtinian justification of critique is a moral one, which is ultimately connected to our immediate ethical concerns in the sphere of practical social intercourse. This is what could be termed Bakhtin's gamble, his 'Pascalian wager'. I conclude this study with a quotation of one of Bakhtin's most evocative passages written only a few years before his death in 1975, a citation which is strongly reminiscent of Walter Benjamin's famous declaration of faith in the 'return of the repressed':

There is neither a first nor a last word and there are no limits to the dialogic context (it extends into the boundless past and the boundless future). Even *past* meanings, that is, those born in the dialogue of past centuries, can never be stable (finalized, ended once and for all) – they will always change (be renewed) in the process of subsequent, future development of the dialogue. At any moment in the development of the dialogue there are immense, boundless masses of forgotten contextual meanings, but at certain moments of the dialogue's subsequent development along the way they are recalled and invigorated in renewed form (in a new context). Nothing is absolutely dead: every meaning will have its homecoming festival.

(1986: 170)

Notes

INTRODUCTION

1 As this study was nearing completion, several important works on Bakhtin appeared that unfortunately came along too late to receive significant attention in the main text of this study, although I occasionally refer to them in the notes. Aside from a collection of Bakhtin's early writings entitled *Art and Answerability* (1990), some of these include: Holquist (1990), Jones (1990), Lodge (1990), Morson and Emerson (eds) (1989), and Stam (1989).

2 Said's comments are contained in an interview entitled 'Media, Margins and Modernity: Raymond Williams and Edward Said', included in Williams (1989).

3 The roots of the by now famous (or infamous) 'authorship question' can be traced to 1971, when the eminent Soviet academician V. V. Ivanov put forward the thesis that at least three key works of this Circle – Medvedev's *The Formal Method in Literary Scholarship* and Voloshinov's *Marxism and the Philosophy of Language* and *Freudianism: A Marxist Critique* – were in fact written by Bakhtin himself. Voloshinov and Medvedev, alleged Ivanov, merely edited or transcribed Bakhtin's own material. Precisely why these books were originally attributed to Voloshinov and Medvedev is unclear, especially given that Bakhtin was simultaneously publishing other works under his own name. The potential political sensitivity of these works may have been a factor – and given that both Voloshinov and Medvedev failed to survive Stalin's purges in the 1930s, it may have been a rather cunningly successful strategy. Or, perhaps less cynically, it may have been the result of Bakhtin's cavalier regard for official recognition as well as the fact that he considered authorship to be a collective and not an individual phenomenon. In any event, the question of whether Bakhtin 'actually' wrote the works formerly attributed to Voloshinov and Medvedev is still very much an open one. Nevertheless, I am sympathetic to Young's (1985–6) contention that the currently widespread impulse to reduce the authorship of these texts to Bakhtin himself contradicts Bakhtin's ethical invective against monologic thinking (to say nothing of his comments vis-à-vis the nature of

authorship), and it ignores very real differences in style and content between the disputed works and those texts which are undeniably Bakhtin's own. The literature on the 'authorship question' is voluminous: Ivanov (1974) and Clarke and Holquist (1984a and 1986) are the principal defenders of the thesis that Bakhtin is responsible for the disputed works, while Todorov (1984) is more cautious and Titunik (1984 and 1986) rejects this suggestion altogether. Following a detailed textual comparison of these texts, Perlina (1983) comes to the conclusion that Bakhtin clearly wrote or dictated parts of the works in question, whilst the hand of Voloshinov or Medvedev can be discerned in other passages. This position strikes me as a very reasonable compromise.

4 In fact, the on-going debate about the 'proper' theoretical status of Bakhtin's texts – Marxist, structuralist, proto-deconstructionist, post-modernist, liberal-humanist – has proved to be one of the major growth areas in the entire 'Bakhtin industry'. See, for instance, Hirschkop (1985 and 1986b), Morson (1986), White (1987–8), and Young (1985–6).

5 As an illustration, a computer search I conducted in 1987 revealed 294 titles on Bakhtin and the Circle listed under the rubric of 'literary theory/criticism', but only 16 under 'linguistics' and 10 under 'sociology'.

6 I borrow the phrase 'hermeneutic nihilism' from Stam (1989).

7 On this point, I would concur entirely with Dominick LaCapra:

Bakhtin is generally not discussed in the context of the history of Marxist thought. [. . .] Indeed when Bakhtin is compared with theorists attempting to relate Marxism and semiotics – including Jürgen Habermas – the distinctiveness of his emphases becomes apparent. One is tempted to conclude that what is needed is more of a 'dialogue' between other Marxists and Bakhtin, whose concerns have relatively little place in Marxist literature.

(1983: 319)

8 Of course, there are many areas where Bakhtin does not easily fit into the mainstream of Western Marxism; for instance, he would have rejected the (re)turn to Hegel envisaged by most members of the Western Marxism tradition (epitomized by Lukács's stated desire to develop a Marxism that was a 'Hegelianism more Hegelian than Hegel'). Nor would he have agreed with the widespread attempt to incorporate psychoanalysis into critical theory.

9 Jacoby (1981) provides an excellent discussion of Korsch and other 'council communists' during this period.

10 For a good discussion of the concept of 'critique' in Western Marxism, see McCarney (1990). See also Max Horkheimer's essay 'Traditional and Critical Theory', included in Connerton (ed.) (1976: 223), where he writes:

[Critical theory] is not just a research hypothesis which shows its value in the ongoing business of men; it is an essential element in the historical effort to create a world which satisfies the needs and powers of men. [This] theory never simply aims at an increase of knowledge as such. Its goal is man's emancipation from slavery.

11 This survey misses out some obvious and important texts, but I will attempt to justify my selection as follows: Bakhtin's earliest writings, the so-called 'architectonic' essays, remained untranslated until this work was nearing completion (now available as *Art and Answerability* 1990). In any event, because they are densely philosophical tracts mainly concerned with the development of a phenomenology of subjectivity and the aesthetics of artistic creation, they are tangential to my concerns here. I have also by-passed Voloshinov's *Freudianism: A Marxist Critique* (1976), not because it is uninteresting, but because most of the crucial insights contained therein (for example, the semiotic basis of human cognition) can be found in *Marxism and the Philosophy of Language*. Likewise, the scattered essays of Voloshinov and Medvedev collected in *Bakhtin School Papers* (1983) more or less recapitulate the central points raised in their larger studies. Finally, I have chosen not to discuss the recent volume *Speech Genres and Other Late Essays* (1986), mainly because these writings exist in the form of rough notes and rather gnomic formulations that are not easily open to systematic exegesis. However, I will refer to the *Speech Genres* material extensively in the second section of the present study, especially in chapter four.

12 Originally from an unpublished manuscript dating from the late 1910s, quoted in Clarke and Holquist (1984b: 306).

13 For instance, as J. B. Thompson has convincingly written:

> If the theory of ideology has been marked since its origins by controversy and dispute, it is only in recent years that this theory has been enriched and elaborated through a reflection on *language*. For increasingly it has been realized that 'ideas' do not drift through the social world like clouds in a summer sky, occasionally divulging their contents with a clap of thunder and a flash of light. Rather, ideas circulate in the social world as utterances, as expressions, as words which are spoken and inscribed. Hence to study ideology is, in some part and in some way, to study language in the social world. [. . .] It is to study the ways in which the multifarious uses of language intersect with power, nourishing it, sustaining it, enacting it.
>
> (1984: 2)

1   THE 1920s WRITINGS

1 Partly because this was one of the first texts of the Bakhtin Circle to be translated into English, but also because it has been widely viewed as a characteristic text of the Circle as a whole, *Marxism and the Philosophy of Language* has received a large amount of critical attention. See, for instance, Jameson (1974), Pateman (1982), Silverman and Torode (1980), and Weber (1985).

2 It is worth stressing that Voloshinov's extension of the notion of 'language competence' to include wider relations of social power and ideology closely resembles Pierre Bourdieu's (1977c) conceptualization of language as a form of 'symbolic capital' (i.e., that any speech-act expresses and reinforces the power relations between different social groups and that each such group possesses a distinct level of linguistic competence and symbolic power).

3 Like Wittgenstein, therefore, Voloshinov rejected the possibility of a private language, and he also felt that language was always-already embedded in the 'stream of thought and life', or forms of purposeful, shared activity. The similarities between Bakhtin/Voloshinov and Wittgenstein are intriguing, and their differences equally telling. Nor is this convergence wholly accidental, given that Nikoli Bakhtin (Mikhail's brother) appears to have been a major source of inspiration for Wittgenstein's *Philosophical Investigations*. Eagleton (1986 and 1987) discusses the connection between Bakhtin and Wittgenstein at some length.

4 Voloshinov felt that these subordinated discursive forms did find expression in situations where such inequities (class or otherwise) were absent or relaxed. A good literary example of this is to be found in Turgenev's *Fathers and Sons*. The nihilist Bazarov (who prides himself on being able to converse with the common man) accosts two peasants and engages them in conversation. When his attempt to interrogate their political opinions is met with deferential, half-mumbled responses, Bazarov leaves in disgust, convinced that the Russian peasant is too slow-witted and subservient to improve his own lot. Immediately upon his departure, the peasants' talk loses all trace of patriarchal deference and acquires a note of self-assured independence. 'A master's always a master', they conclude from this encounter, 'they ain't got much understanding'.

5 In an earlier study of Freud entitled *Freudianism: A Marxist Critique*, (1976), Voloshinov rejected the psychoanalytic tendency to posit the psyche as an entity that was fragmentary and dissolute. This is because he felt that the difference between conscious and unconscious states was ideological and not ontological in nature (see Clarke and Holquist 1984a: 180). What Freud referred to as the 'unconscious' was, in actuality, a combination of biological and biographical factors belonging to the domain of inner signs. Such inner signs were the furthest possible distance from a fully-fledged material and institutional expression. The further these inner signs edged towards social and institutional embodiment, however, the less they could be explained by reference to these biological and biographical factors – and, accordingly, the more overtly 'conscious' and intersubjective they became. The evolution from the infantile ego to adult consciousness was not, therefore, a matter of the repression of ego gratification, as in classical psychoanalytic theory. Rather, it represented the acquisition of different discursive practices. It has often been remarked that this position is akin to the Lacanian assertion that subjectivity is formed through the entry of the (pre-symbolic)

unconscious into the 'Symbolic Order' of language (see Bruss 1976 and Stam 1989). However, Voloshinov would have had little sympathy with the notion that this process was universal and transhistorical, insofar as these discursive practices are radically historical in nature.

6 Voloshinov's insistence that human thought cannot occur outside of the matrix of semiological systems that constitute it and that signification itself is dialogical in nature finds a strong echo in the work of Charles Pierce, the American philosopher and semiotician. For a more detailed account of the similarities between Bakhtin/ Voloshinov and Pierce, see Danow (1984), Francoeur (1985), and Ponzio (1984).

7 Parenthetically, this is palpably similar to J. McCarney's argument that ideological complexes 'embody an assessment or grading of, evince a *pro* or *contra* attitude towards, states of affairs and human activities; towards, that is, particular patterns and arrangements and the practices which seek to modify, preserve, strengthen, undermine, or transform them' (1980: 10).

8 Medvedev has, unfortunately, attracted less attention than the other members of the Bakhtin Circle; at times, he seems to be considered something of a 'poor man's Bakhtin'. Some useful commentaries do exist, however, most notably Clarke and Holquist (1984a), Swingewood (1986), and Tribe (1980).

9 Medvedev was one of the more elusive and mysterious members of the Bakhtin Circle, and the authorship of *The Formal Method* is perhaps the most heavily debated. An ardent Bolshevik sympathizer, after the 1917 revolution Medvedev occupied several important government posts in education and publishing, and wrote prolifically on sociological, literary and linguistic issues. He was arrested in the 1930s during one of Stalin's many purges and 'disappeared' shortly afterwards. For more about Medvedev's life and works and the authorship question, see the 'Foreword' by Godzich and the 'Introduction' by Wehrle in *The Formal Method* (1985 edition).

10 Originally designated by the acronym *Opajaz* (the Society for the Study of Poetic Language), it consisted of a group of scholars, linguists and literary historians of whom Yury Tynyanov, Boris Eichenbaum and Viktor Shklovsky were the major exponents. It also included a number of non-Leningrad members, such as the Muscovite linguist Roman Jakobson, who later left Russia and joined the Prague Linguistic Circle.

11 The suppression of Formalism occurred when the cultural climate in the USSR became more closed and repressive, roughly after the mid-1920s. 'Formalism' was to become a taboo subject for at least the next thirty years in Soviet intellectual circles. On this phase of Soviet intellectual history, see Erlich (1981 and 1984), Pechey (1986), Selden (1984), and Todorov (1987).

12 For instance, in his long essay 'The Problem of Content, Material and Form in Verbal Art' written in 1924, Bakhtin sketches out a general aesthetics in relation to literary poetics through an astute critique of Russian Formalism. In this text, Bakhtin argues that Formalism is

deficient because it restricts textual analysis to the 'material' of the word. But whilst literary production certainly involves the transformation of determinate linguistic materials into more complex discursive structures, this alone cannot account for a much wider spectrum of cognitive, ethical and aesthetic relations between author (or reader) and art-work. A viable literary poetics must therefore encompass not only the analysis of form and its technical realization but also the architectonic construction of a text as a 'lived event' within the wider social, cultural and historical context. Brief summaries of this essay can be found in Clarke and Holquist (1984a: 188–90) and Todorov (1984: 36–7). It is now available in English translation in the volume *Art and Answerability* (1990).

13 In an interesting anticipation of Barthes's notion of the 'death of the author' the Formalists argued that a writer was simply a craftsman or a 'skilled maker of artifacts' who was not ultimately responsible for the artistic or aesthetic qualities of the text. See Shklovsky (1965a).

14 More specifically, it was felt that any literary work could be typified in terms of which textual device constituted the 'dominant' one within a structured system of such devices. Each such device had an indexical 'value', and each operated in terms of a series of inherent transformative 'laws' which could be specified with scientific precision. See Jakobson (1978a).

15 That is, Medvedev argues that Formalism was not a scholarly movement in the typical sense, but a loose collection of artists and intellectuals who closely identified with the modernist innovations and iconoclasm of the Futurists. The Futurists were primarily concerned with the technical aspects of the poetic work and with its potential 'shock effect', and were therefore unconcerned with more traditional issues of textual meaning or aesthetics per se. Through its celebrations of modernism and industrialization, its rejection of traditional forms of mimetic art, and in its wild experimentation with poetic form, rhyme and structure, Futurist writers such as Kamensky, Khlebnikov and Mayakovsky sought to challenge the elitist pretensions of what they took to be a decadent bourgeois society fused with a Tsarist autocracy. The definitive study of Russian Futurism is Markov's (1969), but a more recent study is by White (1990). For a discussion of the historical connection between Russian Futurism and Formalism, see Bennett (1979: 29–37) and Erlich (1981: 42–50).

16 For example, In his *Literature and Revolution* (1970) Trotsky suggested that Formalist analyses might be useful for delineating particular aspects of literary form as an adjunct to the historical materialist study of literature as a social and historical phenomenon. Bukharin echoed Trotsky's view, but Lunacharsky denounced what he took to be the subordination of questions of ethical value and emotional intensity to the system of formal textual devices, and a number of other minor critics unambiguously condemned this new heresy. For an extended discussion of the Marxist reception of the Formalist school in post-revolutionary Russia, see Erlich (1981), Holquist (1985b), and Walton (1981). By contrast, Medvedev agreed with the Formalists that

literature was not simply a 'mirror of reality', and he likewise felt that
the specificity of the 'literary' sphere had to be acknowledged and
adequately theorized. He clearly feared that the task of understanding
the intrinsic qualities of the art-work could be lost under a morass of
crude sociological reasoning conducted by an overly *parti pris*
Marxism. Moreover, Medvedev explicitly praised the Formalists for
pioneering the study of the phonetic and linguistic organization of
literary texts, an aspect he felt to be crucial for grasping the work as a
whole.

17 See, for example, Eichenbaum's essay 'Literary Environment', in
Matejka and Pomorska (eds) *Readings in Russian Poetics* (1978).

18 Erlich (1981: 115), for example, argues that while Medvedev makes
some cogent criticisms vis-à-vis Formalism's asocial poetics, he fails to
broach the gulf between the specificity of literary art and extra-literary
context and, as a result, ultimately ends up reinforcing the methodological distinction he attributes to his Formalist opponents. Frow
(1986: 98), by contrast, finds fault with Medvedev's dogmatism and
inability to grasp the important differences between individual
Formalist theorists, particularly with regard to the question of literary
history.

19 For a detailed account of the numerous editorial changes which have
affected Bakhtin's *Dostoevsky* book, see the 'Editor's Preface' by
Emerson in the 1984 translation, and also chapter eleven of Clarke
and Holquist (1984a). The long middle section on the 'carnivalesque'
and Dostoevsky's relation to that tradition was added in 1961, long
after the original edition was published. This section is the most
substantially reworked part, and it bears the mark of Bakhtin's later
interest in folk laughter and popular culture which eventually came to
fruition in *Rabelais and His World*. Because I examine the latter in the
following chapter, I shall not refer to this part of the text here.

20 For instance, references to the concrete socio-economic conditions of
19th-century Russia are surprisingly few and far between. These are
generally confined to remarks about the historical peculiarities of
capitalist development in Russian society, and how these factors may
have contributed to the perennial theme of the 'outsider' in
Dostoevsky's writings. Perhaps because of this Formalist leaning, the
book was initially greeted by incredulity and hostility on the part of
most Soviet critics. One exception was Anatoly Lunacharsky's often
fulsome review of the original edition entitled 'Dostoyevsky's
"Plurality of Voices"' (1973). Interestingly, Clarke and Holquist
(1984a: 238) argue that Lunacharsky's positive response to the book
was a major factor in getting Bakhtin's initial sentence changed after
his arrest in 1929 from time in a Siberian labour camp to the relatively
milder fate of exile in Kazakhstan. Ironically, it may have been
Bakhtin's lack of deference toward Marxist orthodoxy in the *Dostoevsky*
book (a 'deviation' which was, however, undoubtedly compounded by
his religious predilections) which led to his arrest in the first place.

21 For a detailed discussion of this aspect of Bakhtin's work, see Bagby
(1982) and Danow (1984).

22 Bakhtin's claim that Dostoevsky's artistic method represents a radically new form of authorship has proved to be one of the more contentious elements of his thought, and perhaps the most misunderstood. Wellek (1980), for example, charges that Bakhtin is 'simply wrong' if he thinks that Dostoevsky's heroes are not under his authorial control. Yet Bakhtin is not denying authorial intention or creativity. It is that in the polyphonic novel the author does not assume a privileged epistemological standpoint vis-à-vis the characters but rather allows the latter maximum semantic independence: 'The author is profoundly *active*, but of a special *dialogic* sort' (1984: 285). Of course, this independence is a relative one, subject to the generic constraints of the work as a whole. For more on this issue, see Clarke and Holquist (1984a: 243–6), and Thaden (1987).

23 This is the crux of Bakhtin's aesthetic theory in the early essay 'Author and Hero in Aesthetic Activity', now included in the volume *Art and Answerability* (1990). It is worth noting that in this earlier work Bakhtin envisages a much more central role for the author vis-à-vis the formation of the fictional hero. That is, here Bakhtin speculates that the 'being-outside' of the author with respect to the hero (what he terms the 'surplus of vision') enables the former to 'concentrate' the hero and his/her ethical actions, by which he means imparting to the hero a consummating 'wholeness'. This would seem to be at odds with the main thesis of *Problems of Dostoevsky's Poetics*; namely, that poly—phony equals the hero's autonomous 'power to signify', or at least to maximize the distance between the hero's activities and the directing consciousness of the author. This apparent conceptual tension has not gone unnoticed; see, for example, Markiewicz (1984).

24 Julia Kristeva has argued that Bakhtin's interpretation of the 'I' in Dostoevsky's works prefigures and substantiates the poststructuralist thesis that the 'subject' is not a unified whole but rather a 'decentred', unstable entity. See her essay 'Word, Dialogue and Novel' (1986).

25 Bakhtin's hostility to the 'typification' of literary heroes is therefore fundamentally at odds with the aesthetic theory of the Hungarian Marxist Georg Lukács. Lukács felt that the hallmark of the great novel was its ability to typify the historical contradictions and class-determined world-views characteristic of a particular era. Accordingly, the 18th-century historical novels of Fielding and Richardson occupied the pinnacle of Lukács's literary pantheon. For an extended comparison of the theories of Lukács and Bakhtin, see Aucouturier (1983) and Jha (1985).

26 In one of the more moving passages in *Problems of Dostoevsky's Poetics*, Bakhtin writes:

> ... the major emotional thrust in all Dostoevsky's work, in its form as well as its *content*, is the struggle against a *reification* of man, of human relations, of all human values under the conditions of capitalism. Dostoevsky did not, to be sure, completely understand the deep economic roots of reification; nowhere, as far as we know, did he use the actual term 'reification,' but it is this term precisely

that best expresses the deeper sense of his struggle on behalf of man. With great insight Dostoevsky was able to see how this *reifying devaluation* of man had permeated into all the pores of contemporary life, and even into the very foundations of human thinking.

(1984: 62)

2 THE 1930s AND 1940s WRITINGS

1 I borrow this term from the French historian Braudel (1980).

2 For Bakhtin, chronotopes refer to the 'intrinsic connectedness of temporal and spatial relationships that are artistically expressed in literature' (1981: 84) – that is, the system of interacting time and space indicators that are necessary for any kind of artistic visualization. Different genres incorporate different chronotopic systems. In the epic, real historical time is inverted: the present and the future are fleeting and ephemeral compared to the proposed richness and grandiosity of a mythical past. With the emergence of proto-novelistic literary genres, however, this inversion is itself reversed. Time and space begin to take on concrete rather than abstract qualities, in that the idealistic 'vertical' time-space axis of the epic is replaced by the 'historical' axis of real historical time. By utilizing actual boundaries of time and space in their texts, the novel and its precursors can express the 'real-life possibilities of human development'.

3 Bakhtin's stance on the issue of authorship is remarkably similar to that of Barthes in his brief essay 'The Death of the Author'. Here, Barthes argues that authorship as it has been traditionally understood is a myth, and that meaning is 'plural', heterogeneous, the product of the interaction of many texts and voices that can only be unified at the point of its reception. At one stage, Barthes sounds very much like Bakhtin indeed when he writes: 'a text is made of multiple writings, drawn from many cultures and entering into mutual relations of dialogue, parody, contestation' (1977: 148).

4 B. Anderson largely substantiates Bakhtin's thesis vis-à-vis the linguistic-cultural shift of the late Middle Ages and the early Renaissance. He argues that the decline of the absolute hegemony of the medieval church during this period can be explained by the virtual dissolution of three previously axiomatic beliefs: (i) 'the idea that a particular script-language offered privileged access to ontological truth'; (ii) 'that society was naturally organized around and under high centres – monarchs who were persons apart from other human beings and who ruled by some form of cosmological (divine) dispensation'; (iii) 'a conception of temporality in which cosmology and history were indistinguishable, the origins of the world and of men essentially identical' (1983: 40). In particular, he identifies the explosion of print media and the rapid dissemination of humanist and classical texts in the late 15th- and early 16th-century as being of especial importance in this regard.

5 Bakhtin's phenomenology of the self – which for Clarke and Holquist

is connected to a wider theory of 'architectonics' – bears more than a passing resemblance to the philosophy of Heidegger and the early Sartre as well as Mead's notion of the 'significant Other'. However, Bakhtin's work in this area largely predates these and can be traced to his earliest writings dating from 1919–26, some of which remain unpublished. For more on this aspect of Bakhtin's project, see chapter three of Clarke and Holquist (1984a), Emerson (1986), and Holquist (1985a and 1990).

6 Interestingly, Clarke and Holquist (1984a: 275) mention that the essay 'Discourse in the Novel' was written after a conference on the novel organized by Georg Lukács at the Communist Academy in Moscow in 1934–5. In other words, this text can plausibly be read as a kind of implicit critical commentary on the sociology of the novel that Lukács was then attempting to develop, an approach which is in many ways antithetical to Bakhtin's own. Whereas Lukács sees the novel as a debased form of 'the great epic', Bakhtin was concerned to emphasize the differences between the novel and the epic in the strongest possible terms.

7 In order to trace the genealogy of this conflict, Bakhtin in 'Discourse in the Novel' proposes that the evolution of the novel form be analysed in terms of what he calls 'two stylistic lines of development'. In the 'first line' of novelistic development, dating from the Sophistic rhetorics of Greek antiquity, only a single language and style can be ascertained. Heteroglossia is certainly present, but only in a muted and tangential form. Accordingly, language here is abstract, static, and lifeless: it is prevented from establishing any life-sustaining contact with everyday social existence. The second line (Rabelais, Cervantes, Gogol), by contrast, incorporates this social discourse into the structure of the text without necessarily privileging one linguistic style over another. It thereby subverts the lofty pretensions of 'literary language', by dragging the language of prose down to the 'dregs of an everyday gross reality', and by undermining the hegemony of an 'unmediated and pure authorial discourse'.

8 See Goethe's *Italian Journey* (1962).

9 Good commentaries on Bakhtin's *Rabelais* book include Anchor (1985), Berrong (1985 and 1986), Flaherty (1986), Kinser (1990), and Wilson (1986). An overview of some of this literature can be found in McKinley (1987).

10 A good example of this carnivalesque metamorphosis of pre-given social roles is the folk legend of the *Eulenspiegel*, found throughout Northern Europe in the Middle Ages. This tale concerned a wandering prankster who always appeared in a different guise (doctor, monk, artisan, etc.) and who was a combination of fool and wise man. See Sheppard (1983); also Zijderveld (1982: 83–4).

11 V. V. Ivanov perceptively writes that Bakhtin's concern with the top–bottom oppositions of folk culture in *Rabelais and His World* constitutes the basis of a social semiotics of symbolic forms which pre-figured Lévi-Strauss's analyses of the binary relations within 'primitive' myth and ritual by some twenty years. Ivanov also finds

Bakhtin's semiotics relevant for understanding certain aspects of film (he mentions Eisenstein's *Que Viva Mexico!* in this regard), dramaturgy and ancient myths. As Ivanov puts it:

> Structural analysis of the ambivalence of 'the language of the public square' and of the image led Bakhtin (independently of structural anthropology and earlier than its founders) [to study] the various forms of inversion, of reversal of the relationships between bottom and top – 'displacement of the hierarchical top and bottom' in the carnival.
>
> (1974: 337)

12 See Burke (1978), which contains an excellent discussion of medieval carnival and other festive rituals. It also chronicles the dissolution of carnival after the 16th century as the clergy and the authorities made a more concerted attempt to suppress it – the 'triumph of Lent'.

13 Occasionally, of course, folk culture became more than just symbolically transgressive. For instance, Ladurie (1979) describes a carnival in a small French town in 1580 that degenerated into bloody conflict – albeit one that was manipulated by local merchants who fomented class hatred for personal advantage. Davis (1975) also mentions a celebration which turned into a peasant revolt in Berne, 1513, whilst Burke (1978) talks about the so-called 'evil carnival' in Basel in 1376.

14 For instance, Bakhtin mentions medieval literary parodies, wherein scholastic habits and strict academic rules were transformed into festive games and jokes, such as the so-called 'drunkard's mass', parodies of the Last Supper and other religious events (which were intended to 'travesty the serious and make it ring with laughter'), and the *orationes quodlibetica*, mock debates held by students on ridiculous subjects, which parodied learned discourse and combined high-minded rhetoric with obscenities and scatological references.

15 For a detailed examination of the gloomy eschatology of the medieval church, see Huizinga (1965).

16 Recalling Brecht's notion of 'epic theatre' (which similarly sought to break down the artificial barrier between performer and observer), Bakhtin suggests that carnival 'is not a spectacle seen by the people; they live in it, and everyone participates because its very idea embraces all the people (1968: 7). It is worth mentioning that Bakhtin's juxtaposition of 'carnival' and 'spectacle' in this quotation finds a curious echo in the writings of the Situationist International. The Situationists felt that the modern spectacle (in the form of mass media, political campaigns, sports events, etc.) anaesthetized the observer and turned individuals into passive consumers of images. It was therefore a potent form of social control, but one that could be challenged by various strategies of transgression and subversion (called *détournement*) which bear more than a passing resemblance to Bakhtin's carnivalesque. Like *détournement*, carnival is a form of empowerment, which made possible an expansion of autonomy and creativity. For a representative example of Situationist literature, see Debord (1987), and also a recent collection of Situationist texts edited by Blazwick (1989).

Good discussions of the Situationist movement include Marcus (1989), Plant (1990), and Wollen (1989).

17 A particularly apposite example which is worth mentioning is the famous 'feast of fools'. This celebration occurred in late December, and the central event was the election of a mock bishop or abbot – the 'lord of misrule'. This was followed by dancing, street processions, a mock mass enacted by clergy in women's clothes or dressed back to front, the recital of bawdy songs and verses, card-playing on the altar, and the usual drinking and feasting – especially large blood sausages, an obvious phallic/fertility symbol. As P. Burke (1978: 192) puts it, the feast of fools was a perfect example of the 'literal enactment of the world turned upside down'.

18 See p. 160 of his unfinished fragment 'Paris – the Capital of the Nineteenth Century', included in *Charles Baudelaire* (1983).

19 On this, see Febvre and Martin (1990), which chronicles the dissolution of classical Latin as a pan-European language which resulted from the combined effects of the development of distinct national languages, the triumph of humanism (in the writings of Erasmus, Rabelais, and others), and the massive upsurge in printing in the late 15th and early 16th centuries.

20 Bakhtin emphasizes that this understanding of negation is quite different from the logical relation that connects opposites in dialectical thought of an idealistic or Hegelian sort. In the latter, the connected objects or phenomena are conceptualized as static entities residing on one ontological plane. The folk image, by contrast, is concerned with becoming and ambivalence. Thus, it is an 'elemental' or materialist dialectics, not a formal or abstract one. Bakhtin examines the difference between dialectics and dialogue in more detail in his later philosophical writings, most notably 'From Notes Made in 1970–1' (1986).

21 As Zijderveld points out, the decline of the importance of folk laughter in popular culture can be linked to the consolidation of the bourgeoisie as the dominant class in most of Europe by the 17th century. Although the bourgeoisie originally drew on popular culture to lampoon and mock the aristocracy, once its pre-eminence was secure it substituted 'this-worldly' asceticism and rationality for the 'useful folly' of the early modern era:

> . . . when the bourgeoisie began to emerge in the sixteenth century, fighting for socio-economic and political emancipation from the dominant feudal forces, folly in all its anti-intellectual rudeness would be employed as a weapon. But at the same time, the more self-confident and cocksure this new class became, the more it would reject folly as a force adverse to its economic and political aspirations. When the bourgeoisie had to solidify its socio-economic and political position, the Protestant work ethic served it much better than the loitering ethos of traditional fools.
>
> (Zijderveld 1982: 85)

3 THE BAKHTIN CIRCLE AND THE THEORY OF IDEOLOGY

1 This raises the vexed question of the 'Marxist' status of the works produced by Bakhtin and the Circle – which is, arguably, a derivation of the authorship question itself. For discussions of this issue, see Bakhurst (1990), Carroll (1983), Holquist (1981), and White (1987–8).

2 For good accounts of the mutability of the notion of 'ideology' within Marx's corpus, see Larrain (1979, 1983, and 1989), Márkus (1983), Mészáros (1989), and Williams (1977: 55–71). The issue has received relatively little attention in the literature on Bakhtin and the Circle, but see Bennett (1979: 78), Stewart (1986: 49), and Weber (1985).

3 For examinations of the pre-Marxian Enlightenment roots of *Ideologiekritik*, see Barth (1977) and Head (1985).

4 The Marxist tradition which takes its cue from Marx's writings on commodity fetishism is the Hegelian Marxism of Lukács, Korsch and the Frankfurt School. Yet it also claims contemporary adherents, such as Mepham (1979).

5 Thus, as Parekh (1982) convincingly argues, ideology in the early writings of Marx came to mean both idealism and apologia, and that there is a necessary connection between them. Yet Marx never clarified this linkage, and there is a constant slippage between them in texts like *The German Ideology*. This has served to exacerbate the confusion surrounding the term.

6 In the introduction to the 1970 Lawrence & Wishart edition of *The German Ideology*, Arthur supports this position by arguing that it is possible to 'select certain one-sided formulations, which the authors no doubt resorted to for the purpose of contrasting forcibly their positions from those of the dominant idealist trends, and make these the basis of a fatalistic view which negates human purposefulness and activity'. However, such an interpretation is not adequate because 'the circumstances which are held to shape and form consciousness are not independent of human activity. They are precisely the *social* relations which have been *historically* created by human action' (1970: 21–2). I take this point, but would nevertheless argue that this does not vitiate Williams's (1977) position insofar as he is primarily referring to the overarching impression the text leaves when Marx talks about consciousness as a 'direct efflux' or 'derivation' of the 'real life process' and – perhaps more importantly – the impact these formulations had on the subsequent evolution of Marxist theory at least until the 1960s.

7 For accounts of the emergence of 'Western Marxism' as a distinctive if disparate intellectual movement, see Anderson (1976), Callinicos (1983), Jacoby (1981), Jay (1984a), and Merquior (1986b).

8 There are at least three different positions which have been developed on this score from within the Marxist tradition. Firstly, there has been an attempt to reconstruct the base/superstructure model through the incorporation of such concepts as 'mediation', 'relative autonomy', and so on. See Althusser (1970), although a

non-structuralist example is Sartre (1976). Alternatively, the necessity of this metaphor is rejected altogether, because it is felt to treat complex and dynamic social processes in an undialectical and reductive fashion (Larrain 1986 and Williams 1977). Another (currently fashionable) option is to reject any attempt to develop a grand theory of the social formation as a whole and replace it with a focus on the 'contingent articulation' of particular ensembles of social practices which have no originating centre. This so-called 'post-Marxist' position claims a poststructuralist (but also a Gramscian) pedigree (see Laclau and Mouffe 1985).

9 Also of interest is Kellner (1978).

10 See Callinicos (1983), particularly chapter six; also Laclau (1977) and Swingewood (1977).

11 For more on this, refer to Ricoeur (1981 and 1986) and Zima (1981a).

12 As Voloshinov himself said prophetically in 1929: 'The very foundation of a Marxist theory of ideologies [is] closely bound up with the problem of the philosophy of language' (1973: 9).

13 It worth noting that the Russian term *slovo* utilized by the Bakhtin Circle, which is generally translated as 'word', actually means both word as it is generally understood in English (that is, as a discrete phonetic entity forming a meaningful element of language) as well as the method of putting words to use (their concrete implementation) in actual discourse. It is therefore very similar to the ancient Greek *logos*, which designates 'not merely the capacity for rational discourse but the rational faculty underlying and informing the spoken word in all its forms' (Harris and Taylor 1989: xi).

14 For general discussions of the early Soviet *avant-garde* in relation to linguistic and literary theory, see Gibian and Tjalsma (eds) (1976) and Phillips (1986). Williams discusses the cultural-historical 'moment' of the Bakhtin Circle (or the 'Vitebsk group', as he puts it), bemoaning the fact that the work of the Circle was lost to radical cultural theory for so long. He argues that an earlier appreciation of its output 'could have saved many wasted years' (1986: 26).

15 See Weber's recently-translated review of Voloshinov's *Marxism and the Philosophy of Language* (1985).

16 Larrain's (1983) typology is certainly valuable insofar as it allows us to categorize and understand the various contributions to a theory of ideology throughout the history of Marxist thought. Nevertheless, I would argue that where Larrain errs is on his insistence that a critical approach to the critique of ideology must necessarily maintain such a 'negative' conception of ideological phenomena. For it is entirely possible (as do the Bakhtin Circle, or so I will argue here) to utilize a non-epistemological account of ideology whilst retaining a critical stance vis-à-vis the role of ideology in the maintenance of asymmetrical power relations (see Thompson 1984 and 1987).

17 There are, however, some things we may wish to keep in mind. Firstly, as Larrain (1983) points out, *The German Ideology* was not published in Marx and Engels's lifetime and was in fact not generally available (in the Soviet Union or elsewhere) until the 1930s. Accordingly, the first

generation of European Marxists generally embraced the vaguer and more general notion of 'ideological superstructure' found in the 1859 *Preface* and the work of the later Engels, especially the *Anti-Dühring*. The result was that the concept of ideology gradually lost its initial pejorative connotation, and the 'positive' version was eventually consolidated in the Russian Marxist tradition in the writings of Bukharin, Plekhanov and Lenin. It is reasonable to assume that the Bakhtin Circle would have been more familiar with this Russian tradition than any other, and that this interpretation of ideology would have had a readily recognized meaning in the theoretical discourse of the Soviet left intelligentsia. Perhaps more importantly, however, the negative characterization would have sat uneasily with the general thrust of the Bakhtin Circle's philosophy of language, which lays more stress on the performative or pragmatic functions of language-use than with epistemological considerations.

18 Voloshinov did in fact advance a brief definition in a footnote to his essay 'Literary Stylistics': 'By ideology we have in mind the whole totality of the *reflexions* and *refractions* in the human brain of social and natural reality, as it is expressed and fixed by man in word, drawing, diagram or other form of *sign*' (1983: 113).

19 This is a recurrent criticism of orthodox Marxism made by advocates of structuralist-derived positions. See, for example, Adlam *et al.* (1977), Althusser (1969 and 1971), Hall (1977b), Molina (1977), and Therborn (1980).

20 During the mid- to late 1970s, the work of Althusser and Lacan became increasingly influential with respect to the development of a linguistically-based theory of ideology on the part of the British neo-Marxists. See, for example, Coward and Ellis (1977) and Hirst (1976). The film journal *Screen* has also been significant in the attempt to introject Lacanian themes into the Marxian theory of ideology.

21 It is also worth noting, as Phillips (1986: 52) points out, that Voloshinov's *Freudianism: A Marxist Critique* (1976) had a demonstrable impact on Jakobson and the rest of the Prague Circle, whose writings influenced Lévi-Strauss during his formative years. As Macey (1988) notes, Lacan drew a large amount of inspiration from Lévi-Strauss in turn. One could in fact speculate that Lacan's reconstruction of psychoanalysis was perhaps in some small measure prompted by Voloshinov's original linguistically-based critique of Freud in 1927!

22 Useful accounts of the 'decentring of the subject' appear in Belsey (1980), Harland (1987), Henrique *et al.* (1984), Macdonell (1986), Selden (1984), and Soper (1986).

23 It is worth mentioning the impact on the Bakhtin Circle of the Soviet psychologist Vygotsky (1896–1934), whose career roughly paralleled that of Medvedev and Voloshinov. Reacting against the dominant school of Pavlovian 'reflexology' in Soviet psychology, Vygotsky stressed the need to consider human beings not as physiological organisms who passively responded to external stimuli, but as creative, dynamic beings who actively structured and made meaningful the world around them. As such, he emphasized the role of human

consciousness in this process (although he believed this to be historically and socially determined), particularly the realization of thoughts and motives in the form of social speech and writing. The general process through which the individual acquired an increasing mastery of the external sign-systems was one of Vygotsky's primary concerns. Although Bakhtin and Vygotsky never met, Vygotsky's materialist psychological theories had a demonstrable impact on the Circle (and on the work of Voloshinov in particular). Commentaries on the interconnection between Vygotsky and the Bakhtin Circle include Bakhurst (1990) and Emerson (1986).

24 Parenthetically, one could also mention Voloshinov's (1976) suggestion that there exist substantial conflicts between 'official' or social signs on the one hand and the realm of unofficial or 'inner' speech on the other, resulting in psychic tensions that are analogous to Freud's theories of displacement, censorship, etc. Unlike Freud, however, Voloshinov insists that these conflicts are not 'psychological' or biological but are determined by 'objective material processes' – that is, they are the result of the dialectic of history, not natural drives or impulses.

25 See 'Engels and Free Will' in Timpanaro (1976).

26 I am struck by the similarity between Bakhtin's account of the constitution of language in social practice and A. Giddens's (1979 and 1984) notion of the 'duality of structure': i.e., the thesis that the structural properties of social systems are simultaneously the medium and the outcome of specific forms of action and, therefore, both constrain and enable the purposive activities of social agents. What this implies is that the constitution of agencies and structures (including language and other symbolic systems) are not independent processes, or that one unilaterally constitutes the other; rather, they constitute each other in an ongoing dialectical process. Thus, any viable social or cultural theory must not only be able to account for the nature and functioning of the relatively enduring structural properties of a given social system; it must also explain the actions and experiences of social agents as they produce and reproduce these structures in the light of everyday social praxis. Giddens's theory of structuration is not, however, without its critics: see Callinicos (1987), Clark *et al.* (eds) (1990), and Held and Thompson (eds) (1989).

27 This interest in delineating a middle-ground between the Scylla of a poststructuralist 'discourse fever' and a banal humanism vis-à-vis the issue of the subject has recently received a great deal of attention. See, for example, Callinicos (1987 and 1989), Dews (1987), Geras (1983), Giddens (1987), Soper (1986 and 1990), and two essays by Willis and Corrigan (1980 and 1981).

28 This point is admirably summarized by Bauman:

It belongs to the essence of human existence that it is ever unfinished and inconclusive, open toward the future, lived, evaluated and revised under the auspices of events which exist, so far only ideally, as an end of human effort, as a desirable state, as an ideal pattern, as a nostalgia, a plan, a dream, a threat, a hope, or a danger.

(1976: 34–5)

29 For the Frankfurt School, for example, ideology in the form of mass culture mesmerized the masses and led them to accept false needs which could only be gratified through consumerism. The negation of real human needs and the resultant loss of autonomy and the powers of self-reflection led to the ideological incorporation of the sub-ordinate classes into the status quo: 'The heritage of ideology [is] the totality of what is cooked up in order to ensnare the masses as consumers and, if possible, to mold and constrain their state of consciousness' (The Frankfurt Institute for Social Research, cited in Kellner 1978: 54–5).

30 It is difficult to take issue with most of what Abercrombie and company have to say. However, I would argue that, first of all, their discussion of prominent Marxist theoreticians who are supposed to cleave to this position is somewhat misleading, and not all (e.g. Gramsci's theory of hegemony) subscribe to the DIT. Secondly, it threatens to throw the baby out with the bathwater by rejecting the validity of the concept of ideology en bloc. As A. Callinicos notes (1987), while individuals from subordinate classes may not acquiesce in the dominant ideology in its entirety, this does not preclude the possibility that the dominant belief system may prevent the develop-ment of a coherent oppositional consciousness. In this study, I construe the Bakhtin Circle along the lines of this latter position, and argue that ideology remains a crucial theoretical concept for under-standing the general process by which social agents acquire particular identities and engage in forms of collective and individual action. For further critical discussions of the DIT, see Lodziak (1988), and reviews by Rootes (1981) and Therborn (1984). A counter-response to some of these criticisms and debates can be found by Abercrombie *et al.* (1983) and (eds) (1990).

31 This position is palpably close to Nietzsche's philosophy, which claims contemporary adherents in the form of Michel Foucault's 'genealo-gical' approach in particular and poststructuralism in general. Nietzsche distrusted grand philosophical systems, seeing them as arid metaphysical rationalizations which benefited the hypocrites in power because they repressed 'authentic' passions and desires which sprang from a deep organismic vitality. Weber (1985) suggests that the shadow of Nietzsche falls over much of the work of Voloshinov and Bakhtin, and an extended comparison between them can be found in Curtis (1986).

32 It is difficult to say exactly where this quirky Bakhtinian materialism and stress upon the everyday is derived; Clarke and Holquist (1984a: 84–5) point to the 'kenotic' tradition of the Russian Orthodox Church, wherein the corporeality of Christ and the sacredness of matter (and, incidentally, the importance of community) are strongly affirmed. One could also mention Bakhtin's interest in Acmeist

poetry, which developed a sparse poetic style which emphasized the prosaic and the experiential. Finally, the impact of Marx's own thought cannot be entirely disregarded.

33 Thus, Bakhtin and company are palpably at odds with the Wittgensteinian ethos with tends to pervade most interpretive sociologies of everyday life (e.g. Winch, Garfinkel, etc.). That is, in the *Philosophical Investigations* (1963) Wittgenstein argued that the illusions of metaphysical philosophy could only be averted if one returned to the sphere of 'ordinary language' and the forms of life which corresponded to them. Bakhtin is equally suspicious of grand philosophical systems (he is notably hostile, for example, toward the pretence of Hegelian dialectics to absolute knowledge). Nevertheless, as Eagleton points out (1986), Bakhtin would have rejected Wittgenstein's supposition that ordinary language was somehow removed from the exigencies of class antagonisms and ideological determinations, and he believed that the language of 'everyday life' was already metaphysical.

34 This phenomenon – of ideological self-censorship – is discussed by Medvedev under the rubric of 'speech tact' in *The Formal Method*:

> Speech tact [. . .] gives form to everyday utterances, determining the genre and style of speech performances. Here tact [*taktichnost'*] should be understood in a broad sense, with politeness as only one of its aspects. Tact may have various directions, moving between the two poles of compliment and curse. Speech tact is determined by the aggregate of all the social relationships of the speakers, their ideological horizons, and, finally, the concrete situation of the conversation. Tact, whatever its form under the given conditions, determines all our utterances. No word lacks tact.
>
> (1985: 95)

35 As Crowley has astutely pointed out, monoglossia does not so much represent the total exclusion of difference so much as its extreme hierarchization: social control is effected through the creation of a 'precise pattern of inclusion which place[s] its subjects in certain positions and hierarchical relationships' (1989: 81). Again, compare this to the work of Bourdieu (1977b), particularly the notion of 'doxa'.

36 Or so claim Clarke and Holquist (1984a), Bakhtin's biographers. They remind us that Bakhtin apparently preferred the older and more conservative Symbolist movement (Bely, Blok) to the newer generation of Cubo-futurists, Constructivists and Suprematists. Bakhtin does indeed display pronounced affinities with the Symbolists – as in, for example, the Symbolist desire to de-emphasize the Romanticist importance placed on the role of the individual author in order to explore the poetic nuances and resonances within the sphere of language itself (Mallarmé: 'The pure work implies the elocutory disappearance of the poet'). Moreover, both share a tendency to shift issues of personal emancipation and autonomy to the aesthetic domain, and thus to overemphasize the revolutionary potential of art.

37 For a discussion of Duchamp's anti-aesthetic, see Alexandrian (1970: 3–39). Also of interest is Lewis (1990), and Richter (1965).

38 I was initially drawn to the possibilities of such a comparison whilst reading Polan's essay 'Bakhtin, Benjamin, Sartre: Towards a Typology of the Intellectual Cultural Critic', where he writes:

> We might go so far as to suggest that writing in the case of critics like Bakhtin or Benjamin or Sartre takes on a form that is perspectivalist or cubist, here again becoming part of a particularly modern conception of the relativity of knowledge in space and time.
>
> (1989: 12)

39 For example, it has been plausibly suggested that Bakhtin's apparently 'serious' academic study of folk laughter in *Rabelais and His World* is intended ironically, as a self-conscious parody of scholarly tropes and rhetorical devices which refuses the 'totalizing' (or monologic) vision of the bourgeois intellectual. In support of this Polan (1989) mentions Bakhtin's use of an obscure philological vocabulary to construct an elaborate genealogy of vulgarities and obscene expressions. A similar argument is voiced by White (1983), where he makes the provocative claim that Bakhtin's own dense and abstract style is at odds with the ideal of dialogism – but purposely so. White argues that Bakhtin's own writings are actually multi-levelled parodies of academic discourse, an ironic 'sideways glance' at the methods of scholarship and science. He also suggests that Bakhtin's privileging of dialogical over monological discourse is not grounded in the epistemological distinction between 'truth' as opposed to 'illusion', but rather in the moral distinction between truth and lie.

40 Crowley (1989) takes up this point by suggesting that Bakhtin's implication that the historical movement from mono- to heteroglossia is (more or less) necessarily accompanied by increased pluralism and self-reflection is deeply flawed because it allows an ethical valorization of heteroglossia to ride roughshod over specific historical considerations, and that therefore Bakhtin maintains an overly optimistic assessment of modernity. Hirschkop (1989a) also takes issue with Bakhtin's construal of modern heteroglossia as an ethical ideal rather than a historical reality: for example, Dostoevsky's Russia does not even remotely approximate the situation of free and familiar 'heterolanguagedness' that Bakhtin finds so attractive (although the NEP period of the 1920s was a far more propitious era, it must be said). I return to this issue in more detail in the final chapter.

4 BAKHTIN'S CRITICAL HERMENEUTICS

1 For good discussions of the relationship between Nietzsche and the theory of ideology, see Minogue (1989), and Warren (1984).

2 On the impact of Nietzsche's philosophy on poststructuralist thought,

see Callinicos (1982 and 1989), Dews (1987) and, for primary sources, Derrida (1979) and Foucault (1984).

3 Useful introductions to the history of hermeneutic thought include Bauman (1978) and Bleicher (1980).

4 Illuminating accounts of these intellectual and historical developments can be found in Hughes (1959), Outhwaite (1975) and Swingewood (1984).

5 There have been a couple of other attempts to construe Bakhtin as a hermeneutic thinker: in particular, see Pirog (1987), and chapter two of Todorov (1984). Most commentators on Bakhtin have, however, tended to stress his connection with semiology and literary theory.

6 The religious or quasi-spiritual overtones of this formulation are self-evident; it has affinities with both the peculiarities of the Russian Orthodox faith and certain Jewish philosophers and theologians, such as Herman Cohen, Martin Buber and Emmanuel Levinas. Interested parties may wish to consult Clarke and Holquist's biography (1984a), which focuses on this aspect of Bakhtin's world-view in some detail; also of interest is Perlina (1984), Shukman (1984), and Todorov (1984).

7 Useful accounts of the impact of positivism on modern social thought include Aronowitz (1988), Giddens (ed.) (1974), Simon (1963), and Swingewood (1984).

8 Bakhtin rarely addresses why scientific rationalism has been such a pervasive aspect of the dominant intellectual culture since the Enlightenment, except that it can be implicated in the general hegemonic desire on the part of elites to centralize and unify the social world. However, Taylor (1985) suggests that the ubiquity of the paradigm of naturalism can be (at least partially) explained by the fact that it has a strong elective affinity with the image of man as a free, autonomous agent with the capacity to ascertain 'truth' from an objective, disengaged standpoint. This conception of the agent emerged from the cosmological revolutions of the 17th century and still retains strong roots in our present-day culture. Naturalism – the desire to garner an objective, disinterested knowledge of the social world using the natural sciences as a heuristic – is therefore the logical extension of this flattering (if debateable) view of the self.

9 See, for example, Geertz (1973), Ricoeur (1981) and Taylor (1985). Also of relevance is Thompson's (1984) critique of Ricoeur's analogy between text and action.

10 This demonstrates Bakhtin's convergence with contemporary reception theory (Jauss, Iser, etc.). There has been very little work done on the affinities between reception theory and Bakhtin's reader-oriented dialogism except Shepherd (1989). With respect to reception theory a useful guide is Holub (1984).

11 Zima (1981a) suggests that there is an interesting affinity between Adorno's critique of 'identity thinking', which sought to avoid the abstraction and hierarchization of instrumental reason through a 'paratactic' or essayistic writing style which resisted simplification and

paraphrase, and Bakhtin's monologic/dialogic distinction and his self-parodic, open-ended prose form. Both Bakhtin and Adorno felt that one of the most pernicious aspects of ideology was its pretence that a particular word or concept was wholly adequate to the thing it claimed to represent. Good discussions of Adorno's style can be found in chapter thirteen of Eagleton (1990), the introductory chapter to Jay (1984b), and chapter two of Rose (1978).

12 As Shukman has written:

> Bakhtin's theory of the novel is based on discourse rather than the represented world, yet for him behind each 'voice' that makes up the plural novel-text is a 'consciousness' which is the ultimate reality; and Kristeva's epistemological void is alien to Bakhtin's personalism, steeped as it is in Western humanist values.
>
> (1980: 222–3)

13 Gadamer's hankering for a pre-modern re-integration of different human skills and knowledge-forms is well demonstrated by the following quotation:

> When Aristotle, in the sixth book of the *Nicomachean Ethics*, distinguishes the manner of 'practical' knowledge from theoretical and technical knowledge [...] he expresses, in my opinion, one of the greatest truths by which the Greeks throw light upon the 'scientific' mystification of modern society.
>
> (1979: 107)

14 Gadamer is not entirely forthcoming on such epistemological issues. As Bernstein (1986) convincingly argues, Gadamer rarely speaks about 'truth' as such but rather the 'claims to truth' that tradition makes upon us. We therefore judge and evaluate such claims on the basis of relevant procedures and standards that our relation to tradition makes possible. The problem for Bernstein is that Gadamer never addresses what standards and values are relevant to us in the adjudication of claims in the here and now. Gadamer's philosophy gives us no guidelines on which to base our critical judgements, a warrant to what is actually valid in tradition.

15 See Hekman's (1986: 101) discussion of Gadamer and Heidegger on this point. Gadamer draws extensively on Heidegger's philosophy, and requires no particular elucidation, but it is interesting to note that the late Bakhtin did occasionally refer to Heidegger, and generally in a complimentary manner. In a discussion of the I/Thou relationship in 'From Notes Made in 1970–1', for instance, Bakhtin writes 'Another route [to Dostoevsky's polyphony or something like it] would be to cause the world to begin speaking and to listen to the word of the world itself (Heidegger)' (1986: 149).

16 Bakhtin argues that the 'roots' of any text or art-work extend into the 'distant past', and they have a particular resonance for future generations: 'Works break through the boundaries of their own time, they live in centuries, that is, in *great time* and frequently (with great works,

always) their lives there are more intense and fuller than their lives within their own time' (1986: 4).

17 Interestingly, in an early work entitled 'Author and Character in Aesthetic Activity' (written between 1922 and 1924), Bakhtin explicitly rejects the metaphor of 'fusion'. The point is that for Bakhtin the I/Thou relation should be a reciprocal, mutually-enlightening one, but in which neither party is subordinated to the will or power of the other. A plurality of unmerged (yet interacting) consciousnesses is Bakhtin's ideal, not some kind of Hegelian synthesis. To quote Bakhtin:

> In what way will the event be enriched if I succeed in fusing with the other? If instead of two, there is one? What do I gain by having the other fuse with me? [. . .] Let him rather stay on the outside because from there he can know and see what I cannot see or know from my vantage point, and he can enrich the event of my life. In a *mere* fusion with someone else's life, I can only deepen its tragic character, literally double it.
>
> (cited in Todorov 1984: 108)

18 See, in particular, Gadamer's essay 'On the Scope and Functioning of Hermeneutical Reflection' (1976).

19 In fact, Gadamer seems to regard ideology as something analogous to the 'misunderstanding' of the unacknowledged assumptions and pre-conceptions that constitute a particular world-view and is therefore analogous to 'blind prejudice'. However, as Warnke (1987: 115) points out, there is a significant difference between 'ideology' (at least as it has been conceptualized within the tradition of Western Marxism) and the cultural-historical situatedness of a particular belief or assumption. This explains Habermas's charge that if social inquiry remains at the 'surface level' of the self-understanding of society, then the systematic distortion of this self-understanding and its connection to relations of power and domination cannot be explicated.

20 The fallacy in Gadamer's stance here for Warnke (1987: 136) is that although we may have no absolute grounds whence to criticize tradition as illegitimate, neither can tradition be shown to be superior and legitimate with recourse to some form of reasoned assertion. Thus, we can talk about 'ideology' as a mode of discourse which conforms to the interests and limited perspective of a given class or social groups without resorting to the justification of the critique of this ideology by recourse to a foundationalist epistemology. As Nielsen has written: 'That we do not have the absolute truth or the uniquely true, all-embracing perspective does not mean that some perspectives do not yield more truth, give a more adequate account, than others' (1989: 166).

21 For a full account of the Habermas–Gadamer debate, see Hekman (1986), Jay (1982) and McCarthy (1978).

22 As Habermas writes: 'The distortion of the dialogic relation is subject to the causality of split-off symbols and reified grammatical relations:

that is, relations that are removed from public communication, prevail only behind the backs of subjects, and are also empirically coercive' (1978: 59). In other words, ideology for Habermas represents a communicative disorder which prevents the mutual recognition of subjects. As Ricoeur (1986) has pointed out, 'class struggle' in Habermas's terminology does not designate revolutionary action, but rather a process of mutual recognition between antagonists whereby the necessity for violent struggle is superseded – a position that is ultimately derived from Hegel's master–slave dialectic.

23 See Habermas (1970a, 1970b and 1979). A good discussion of this element of Habermas's work can be found in Held and Thompson (eds) (1982) and Thompson (1984). Briefly, Habermas argues that communicative interaction is intrinsically oriented towards the attainment of an 'ideal speech situation' in which consensus and truth are achieved dialogically. Speech is therefore inherently regulated by a complex of 'dialogue-constitutive universals' which establish a common grid of reference between speakers vis-à-vis distinctions of time and space, being and appearance, various normative claims, and so on. These universal features of speech make possible (i) the rational attainment of consensus; (ii) the achievement of intersubjective understanding; and (iii) a mutual recognition by the participants concerned of the right of all to enter into and shape the outcome of this discursively-achieved consensus.

24 For broader (though often sympathetic) critiques of Habermas's critical theory, see Callinicos (1989), Giddens (1977 and 1982), and Held (1980). A good defence of Habermas can be found in Outhwaite (1987).

25 On this question of the hermeneutic status of the natural sciences, see Lyotard (1984), Mulkay (1979), Rorty (1979), and Toulmin (1982).

26 The central texts are in Ricoeur (1981 and 1986). Also of interest is Thompson (1981 and 1984) and Williams (1988).

27 It should be noted, however, that Ricoeur does occasionally over-emphasize the integrative aspects of ideology, at least from a Bakhtinian point of view. Ricoeur contends that the very existence of a group is predicated on its ability to formulate a series of images of itself which link it with the past, images which are collectively shared and which serve to integrate the group in question. The integrative features of ideology are, moreover, manifested in any social group regardless of size or complexity. Yet, as Thompson (1984) rightly points out, considerable evidence suggests that it is extremely doubtful that all (or most) members of a large industrial society (such as contemporary Britain) share an underlying stratum of beliefs and values. Insofar as complex societies require some degree of 'integration' in order to reproduce themselves over time, it is more likely that this is made possible by the creation of divisions and wide-spread dissensus which undercuts the efficacy of oppositional movements – which suggests that we should make a distinction between system integration and normative integration. Accordingly, it is doubtful that ideology can be profitably understood as a shared matrix of images that promotes social cohesion.

28 It is important to clarify just what Ricoeur has in mind by 'critique', insofar as he is openly contemptuous of Marxist-Leninist notions of 'class war'. Following Habermas, he asserts (1986: 261–3) that the object of 'class struggle' is not the destruction of the enemy but the achievement of mutual recognition and tolerance between adversaries. Thus, the critique of ideology must aim at the negation of its distorting or dissimulating functions, but not at the expense of its integrative role in the symbolic constitution of a social group's self-image. More specifically, the role of a critical hermeneutics is to mediate between the plurality of belief systems that tend to proliferate in the 'open conflictual situation of modernity' and to articulate a (necessarily utopian) vision of a more just society.

29 For Ricoeur's views on utopia, see (1976a, 1976b and 1981).

30 See Castoriadis's 'The Imaginary Institution of Society', in Fekete (ed.) (1984).

31 On the subject of the moral-practical implications of dialogic understanding, Bakhtin wrote in an early text entitled 'Author and Character in Aesthetic Activity' that understanding was not a 'question of an exact and passive reflection' but rather a matter of 'translating the experience into an altogether different axiological perspective, into new categories of evaluation and formation' (cited in Todorov 1984: 22).

32 In *The Rule of Metaphor*, for example, Ricoeur writes that 'objective meaning is not something hidden behind the text. Rather it is a requirement addressed to the reader. The interpretation accordingly is a kind of obedience to this injunction starting from the text' (1978: 319).

33 For more on this, see Hekman (1986: 144).

34 Moreover, as Voloshinov stresses in his important essay 'Discourse in Life and Discourse in Art' (1976), artistic discourse differs from the spoken utterance because it is not as heavily dependent on extraverbal context for the conveyance of meaning – that is, there is no immediate social environment and no common spatial or ideological purview for artistic discourse to refer to.

35 Thompson (1984) also identifies this as an important weakness in Ricoeur's theory of the text and distanciation. He takes issue with Ricoeur's claim that the written text (in contradistinction to spoken utterances) must be understood as an autonomous entity which is abstracted from the social-historical conditions of production. Ricoeur asserts that the text, unlike the speech-act, is not addressed to an audience but to potentially anyone. Thompson, however, feels that this is an exaggeration – indeed, the anticipation of a projected audience directly influences what is written. Moreover, texts are not only written works but commodities; they are designed to be consumed in an economic system dominated by market forces and the transfer of exchange-values. Thus, the supposed autonomy of the text is limited in important ways.

36 It is interesting to note that Bakhtin's textual politics is echoed in the work of a number of prominent Marxist theorists. For instance,

Bennett argues that because textual meaning is regulated by the 'reading formation' that structures the interaction between interpreter and interpretand, alternative readings are just as 'ontologically secure' (if less culturally powerful) than are dominant ones. Accordingly, Marxism should not be concerned to reveal the unitary 'meaning' of a given text (on dubious epistemological grounds), but to 'make [texts] human and reverberate to (ideally) the full range of meanings and effects which they have been furnished a site for' (1987: 75).

37 In his late essay 'From Notes Made in 1970–1', for instance, Bakhtin suggests that whilst rhetoric is only concerned with securing victory over an opponent, true dialogue is interested in the pursuit of truth. Through dialogue, he argues, 'one can reach solutions to questions that are capable of temporal solutions, but not to ultimate questions' (1986: 152). This quotation, however, indicates a significant gap between Bakhtin's dialogism and Habermas's 'discursively achieved consensus'. For Habermas, to cure the 'pathology' of systematically distorted communication takes the form of a resolution of conflicting interests and viewpoints. For Bakhtin, by contrast, no 'final word' can be spoken – the clash of utterances in the dialogic encounter, even if motivated by a 'will to agreement', cannot be totally reconciled; otherwise, the creativity of language (amongst other things) would calcify, become sterile and lifeless. It is impossible – and, indeed, undesirable – to eliminate all misunderstanding, all dissent. As Wellmer has recently put it:

The ideal communication community would be beyond error, dissent, non-understanding and conflict, but only at the cost of bringing language to a halt, of a dying-out of its productive energies and this means at the cost of a cancellation of the linguistic-historical life-form of human beings.

(cited in Dews 1987: 223)

38 As Bakhtin writes:

The dialogic relationship as the only form of relationship toward the human being-personality preserving its freedom and open-endedness. Criticism of all *external* forms of relationship and interaction, from violence to authority; artistic finalization as a variety of violence. [. . .] One cannot force or pre-shape *confessions* (Ippolit). Persuasion through love.

(1984: 291–2)

39 For a good discussion of the utopian tradition within Marxism, see Geoghegan (1987), Levitas (1990), and Lukes (1984).

40 On this topic, see Eagleton (1990) and Gardiner (1992).

41 I think it could be said that Bakhtin's historical schema is teleological in the sense that he evinces a definite movement toward increased self-reflexiveness in the modern era, which is based on specific linguistic-ideological possibilities and resources – i.e., the increasing plurality and differentiation of language-games, ideological

perspectives, etc. However, he is not a teleological thinker in the sense that he envisages a specific, definable end-goal in this movement, examples being Hegel's absolute knowledge as garnered by the world-spirit in its final stages of self-realization, or the orthodox Marxist notion of the inevitable triumph of a classless, communistic society. Rather, like Marx (and rather unlike impoverishing parodies of Marx's thought), Bakhtin saw the potentialities inherent in real social transformations and processes, without ever suggesting that the possibility of their realization (on however partial a basis) was inevitable or pre-figured in advance without the intervention of concerted collective action.

42 See, in particular, the work of the American cultural theorist Jameson (1976, 1979 and 1981).

5 BAKHTIN, IDEOLOGY AND NEO-STRUCTURALISM

1 Due to considerations of space and time, I have been forced to ignore or by-pass many important developments in the area of ideology and language. For a substantial overview of this area, see Larrain (1979), Macdonell (1986), Sumner (1979), Thompson (1984), Threadgold (1986), and Zima (ed.) (1981a and 1981b).

2 As Marx and Engels wrote:

> Language is as old as consciousness, language is practical conscious-ness that exists also for other men, and for that reason alone it really exists for me personally as well; language, like consciousness, only arises from the need, the necessity, of intercourse with other men.
>
> (1978: 158)

Musselwhite (1977) convincingly argues that this passage represents a decisive break with a crude materialism and expresses the 'very germ of a materialist, social and dialectical theory' of language.

3 It is indicative of this situation that one of the most influential texts with respect to Marxist theory and language was Joseph Stalin's short essay *Marxism and Problems of Linguistics*, originally published in *Pravda* in 1950. It was intended to settle a theoretical dispute between N. Y. Marr and a number of other Soviet linguists. Another more notable exception was the work of the Polish philosopher Schaff (1962), who was concerned with criticizing conventionalist theories of language (e.g. Carnap) and the 'picture theory' of Wittgenstein's *Tractatus* period, whilst developing a more dialectical theory of reflection. However, Schaff did not consider the ideological properties of language.

4 See, for example, Culler (1976), and Lévi-Strauss (1968). Also of note in this regard are Harland (1987), Harris (1987), and R. Hawkes (1977).

5 For a discussion of Lévi-Strauss's influences upon the structuralist Marxism of Althusser, see Glucksmann (1974).

6 See Lévi-Strauss's discussion of modern myths (1968: 209–10).
7 For more on the distinction between denotation and connotation, see Barthes (1967).
8 As Hall has written, after Barthes's intervention 'it was the social, ideological nature of language which came under scrutiny, replacing the primacy of the individual utterance with an interest in its location in the inter-textuality of codes' (1977b: 4).
9 On this issue, see Abercrombie *et al.* (1980), Mann (1970 and 1973) and Therborn (1980).
10 It may be remarked, parenthetically, that it is not clear whether Barthes means by this that structural linguistics provides the master key for semiological analysis or whether non-linguistic signifying systems are simply mediated by language. See Chambers (1974) on this point.
11 Good critiques of structuralism along these general lines include Hall (1985a), Hodge and Kress (1988), Morley (1980), and Sumner (1979).
12 That is, Barthes seems to be implying that while the 'masses' are easily beguiled by myth, the semiotician can somehow escape this particular form of 'false consciousness', presumably because semiology is a branch of objective science: 'when a myth reaches the entire community, it is from the latter that the mythologist must become estranged if he wants to liberate the myth' (1973: 157). Yet how this form of 'estrangement' or critical distance is possible – which would, presumably, limit the ideological 'contamination' of a knowledge of mythical systems – is never addressed by Barthes.
13 To quote Thompson:

> ... the meaning of what is said – what is *asserted* in spoken or written discourse as well as that *about which* one speaks or writes – is infused with forms of power; different individuals or groups have a differential capacity to *make a meaning stick.* It is the infusion of meaning with power that lends language so freely to the operations of ideology. Relations of domination are sustained by a *mobilization of meaning* which legitimates, dissimulates or reifies an existing state of affairs; and meaning can be mobilized because it is an essentially open, shifting indeterminate phenomenon.
>
> (1984: 132)

14 See Callinicos (1982) and Smart (1983) for useful discussions of the socio-political background of the emergence of poststructuralism.
15 Julia Kristeva and the *Tel Quel* group, for example, rejected the structuralist position that meaning was a simple expression of an underlying 'pure' structure. Instead, they emphasized the state of play in textual production and the multiplicity of potentially transgressive readings that this textual instability made possible. Similarly, Derrida radicalized Saussure's notion of 'difference' by concentrating on force rather than form, in order to conceptualize meaning as lacking a presence or centre. His stricture in *Writing and Difference* (1978) that 'the absence of an ultimate meaning opens an unbounded space for

the play of signification' can serve as the *leitmotiv* of poststructuralism as a whole.

16 On the one hand, he acknowledges an intellectual debt towards Marx's approach to historical analysis, and insists that one cannot 'write history at the present time without using a whole range of concepts directly or indirectly linked with Marx's thought and situating oneself within a horizon of thought which has been defined and described by Marx' (1980: 53). Moreover, in *The Archaeology of Knowledge* (1977a), Foucault reveals that he is sympathetic to the notion of the 'epistemological break' in Marx's work – i.e., the Althusserian suggestion that the 'mature' Marx dispensed with the attempt to ground social inquiry in the rational subject and embraced a 'decentred' history involving the analysis of modes of production, class struggles, and so on. What is clear, however, is that Foucault does not relegate Marxism *en bloc* to the dust-heap of history as do his *Nouvelle Philosophie* counterparts Glucksmann and Levy. On this, see Dews (1979 and 1980).

17 Thus, while there can be different forms of this power-struggle, there is no possibility of ultimate escape. This helps explain why Foucault is so critical of the traditional Marxian notion of 'liberation' or 'emancipation', insofar as it assumes that mankind can somehow escape the matrix of power/knowledge relations which is an intrinsic feature of sociality itself:

> We must cease once and for all to describe the effects of power in negative terms: it 'excludes', it 'represses', it 'censors', it 'abstracts', it 'masks', it 'conceals'. In fact, power produces; it produces domains of objects and rituals of truth. The individual and the knowledge that may be gained of him belong to this production.
>
> (Foucault 1977b: 194)

18 Callinicos (1982), for example, has responded to the 'Foucauldian threat' by eloquently but forcefully re-stating the case for classical Marxian analysis. Merquior is genuinely hostile towards Foucault, at one point engaging in such iconoclastic statements as 'as far as I can see, nothing he says seems to be in contradiction with the best available scholarship on the subject' (1985: 137). Poster (1984) and Smart (1983 and 1985) have, on the other hand, been much more sympathetic towards Foucault. They acknowledge that the 'crisis of Marxism' is very real, and they assert that his work represents a new form of 'critical theory' that solves many of these entrenched conceptual lacunae. Poulantzas's (1978) position lies somewhere between these two extremes: he suggests that Foucault's concepts of epistemic structures and power/knowledge relations help to avoid the twin errors of 'statism' and 'economism', and he credits Foucault with extending the analysis of power into previously uncharted areas of the social field. Nevertheless, he ends up by arguing that power must have a specific ground or basis, otherwise the possibility of resistance is inconceivable, and that this basis must ultimately be located in the relations of production and the modalities of class struggle.

19 On the affinity between Gramsci and Foucault, see Mouffe (1979), Radhakrishnan (1990) and Smart (1986).

20 Perhaps the most convincing and comprehensive discussions of the poststructuralist tradition on these matters can be found in Callinicos (1989), but see also Dews (1987), Dreyfus and Rabinow (1982), Fraser (1981), Gane (ed.) (1986), and Hoy (ed.) (1986).

21 I have by-passed the work of the late Foucault on the history of sexuality, where he does a rather dramatic *volte-face* with respect to the question of agency and comes close to advocating a conception of the self-reflexive agent. For this development in Foucault's philosophy, see Callinicos (1989: 87), and Dews (1989).

22 P. Willis's (1981) study of the informal, profane culture of working class schoolboys indicates some of the ways this form of culture resistance operates, and how it can partially deconstruct the latent ideological content of dominant discourses. See also Willis and Corrigan (1980 and 1981)

23 On this, see Barker (1989: 272) and Frow (1985).

24 The major exception to this is the work of the (now defunct) Centre for Contemporary Cultural Studies based at the University of Birmingham. In a series of path-breaking empirical and theoretical studies in the 1970s and early 1980s, the CCCS examined the cultural dynamics of (albeit often unconscious) cultural and political refusal on the part of various subaltern groups in modern British society (working-class youth, women, blacks, youth subcultures, etc.). Three excellent collections of the Centre's output are Clarke *et al.* (eds) (1979), Hall and Jefferson (eds) (1976), Hall *et al.* (eds) (1980), and a representative study is Hebdige (1979).

25 Considerations of time and space have forced me effectively to by-pass the work of Althusser and Michel Pêcheux on the theory of ideology; on this issue, however, there are some interesting parallels. Pêcheux argues that 'meaning' is an effect of the position of given words and utterances within particular discursive formations which are connected to class struggles in the various economic, political and ideological spheres. Subjects 'find themselves' embedded within particular, antagonistic discursive formations, and each such formation has its own rules which regulate the production of discourse. A word or phrase uttered within one discursive formation may have a completely different meaning in another; and, conversely, different words may have the same semantic content within another discourse. In other words, Pêcheux maintains what could be termed a 'functional' or processual account of meaning which is in many respects akin to that of Bakhtin and Voloshinov. Interested readers may wish to consult, besides Pêcheux's own writings (1978 and 1982), Cousins (1985), Thompson (1984), and Woods (1977).

26 It is worth considering at this point Voloshinov's curious three-part article 'The Stylistics of Verbal Art', published in the popular journal *Literary Study* in the 1930s (and contained in the collection *Bakhtin School Papers* 1983, though not in its full form). It is interesting for two main reasons: firstly, Parrott (1984) claims that this text is actually a

thinly-veiled parodic attack on the progressive intrusion of RAPP (the Russian Association of Proletarian Writers) into literary-cultural life, as well as the general political consolidation of Stalinism. Voloshinov uses Gogol's *Dead Souls* to draw obvious parallels between the Tsarist and Stalinist bureaucratic castes – even at one point evoking the mediocrity of Stalin himself (1983: 140). He also noted that the sign became reactionary under any ruling class (a 'reactionary codifier') – with the clear implication that Soviet society was not exempt. In other words, it is a good example of the kind of 'Aesopian' writing Bakhtin in particular was adept at. Secondly, at the conclusion of the essay, Voloshinov supplies three extracts about the infamous 'Bloody Sunday' massacre which occurred in 1905 in St Petersburg. In an audacious move, Voloshinov requested his readers to respond to the different class ideologies contained in the extracts and send in their 'decodings' to the journal which were to be reproduced in a future issue (although the journal went defunct and Voloshinov was arrested before a follow-up issue could appear). This strikes one as quite innovative for the time – an attempt to solicit responses to a text in an academic journal from a (largely non- academic) readership.

27 I borrow the term 'reading formation' from Bennett (1987 and 1989).

28 As Polan astutely notes:

> Bakhtin seems to indicate that any celebration of tradition, even a counter-tradition, ends up spatializing knowledge in a reified way. For Bakhtin, tradition itself should be studied dialogically, any single strand transformed by a montagist juxtaposition of any one tradition to another.
>
> (1989: 11–12)

29 On this, see Nonnekes (1987: 136).

30 At this point I draw on a recent essay by Hunter, which I feel largely vindicates Bakhtin's position. Hunter convincingly argues that experience cannot be reduced to linguistic meaning. Both structuralists and philologists consider 'meaning' to be something that one finds in a dictionary (i.e., in formal definition). The problem with this is that social agency 'has no general form (subjectivity) whose structure can be read off from a theoretical analysis of meaning of the 'subject positions' made available by a linguistic system'. As such, there is no requirement that we posit a 'general mechanism in which experienced objects and events are represented in language' (1989: 191). His conclusion is that the constitution of the subject involves a range of cultural, linguistic, non-linguistic and natural relations, all of which must be taken into account when talking about 'subjectivity' and 'agency'.

31 For Bourdieu, the logic of practice that results from our reflexive apprehension of external structural forces results in a series of relatively stable sets of dispositions and orientations – what he calls the habitus. The structure of the habitus is ultimately derived from the shared material experiences and capacities of particular social groups, in which socio-economic class is a particularly important factor. He

argues that practice is oriented towards achieving instrumental success on the basis of past successes and failures as mediated through the habitus, which skews particular action-strategies in certain subtle ways. Different class positions will be subject to different conditions, experiences and life-chances, and thus will manifest distinctive habitus-forms, which will in turn regulate the different forms of rationalized action-strategies. This can be seen in class-specific patterns of consumption and appropriation, 'taste', bodily disposition, and of course language. See Bourdieu (1977a, 1977b, 1977c and 1990). The many significant affinities between Bakhtin and Bourdieu have not, at least to my knowledge, received the attention they deserve.

6 TOWARDS A DIALOGICAL IDEOLOGICAL CRITICISM

1 For more on this question, see the essays by Dreyfus and Habermas and Rabinow in Hoy (ed.) (1986). Also of interest is Habermas's (1987) critique of the Nietzschean strain within poststructuralism.

2 This also, I think, demonstrates the essentially Kantian ethics which Bakhtin operates with – i.e., the categorical imperative to treat the other as a fellow-subject (an end in itself) rather than as an object (as a means to an end). Moreover, one could argue that Bakhtin's stress on the unfinalizability of humankind is derived from Kant's world of free subjectivity, which is grounded in the (unpredictable and un-knowable, at least in the scientific sense) noumenal realm. This can be contrasted with the phenomenal realm of natural, causal processes, which can in principle be known through the methods of empirical science.

3 This has been well documented in McFarlane (1976). For an examination of the impact of positivism on Russian intellectual history, see Walicki (1979).

4 In *Dialectic of Enlightenment* (1972), Adorno and Horkheimer argued that the theory of knowledge promoted by the Enlightenment was based on the empiricist/pragmatist premise that human beings could only understand and know something if they could control it. What could not be 'understood' in this manner was simply ignored, or described as 'cognitively meaningless'. Thus, this form of knowledge actively encouraged the manipulation of objects and events, thereby perfecting humanity's domination of (and alienation from) nature. To Horkheimer and Adorno, this was symptomatic of reified thinking in a society increasingly dominated by exchange-value, which had reduced people and dynamic social processes to abstractions within a mechanical system.

5 In his discussion of Marx and romanticism, Löwy (1987) suggests that (given that certain elements or romanticism can be found in Marx's world-view) one of the major things that distinguishes these philo-sophies is the failure of the latter to come to grips with the specificity of capitalism in any systematic fashion. The net result is that the

romantic denunciation of capitalism (as articulated by the likes of Ruskin, Morris or Fourier) failed to comprehend capitalism dialectically – that is, to see the actual potentialities for progressive development gestating within the capitalist mode of production as well as the obvious deficiencies. One could argue that Bakhtin's critiques of the reification and objectification of humanity suffer from a similar inability to graft this social and cultural criticism onto a more sociological or historiographic analysis of capitalist social relations, and in this sense he remains a 'romantic anti-capitalist'. This conclusion might be somewhat over-hasty, however, given that there are countervailing tendencies that can also be found in Bakhtin's texts. In *Problems of Dostoevsky's Poetics*, for example, he writes:

> The materialization of man under conditions of class society, carried to its extreme under capitalism. This materialization is accomplished (realized) by external forces acting on the personality from without and from within; this is violence in all possible forms of its realization (economic, political, ideological), and these forces can be combated only from the outside and with equally externalized forces (justified revolutionary violence); the goal is personality.

(1984: 298)

6 Bakhtin's phenomenological stress on lived experience can be further elaborated by examining his attitude toward the question of 'truth' in discourse. For the dogmatic ideologue, truth and falsity are derived directly from the axiomatic premises contained within a unified belief system. It is a process of purely logical deduction, of abstract conceptual linkages ('no-man thoughts') which never become embodied or 'personified' in the form of a particular individual or socio-ideological point of view. For Bakhtin, 'real' or practical truth could only emerge from the free dialogic interaction between individuals who 'embodied' in the fullest sense of the word the points of view they espoused, who invested all of their moral, ethical and even physical being in the dialogues they engaged in and the ideas they sought to interrogate.

7 Derrida, of course, feels that such 'phonocentrism' succumbs to a metaphysics of 'presence' (logocentrism), in that speech gives the appearance of immediate meaning but, since meaning is constantly deferred through an infinite network of 'traces' or textual sublimations, this is only illusory. This is the crux of his critique of Saussure, whom he links up with the metaphysical tradition in Western philosophy – see, for example, his *Of Grammatology* (1977). Of course, too much can be made of Bakhtin's 'phonocentrism': he also denies that meaning is 'self-present' in the utterance (written or spoken), because meaning is constructed in the dialogic space between individuals and in the intertextual references that adhere to a given utterance's usage which is both recursive and anticipatory.

8 See chapter four of Berman (1983), where he discusses literary modernism in St Petersburg in the 19th and early 20th centuries.

9 As Lowe writes:

> Typographic standardization shifted the knowable entirely to the 'content.' This meant a formalization of the known as content, detached from the knower. Previously, it was very difficult to separate the two, and certain bodies of knowledge depended on personal transmission of a master. But now formalized, i.e., depersonalized, content in print could be accessible by any competent, qualified reader. This typographic standardization made possible the new ideal of objective knowledge.
>
> (1982: 4)

10 In his essay 'The Work of Art in the Age of Mechanical Reproduction' (1969), Benjamin argued that the 'aura' of a cultural or artistic product was the 'unique nimbus' that permeated an original work, a singular essence that transferred to the object a sense of authenticity. However, this mystique or aura could not be preserved if it was reproduced by mechanical means. Under such conditions, the reproduced object would no longer be 'embedded in the fabric of tradition'. Thus, the loss of aura signalled a distinct cultural crisis in modern society. However, Benjamin and the central members of the Frankfurt School diverged sharply as to the interpretation of this perceived cultural crisis. Benjamin, although he mourned this loss of aura in artistic/cultural production, followed Brecht's lead in recognizing the progressive or even potentially revolutionary capacities of a politicized, collectivized art and culture – particulary in film and recordings – which could raise standards of critical awareness. The loss of aura de-reified and de-mystified art, encouraging the 'masses' to participate in the control and understanding of cultural/artistic production and consumption. For good discussions of this debate, see Lunn (1982) and Slater (1977).

11 The pervasive gloominess of the Frankfurt School's theories of the 'culture industry' et al can perhaps be explained in part by the Institute's proximity to Nazism, the Stalinization of Soviet Marxism, and the experience of culture shock upon arriving in America after their expulsion from Germany. On this topic, see Anderson (1976), Held (1980), and Jay (1973).

12 As Dews succinctly writes:

> An assessment of the modern subject [. . .] which would avoid the oscillation between irrationalist rebellion and resignation characteristic of the French philosophy of the seventies must begin by acknowledging in capitalist modernity an interplay of progressive and regressive elements far more complex than anything post-structuralism appears able to envisage.
>
> (1984: 95)

13 Useful commentaries on Benjamin's philosophy of history include Eagleton (1981), which also contains a chapter on Bakhtin and Brecht, and Roberts (1983).

14 It should be recalled, for example, that Bakhtin insists that the

carnivalesque as a mode of social critique must in a pendulum-like movement (or 'grotesque swing') encompass both the negative or deconstructive and the positive or utopian. This in fact reminds one of F. Jameson's stricture that Marxist cultural analysis cannot

. . . be content with its demystifying vocation to unmask and to demonstrate the ways in which a cultural artifact fulfils a specific ideological mission, in legitimating a given power structure, in perpetuating and reproducing the latter, and in generating specific forms of false consciousness (or ideology in the narrower sense). It must not seek to practise this essentially negative hermeneutic function (which Marxism is virtually the only current critical method to assume today) but must also seek, through and beyond this demonstration of the instrumental function of a given cultural object, to project its simultaneously Utopian power as the symbolic affirmation of a specific historical and class form of collective unity. This is a unified perspective and not the juxtaposition of two options or analytic alternatives: neither is satisfactory in itself.

(1981: 291)

15 Pechey (1990) convincingly suggests that Bakhtin's affinity with modernism lies primarily on a philosophical rather than a cultural plane. On the other hand, Polan argues that in order to evoke modern experience one does not need to refer directly to modernity but rather make writing itself modern (1989: 11).

16 For good discussions on the role of Romanticist philosophy in Marx's thought, see Anderson (1976), Berman (1982), Gouldner (1980), Löwy (1987), and Stedman-Jones (1977).

17 Bakhtin's emphasis on the secularization of language and consciousness in the contemporary age is remarkably similar to Habermas's (1971) argument that whereas in traditional societies domination is exercised through mythical or religious systems 'from above', the process of modernity and modernization shifts the basis of legitimation to the formal, contractual relation between individuals in the market. Authority comes to be transmitted through the institutions of the public sphere, wherein the pressing concerns of social and political life are discussed via standards of critical reason. See also Gouldner (1976), who attempts to portray ideology as a deep structure which enables a modern form of rational argumentation and justification.

18 See Hirschkop (1989a: 27) on this point.

19 As Hirschkop writes:

A social theory unable to conceive of social connection in terms other than the interaction of consciousness [would] fatally overestimate the power of the natural form of social interaction – dialogism – and underestimate the power of monologism, whose hegemonic mode of domination it cannot comprehend.

(1986c: 106)

20 See Larrain (1989: 108–9) in relation to this issue.

21 For an interesting discussion of Lunacharsky's rather idiosyncratic brand of Marxism, see Tait (1986).

22 Besides utilizing folk themes (both in terms of artistic styles and cultural references but also in the appearance of street theatre, puppet shows, jesters, circus acts, satirical-grotesque performances, and so on), these festivals also incorporated revolutionary themes by allegorically 'plundering' the history of past mass struggles such as the Paris Commune and the French Revolution. These events had official sponsorship (but were marked by a high degree of popular enthusiasm and mass participation, until Stalin usurped them for narrowly political ends in the 1930s), and they were strongly supported by the Soviet commissar for culture Anatoly Lunacharsky. For an excellent discussion of this and other carnivalesque phenomena in post-revolutionary Russia, see Stites (1989 and 1990). Also of interest is *Street Art of the Revolution*, Tolstoy *et al.* (eds) (1990). Stills and objects from this period were also shown at the Cornerhouse gallery in Manchester as part of the 'Leningrad in Manchester' exhibition, June 16 – July 22, 1990.

23 There were also many lesser known groups and movements, such as the fascinating 'Oberiu' collective which included the absurdist writers and dramatists D. Kharms and A. Vvedensky, who seem to have invented Dada all by themselves without foreknowledge of their Western counterparts. Their playful assault on traditional language usage and their comic and often bizarre theatrical spectacles have clearly carnivalesque elements, and could certainly be studied in more detail using Bakhtinian categories. See *Russia's Lost Literature of the Absurd*, a collection of Oberiu writings, with a useful introduction by the editor Gibian. Also of interest is Kelly's (1989) intriguing study of folk-festive aspects of Soviet agit-prop puppet theatre in the early years following the revolution.

24 On this episode in Soviet cultural history, see Barry (1989). For a Bakhtinian theory of music, see Hirschkop (1989c).

25 For instance, in his justly famous *The Cheese and the Worms*, Carlo Ginzburg acknowledges the originality of Bakhtin's writings on medieval popular culture, but also charges that Bakhtin makes a number of controversial claims about the nature of this culture on the basis of learned, mainly literary texts which were not of popular origin. Likewise, Berrong (1985 and 1986) faults Bakhtin for imposing his utopian vision on a historical period which simply does not live up to his conception of a revolutionary carnival culture.

26 Burke (1978), although not specifically addressing Bakhtin's theories, gives the example of the May Day festival in London in 1512 that resulted in the massacre and expulsion of foreigners. Le Roy Ladurie's (1979) study of the carnival in Romans in 1580 demonstrates that what started off as a peasant revolt against excessive taxation ended up as a sectarian bloodbath manipulated by the town's elites for political advantage. Moreover, as Byrd (1987) points out, both Freud and Bakhtin valorize humour and laughter as healthy, subversive, and so on – but both ignore the potential for humour to

reinforce social stereotypes (women, ethnic minorities) and to aid social control of said groups. Humour can help support certain reactionary hierarchies (patriarchy, racism), and cannot be considered as *ipso facto* liberating or emancipatory – a good example being the Nazi's penchant for crude jokes in the mobilization of anti-Semitic feeling. Hence, Bakhtin's precept that laughter 'is never used by violence and authority' is clearly wrong. Laughter, like any other cultural practice, is not intrinsically liberatory, and its significance and effects depend on the concrete social and cultural practices within which it is embedded.

27 An example Davis (1975) discusses in some detail is the 'charivari', instances of public humiliation and mockery administered by so-called 'youth-abbeys' (a sort of medieval youth gang) when breaches of social etiquette or marriage customs occurred. Proponents of this 'carnival as safety valve' view also point to the work of such anthropologists as Max Gluckman and Victor Turner (1974), who have studied similar 'rites of protest' in non-Western societies (involving status reversals, symbolic inversions, etc.). The latter have generally concluded that such transgressions ultimately strengthen the status quo and existing social norms rather than subvert them: 'By making the low high and the high low, they reaffirm the hierarchical principle' (Gluckman 1963). This stance also has supporters on the left, such as Bernstein (1986) and Eagleton (1981). Eagleton, otherwise clearly sympathetic to Bakhtin's approach, suggests that carnival has a primarily cathartic, re-integrating function: 'Carnival, after all, is a licensed affair in every sense, a permissible rupture of hegemony, a contained popular blow-off as disturbing and relatively ineffectual as a work of art. As Shakespeare's Olivia remarks, there is no slander in an allowed fool' (1981: 148).

28 For example, Davis (1975: 118) discusses a case in Lyons in the 1580s where carnival criticism was directed toward such obviously political concerns as the folly of foreign war and the lack of affordable foodstuffs. The resulting social unrest was only quelled after a period of intense and violent repression. It is worth noting that peasant revolts were a particular interest of Engels, who wrote a book on the German Peasant War of 1524–5. Also of interest in this context is Cohn (1970).

29 As Stallybrass and White suggest, carnival is not an either/or phenomenon – it is not essentially a counter-hegemonic practice nor a tool of social regulation. The actual features of carnival are dependent on the particular social and historical conjuncture within which it occurs: 'carnivals are [not] *intrinsically* radical or conservative. [While] carnival may be a stable and cyclical ritual with no noticeable politically transformative effects, it may often act as the *catalyst* and *site of actual and symbolic struggle*' (1986: 14). This point is reiterated at length by White (1987–8).

30 See Lombardi-Satriani (1974). Also of interest are Cirese (1982), and a recent collection of Gramsci's cultural and linguistic writings (1985).

31 On this, see Salamini (1981). Also of relevance are Gramsci's 'Notes

on Language' (1984) and Mansfield (1984). Crowley (1987) has attempted to utilize Gramsci's theory of hegemony and language for an understanding of the dynamics of linguistic centralization in Victorian Britain.

32 As Gramsci wrote:

> Every time the question of language surfaces in one way or the other, it means that a series of other problems are beginning to emerge: the formation and expansion of the ruling class, the necessity of establishing closer and firmer ties between the leading groups and national-popular masses, that is of reorganizing the cultural hegemony.
>
> (1985: 2)

33 Bakhtin notes, for example, that the popular distrust of authority and its love of blasphemous laughter could only be partial and utopian, groping towards but never quite achieving the status of a 'critical and clearly defined opposition'. Folk culture and the truth of laughter it expressed were therefore marked by a 'spontaneous, elemental character'. Fear and weakness still held the upper hand in medieval society: 'Freedom granted by laughter often enough was mere festive luxury' (1968: 95).

34 Other interpreters of Bakhtin argue against this view. See, for instance, Carroll (1983: 83) and Polan (1989: 16).

35 As Pechey accurately notes, for Bakhtin the 'contending forces seem to be starkly polarized and to operate in abstraction from the institutional sites in which complex relations of discourse and power are actually negotiated' (1989: 52).

36 Here, I draw liberally on the points raised by Swingewood (1977) and in part three of Held (1980).

37 Crucial to understanding Bakhtin's neglect of key institutional and social factors in his various studies is the cultural and political context of intellectual production in the Soviet Union *circa* 1917–40. Drawing on the seminal work of Boris Kagarlitsky (1988) and others on the intellectual culture of Tsarist and Soviet Russia, I suggest that many of the particularities of Bakhtin's inflation of the subversive potential of 'novelness' and his theoretical neglect of the socio-political sphere must be traced to the situation of the dissident intellectual stratum in the historical context of Stalinist Russia. Kagarlitsky convincingly argues that because the members of the radical intelligentsia were unable to address pressing contemporary political and social issues directly due to the threat of censorship or direct political repression, a frequently-pursued alternative was to examine these questions in a largely allegorical fashion – a practice that continued more or less unhindered well into the Soviet period. Studies of this type would largely escape censorship, and could easily be 'decoded' by other intellectuals of an oppositional temperament. Such an 'Aesopian' approach also helps explain why the formulation of vital political issues in primarily cultural and literary terms was such a common intellectual practice in both Tsarist and Stalinist Russia.

38 Some of the more successful and creative attempts to appropriate Bakhtin for empirical study include Stam (1988 and 1989), who utilizes Bakhtinian categories for the purposes of film, televisual and media analysis, Roberts's (1990) use of Voloshinov's semiotic theory to critique postmodern art practice, and the numerous attempts to wed Bakhtin's conception of the carnivalesque and the grotesque body with feminist discourse (see, for example, Holden 1985, and Willis 1989).

39 In Dostoevsky's works, argues Bakhtin, people are deprived of a decent existence and strive to regain one. Hence, Dostoevsky's heroes are

> ... motivated by the utopian dream of creating some sort of human community that lies beyond existing social forms. [. . .] Communion has been deprived, as it were, of its real-life body and wants to create one arbitrarily, out of purely human material. All this is a most profound expression of the social disorientation of the classless intelligentsia, which feels itself dispersed throughout the world and whose members must orient themselves in the world one by one, alone and at their own risk. [. . .] The solitary person finds that his own voice has become a vacillating thing, his own unity and his internal agreement with himself has become a postulate.
>
> (1984: 280–1)

Bibliography

Abercrombie, N. (1980) *Class, Structure and Knowledge*, Oxford: Basil Blackwell.

Abercrombie, N., Hill, S. and Turner, B.S. (1980) *The Dominant Ideology Thesis*, London: George Allen & Unwin.

——(eds) (1990) *Dominant Ideologies*, London: Unwin Hyman.

——(1983) 'Determinacy and Indeterminacy in the Theory of Ideology', *New Left Review* 142: 55–66.

Adlam, D., Henriques, J. Rose, N., Salfield, A. Venn, A. and Walkerdine, V. (1977) 'Psychology, Ideology and the Human Subject', *Ideology & Consciousness* 1: 5–56.

Adorno, T. and Horkheimer, M. (1972) *Dialectic of Enlightenment*, New York: Herder & Herder.

Alexandrian, S. (1970) *Surrealist Art*, London: Thames and Hudson.

Althusser, L. (1971) *Lenin and Philosophy and Other Essays*, trans. B. Brewster, New York: Monthly Review Press.

——(1969) *For Marx*, trans. B. Brewster, London: Verso.

——and Balibar, E. (1970) *Reading Capital*, trans. B. Brewster, London: Verso.

Anchor, R. (1985) 'Bakhtin's Truths of Laughter', *Clio* 14, 3: 237–57.

Anderson, B. (1983) *Imagined Communities: Reflections on the Origin and Spread of Nationalism*, London: Verso.

Anderson, P. (1983) *In the Tracks of Historical Materialism*, London: Verso.

——(1976) *Considerations on Western Marxism*, London: Verso.

Aronowitz, S. (1988) *Science as Power: Discourse and Ideology in Modern Society*, London: Macmillan.

Arthur, C. J. (1970) 'Editor's Introduction', in C. J. Arthur (ed.), *The German Ideology*, London: Lawrence & Wishart.

Aucouturier, M. (1983) 'The Theory of the Novel in Russia in the 1930s: Lukács and Bakhtin', in J. Garrard (ed.) *The Russian Novel From Pushkin to Pasternak*, New Haven: Yale University Press.

Bagby, L. (1982) 'Mikhail Bakhtin's Discourse Typologies: Theoretical and Practical Considerations', *Slavic Review* 41, 1: 35–58.

Bakhtin, M. (1990) *Art and Answerability: Early Philosophical Essays by M. M. Bakhtin*, M. Holquist and V. Liapunov (eds), trans. and notes V.

Liapunov, supplement trans. K. Brostrom, Austin: Texas University Press.

—— (1986) *Speech Genres and Other Late Essays*, C. Emerson and M. Holquist (eds), trans. V. W. McGee, Austin: Texas University Press.

—— (1984) *Problems of Dostoevsky's Poetics*, ed. and trans. C. Emerson, Manchester: Manchester University Press.

—— (1981) *The Dialogic Imagination: Four Essays by M. M. Bakhtin*, M. Holquist (ed.), trans. C. Emerson and M. Holquist, Austin: Texas University Press.

—— (1974) 'The Art of the Word and the Culture of Folk Humor', in H. Baran (ed.) *Structuralism and Semiotics: Readings from the Soviet Union*, White Plains: International Arts and Sciences Press, Inc.

—— (1968). *Rabelais and His World*, trans. H. Isowolsky, Cambridge (Mass.): The MIT Press.

—— and Medvedev, P. N. (1985) *The Formal Method in Literary Scholarship: A Critical Introduction to Sociological Poetics*, trans. A. J. Wehrle, Cambridge (Mass.): Harvard University Press.

Bakhurst, D. (1990) 'Social Memory in Soviet Thought', in D. Middleton and D. Edwards (eds) *Collective Remembering*, London: Sage Publications.

Barker, M. (1989) *Comics, Ideology and the Critics*, Manchester: Manchester University Press.

Barry, M. (1989) 'Ideology and Form: Shostakovich East and West', in C. Norris (ed.) *Music and the Politics of Culture*, London: Lawrence & Wishart.

Barth, H. (1977) *Truth and Ideology*, Berkeley: University of California Press.

Barthes, R. (1977) *Image–Music–Text*, ed. and trans. S. Heath, London: Fontana.

—— (1973) *Mythologies*, London: Granada Publishing.

—— (1967) *Elements of Semiology*, trans. A. Lavers and C. Smith, London: Jonathan Cape.

Bauman, Z. (1978) *Hermeneutics and Social Science*, London: Hutchinson.

—— (1976) *Socialism: The Active Utopia*, London: George Allen & Unwin.

Belsey, C. (1980) *Critical Practice*, London: Methuen.

Benjamin, W. (1983) *Charles Baudelaire: A Lyric Poet in the Era of High Capitalism*, trans. H. Zohn, London: Verso.

—— (1973) *Understanding Brecht*, trans. A. Bostock, London: Verso.

—— (1969) *Illuminations: Essays and Reflections*, H. Arendt (ed.), trans. H. Zohn, New York: Schocken Books.

Bennett, T. (1989) 'Texts, Readers, Reading Formations', in P. Rice and P. Waugh (eds) *Modern Literary Theory: A Reader*, London: Edward Arnold.

—— (1987) 'Texts in History: The Determinations of Readings and their Texts', in D. Attridge, G. Bennington and R. Young (eds) *Post–Structuralism and the Question of History*, Cambridge: Cambridge University Press.

—— (1979) *Formalism and Marxism*, London: Methuen.

Berger, P. and Luckmann, T. (1966) *The Social Construction of Reality: An Essay in the Sociology of Knowledge*, Garden City: Doubleday.

Berman, M. (1983) *All That is Solid Melts into Air: The Experience of Modernity*, London: Verso.

Bernstein, M.A. (1986) 'When the Carnical Turns Bitter: Preliminary Reflections on an Abject Hero', in G.S. Morson (ed.) *Bakhtin: Essays and Dialogues on His Work*, Chicago: The University of Chicago Press.

Bernstein, R. (1986) *Philosophical Profiles*, Cambridge: Polity.

Berrong, R. (1986) *Rabelais and Bakhtin: Popular Culture in 'Gargantua and Pantagruel'*, Lincoln and London: University of Nebraska Press.

——(1985) 'The Presence and Exclusion of Popular Culture in "Pantagruel and Gargantua" (or Bakhtin's Rabelais Revisited)', *Etudes Rabelaisiennes* 18: 19–56.

Bhaskar, R. (1979) *The Possibility of Naturalism: A Philosophical Critique of the Contemporary Human Sciences*, Brighton: Harvester.

Billington, J. (1966) *The Icon and the Axe: An Interpretive History of Russian Culture*, London: Weidenfeld and Nicolson.

Blazwick, Iwona (ed.) (1989) *An Endless Adventure . . . An Endless Passion . . . An Endless Banquet: A Situationist Scrapbook*, London: Verso.

Bleicher, J. (1980) *Contemporary Hermeneutics: Hermeneutics as Method, Philosophy and Critique*, London: Routledge & Kegan Paul.

Bottomore, T. (ed.) (1983) *A Dictionary of Marxist Thought*, Cambridge (Mass.): Harvard University Press.

Bourdieu, P. (1990) *In Other Words: Essays Towards a Reflexive Sociology*, trans. M. Adamson, Cambridge: Polity.

——(1977a) 'Symbolic Power', in *Two Bourdieu Texts*, trans. Richard Nice, CCCS Stencilled Occasional Paper 46.

——(1977b) *Outline of a Theory of Practice*, trans. R. Nice, Cambridge: Cambridge University Press.

——(1977c) 'The Economics of Linguistic Exchanges', *Social Science Information* 16, 6: 645–68.

Braudel, F. (1980) *On History*, trans. S. Matthews, Chicago: Chicago University Press.

Bruss, N. (1976) 'V. N. Voloshinov and the Structure of Language in Freudianism', in V. N. Voloshinov, *Freudianism: A Marxist Critique*, N. Bruss and I. R. Tikunik (eds), trans. I. R. Tikunik, New York and London: Academic Press.

Burke, K. (1984) *Attitudes Toward History*, Berkeley: University of California Press.

Burke, P. (1978) *Popular Culture in Early Modern Europe*, New York: New York University Press.

Byrd, C. (1987) 'Freud's Influence on Bakhtin: Traces of Psychoanalytic Theory in *Rabelais and His World*', *Germano-Slavica* 5, 5–6: 223–30.

Callinicos, A. (1989) *Against Postmodernism: A Marxist Critique*, Cambridge: Polity.

——(1987) *Making History*, Cambridge: Polity.

——(1985) 'Postmodernism, Post-Structuralism, Post-Marxism?', *Theory, Culture and Society* 2, 3: 85–101.

——(1983) *Marxism and Philosophy*, Oxford: Oxford University Press.

——(1982) *Is There a Future for Marxism?*, Atlantic Highlands: Humanities Press.

Carroll, D. (1983) 'The Alterity of Discourse: Form, History, the Question of the Political in M. M. Bakhtin', *Diacritics* 13, 2: 65–83.

Castoriadis, C. (1984) 'The Imaginary Institution of Society', in J. Fekete (ed.) *The Structural Allegory: Reconstructive Encounters with the New French Thought*, Manchester: Manchester University Press.

Certeau, M. de (1984) *The Practice of Everyday Life*, trans. S. F. Randall, Berkeley: University of California Press.

Chambers, I. (1974) 'Roland Barthes: Structuralism/Semiotics', *Working Papers in Cultural Studies* 4: 49–68.

Cirese, A. (1982) 'Gramsci's Observations on Folklore', in A. S. Sassoon (ed.) *Approaches to Gramsci*, London: Writers & Readers.

Clarke, J., Modgil, C. and Modgil, S. (eds) (1990) *Anthony Giddens: Consensus and Controversy*, London: The Falmer Press.

Clarke, J., Chritcher, C. and Johnson, R. (eds) (1979) *Working Class Culture: Studies in History and Culture*, London: Hutchinson.

Clarke, K. and Holquist, M. (1986) 'A Continuing Dialogue', *Slavic and Eastern European Journal* 30, 1: 96–102.

——(1984a) *Mikhail Bakhtin*, Cambridge (Mass.) and London: Harvard University Press.

——(1984b) 'The Influence of Kant in the Early Work of M. M. Bakhtin', in J. Strelka (ed.) *Literary Theory and Criticism*, New York: Peter Lang.

Cohn, N. (1970) *The Pursuit of the Millennium: Revolutionary Millenarians and Mystical Anarchists of the Middle Ages*, London: Temple Smith.

Connerton, P. (1989) *How Societies Remember*, Cambridge: Cambridge University Press.

Cousins, M. (1985) 'Jokes and Their Relationship to the Means of Production', *Economy and Society* 14: 95–112.

——and Hussain, A. (1986) 'The Question of Ideology: Althusser, Pêcheux and Foucault', in J. Law (ed.) *Power, Action and Belief: A New Sociology of Knowledge?*, London: Routledge & Kegan Paul.

Coward, R. and Ellis, J. (1977) *Language and Materialism: Developments in Semiology and the Theory of the Subject*, London: Routledge and Kegan Paul.

Crowley, T. (1989) 'Bakhtin and the History of the Language', in K. Hirschkop and D. Shepherd (eds) *Bakhtin and Cultural Theory*, Manchester: Manchester University Press.

——(1987) 'Language and Hegemony: Principles, Morals and Pronunciation', *Textual Practice* 1, 3: 278–96.

Culler, J. (1983) *Barthes*, London: Fontana.

—— (1976) *Saussure*, London: Fontana.

—— (1975) *Structuralist Poetics: Structuralism, Linguistics and the Study of Literature*, London: Routledge and Kegan Paul.

Curtis, J. M. (1986) 'Mikhail Bakhtin, Nietzsche, and Russian Pre-revolutionary Thought', in B. G. Rosenthal (ed.) *Nietzsche in Russia*, Princeton: Princeton University Press.

Danow, D. (1984) 'M. M. Bakhtin's Concept of the Word', *American Journal of Semiotics* 3, 1: 79–97.

Danto, A. C. (1965) *Nietzsche as Philosopher*, New York: The Macmillan Company.

Davis, N. Z. (1975) *Society and Culture in Early Modern France*, London: Duckworth.

Debord, G. (1987) *Society of the Spectacle*, Exeter: Rebel Press.

Dejean, J. (1984) 'Bakhtin in/and History', in L. Dolezel and I. R. Tikunik (eds) *Language and Literary Theory*, Ann Arbor: Michigan Slavic Publications.

Derrida, J. (1979) *Spurs: Nietzsche's Style*, trans. B. Harlow, Chicago: Chicago University Press.

——(1978) *Writing and Difference*, trans. A. Bass, London: Routledge & Kegan Paul.

——(1977) *Of Grammatology*, trans. G. C. Spivak, Baltimore: Johns Hopkins University Press.

Dews, P. (1989) 'The Return of the Subject in Late Foucault', *Radical Philosophy* 51: 37–41.

——(1987) *Logics of Disintegration: Post–Structuralist Thought and the Claims of Critical Theory*, London: Verso.

——(1984) 'Power and Subjectivity in Foucault', *New Left Review* 144.

——(1980) 'The "New Philosophers" and the End of Leftism', *Radical Philosophy* 24: 2–11.

——(1979) 'The Nouvelle Philosophie and Foucault', *Economy and Society* 8.

Dreyfus, H. (1980) 'Holism and Hermeneutics', *Review of Metaphysics* 34: 3–23.

—— and Rabinow, P. (1982) *Michel Foucault: Beyond Structuralism and Hermeneutics*, Brighton: Harvester.

——(1986) 'What is Maturity? Habermas and Foucault on Modernity', in D. C. Hoy (ed.) *Foucault: A Critical Reader*, Oxford: Basil Blackwell.

Eagleton, T. (1990) *The Ideology of the Aesthetic*, Oxford: Basil Blackwell.

——(1987) *Saints and Scholars*, London: Verso.

——(1986) 'Wittgenstein's Friends', in *Against the Grain: Selected Essays*, London: Verso.

——(1981) *Walter Benjamin: Or Towards a Revolutionary Criticism*, London: Verso.

Eco, U. (1987) *Travels in Hyperreality*, London: Picador.

——(1979) *The Role of the Reader: Explorations in the Semiology of Texts*, Bloomington: Indiana University Press.

Eichenbaum, B. (1978) 'Literary Environment', in L. Matejka and K. Pomorska (eds) *Readings in Russian Poetics*, Ann Arbor: Michigan Slavic Publications.

Emerson, C. (1986) 'The Outer Word and Inner Speech: Bakhtin, Vygotsky, and the Internalization of Language', in G. S. Morson (ed.) *Bakhtin: Essays and Dialogues on his Work*, Chicago: Chicago University Press.

——(1984) 'Editor's Preface', in *Problems of Dostoevsky's Poetics*.

Engels, F. (1956) *The German Peasants' War*, Moscow: Progress Publishers.

Erlich, V. (1984) 'Formalism and Russian Literary Culture of the 1920s', in J. P. Strelka (ed.) *Literary Theory and Criticism*, New York: Peter Lang.

——(1981) *Russian Formalism: History/Doctrine*, 3rd edition, New Haven, Yale University Press.

Febvre, L. and Martin, H.-J. (1990) *The Coming of the Book: The Impact of Printing 1450–1800*, trans. D. Gerard, London: Verso.

Flaherty, P. (1986) 'Reading Carnival: Towards a Semiotics of History', *Clio* 15, 4: 411–28.

Forgacs, D. (1982) 'Marxist Literary Theories', in A. Jefferson and D. Robey (eds) *Modern Literary Theory: A Comparative Introduction*, London: Batsford.

Foucault, M. (1984) *The Foucault Reader*, P. Rabinow (ed.), New York: Pantheon Books.

——(1981) *The History of Sexuality Vol. One: An Introduction*, trans. R. Hurley, Harmondsworth: Penguin.

——(1980) *Power/Knowledge: Selected Interviews and Writings 1972–77*, ed. and trans. C. Gordon, New York: Pantheon Books.

——(1977a) *The Archaeology of Knowledge*, trans. A. Sheridan, London: Tavistock.

——(1977b) *Discipline and Punish*, trans. A. Sheridan, Harmondsworth: Penguin.

——(1971) *The Order of Things*, trans. A. Sheridan, New York: Vintage Books.

Francoeur, L. (1985) 'The Dialogical Semiosis of Culture', *American Journal of Semiotics* 3, 3: 109–30.

Fraser, N. (1981) 'Foucault on Modern Power: Empirical Insights and Normative Confusions', *Praxis International* 1: 272–87.

Frow, J. (1985) 'Discourse and Power', *Economy and Society* 14, 2.

——(1986) *Marxism and Literary History*, Oxford: Basil Blackwell.

Gadamer, H.-G. (1979) 'The Problem of Historical Consciousness', in P. Rabinow and W. M. Sullivan (eds) *Interpretive Social Science: A Reader*, Berkeley: University of California Press.

——(1979, 1975) *Truth and Method*, 2nd English edition, London: Sheed and Ward.

——(1976) 'On the Scope and Functioning of Hermeneutic Reflection', in *Philosophical Hermeneutics*, ed. and trans. David E. Linge, Berkeley: University of California Press.

Gane, M. (ed.) (1986) *Towards a Critique of Foucault*, London: Routledge & Kegan Paul.

Gardiner, M. (1992) 'Bakhtin's Carnival: Utopia as Critique', *Utopian Studies* 3, 2.

Garrard, J. (1983) 'Introduction: The Rise of the Novel in Russia', in J. Garrard (ed.) *The Russian Novel from Pushkin to Pasternak*, New Haven: Yale University Press.

Gasparov, M. L. (1984) 'M. M. Bakhtin in Russian Culture of the Twentieth Century', *Studies in Twentieth Century Literature* 9, 1: 169–76.

Geertz, C. (1973) *The Interpretation of Cultures*, New York: Basic Books.

Geoghegan, V. (1987) *Utopianism and Marxism*, London: Methuen.

Geras, N. (1983) *Marx and Human Nature: Refutation of a Legend*, London: Verso.

Geyer-Ryan, H. (1988) 'Counterfactual Artefacts: Walter Benjamin's Philosophy of History', in E. Timms and P. Collier (eds) *Visions and Blueprints: Avant-Garde Culture and Radical Politics in Early Twentieth Century Europe*, Manchester: Manchester University Press.

Gibian, G. (ed.) (1971) *Russia's Lost Literature of the Absurd: A Literary Discovery*, Ithaca: Cornell University Press.

——and Tjalsma, H. W. (eds) (1976) *Russian Modernism: Culture and the Avant-Garde*, 1900–1930, Ithaca: Cornell University Press.

Giddens, A. (1987) *Social Theory and Modern Society*, Cambridge: Polity.

——(1984) *The Constitution of Society*, Berkeley and Los Angeles: University of California Press.

——(1983) 'Four Theses on Ideology', *Canadian Journal of Political and Social Theory* 7: 2–3.

——(1982) *Profiles and Critiques in Social Theory*, Berkeley: University of California Press.

——(1979) *Central Problems in Social Theory*, Berkeley: University of California Press.

——(1977) *Studies in Social and Political Theory*, London: Hutchinson.

——(1976) *New Rules of Sociological Method*, London: Hutchinson.

——(ed.) (1974) *Positivism and Sociology*, London: Heinemann.

Ginzburg, C. (1980) *The Cheese and the Worms: The Cosmos of a Sixteenth-Century Miller*, trans. J. and A. Tedeschi, London: Routledge & Kegan Paul.

Glazener, N. (1989) 'Dialogic Subversion: Bakhtin, the Novel and Gertrude Stein', in K. Hirschkop and D. Shepherd (eds), *Bakhtin and Cultural Theory*, Manchester: Manchester University Press.

Gluckman, M. (1963) *Custom and Conflict in Africa*, Oxford: Basil Blackwell.

Glucksmann, M. (1974) *Structuralist Analysis in Contemporary Social Thought: A Comparison of the Thought of Claude Lévi-Strauss and Louis Althusser*, London: Routledge and Kegan Paul.

Goethe, J. (1962) *Italian Journey 1786–1788*, trans. W. H. Auden and E. Mayer, Harmondsworth: Penguin.

Goffman, E. (1959) *The Presentation of the Self in Everyday Life*, Harmondsworth: Penguin.

Gouldner, A. W. (1980) *The Two Marxisms: Contradiction and Anomalies in the Development of Theory*, New York: The Seabury Press.

——(1976) *The Dialectic of Ideology and Technology: The Origins, Grammar and Future of Ideology*, Oxford: Oxford University Press.

Gramsci, A. (1985) *Selections from Cultural Writings*, D. Forgacs and G. Nowell–Smith (eds), trans. W. Boelhower, London: Lawrence & Wishart.

——(1984) 'Notes on Language', *Telos* 59: 127–50.

——(1979) *Letters From Prison*, London: Quartet Books Ltd.

——(1971) *Selections from the Prison Notebooks*, ed. and trans. Q. Hoare and G. Nowell–Smith, New York: International Publishers.

Grossberg, L. (1984) 'Strategies of Marxist Cultural Interpretation', *Critical Studies in Mass Communications* 1: 392–421.

Habermas, J. (1987) *The Philosophical Discourse of Modernity: Twelve Lectures*, trans. F. Lawrence, Cambridge: Polity.

——(1986) 'Taking Aim at the Heart of the Present', in D. C. Hoy (ed.) *Foucault: A Critical Reader*, Oxford: Basil Blackwell.

——(1979) *Communication and the Evolution of Society*, trans. T. McCarthy, London: Heinemann.

——(1978) *Knowledge and Human Interests*, 2nd edition, trans. J. Shapiro, London: Heinemann.

——(1977) 'A Review of Gadamer's *Truth and Method*', in F. Dallmayr and T. McCarthy (eds) *Understanding and Social Inquiry*, Notre Dame: University of Notre Dame Press.

——(1971) *Towards a Rational Society: Student Protest, Science and Politics*, trans. J. Shapiro, London: Heinemann.

——(1970a) 'On Systematically Distorted Communication', *Inquiry* 13: 205–18.

——(1970b) 'Towards a Theory of Communicative Competence', *Inquiry* 13: 360–75.

Hall, S. (1985a) 'The Rediscovery of Ideology: Return of the Repressed in Media Studies', in V. Beechey and J. Donald (eds) *Subjectivity and Social Relations*, Milton Keynes: The Open University Press.

——(1985b) 'Signification, Representation, Ideology: Althusser and the Post–Structuralist Debates', *Critical Studies in Mass Communications* 2, 2: 91–114.

——(1980) 'Encoding/Decoding', in S. Hall, D. Hobson, A. Lowe and. P. Willis (eds) *Culture, Media, Language*, London: Hutchinson.

——(1977a) 'Culture, the Media and the "Ideological Effect"', in J. Curran, M. Gurevitch and J. Woollacott (eds) *Mass Communication and Society*, London: Edward Arnold.

——(1977b) 'A Critical Survey of the Theoretical and Practical Achievements of the Past Ten Years', in F. Barker, J. Coombs, P. Hulme, C. Mercer and D. Musselwhite (eds) *Literature, Society and the Sociology of Literature*, Colchester: University of Essex.

——and Jefferson, T. (eds) (1976) *Resistance Through Rituals*, London: Hutchinson.

Harland, R. (1987) *Superstructuralism: The Philosophy of Structuralism and Post–Structuralism*, London: Methuen.

Harris, R. (1987) *Reading Saussure*, London: Duckworth.

——and Taylor, T. (1989) *Landmarks in Linguistic Thought*, London: Routledge.

Hawkes, T. (1977) *Structuralism and Semiotics*, London: Methuen.

Head, B. W. (1985) *Ideology and Social Science: Destutt de Tracy and French Liberalism*, Dordrecht: Martinas Nijhoff.

Hebdige, D. (1979) *Subculture: The Meaning of Style*, London: Methuen.

Hekman, S. (1986) *Hermeneutics and the Sociology of Knowledge*, Cambridge: Polity.

Held, D. (1980) *Introduction to Critical Theory*, Berkeley: University of California Press.

——and Thompson, J. B. (1989) *Social Theory of Modern Society: Anthony Giddens and His Critics*, Cambridge: Cambridge University Press.
——(1982) *Habermas: Critical Debates*, Cambridge (Mass.): The MIT Press.
Henrique, J., Holloway, W., Urwin, C., Venn, C. and Walkerdine, V. (eds) (1984) *Changing the Subject: Psychology, Social Regulation and Subjectivity*, London: Methuen.
Hirschkop, K. (1989a) 'Introduction: Bakhtin and Cultural Theory', in K. Hirschkop and D. Shepherd, *Bakhtin and Cultural Theory*, Manchester, Manchester University Press.
——(1989b) 'Dialogism as a Challenge to Literary Criticism', in C. Kelly, M. Makin and D. Shepherd (eds) *Discontinuous Discourses in Modern Russian Literature*, London: Macmillan.
——(1989c) 'The Classical and the Popular: Musical Form and Social Context', in C. Norris (ed.) *Music and the Politics of Culture*, London: Lawrence & Wishart.
——(1986a) 'A Response to the Forum on Mikhail Bakhtin', in G. S. Morson (ed.) *Bakhtin: Essays and Dialogues on his Work*, Chicago: Chicago University Press.
——(1986b) 'The Domestication of M. M. Bakhtin', *Essays in Poetics* 11, 1: 76–87.
——(1986c) 'Bakhtin, Discourse and Democracy', *New Left Review* 160: 92–113.
——(1985) 'The Social and the Subject in Bakhtin', *Poetics Today* 5, 4: 769–75.
Hirst, P. (1976) 'Althusser and the Theory of Ideology', *Economy and Society* 5.
Hodge, R. and Kress, G. (1988) *Social Semiotics*, Cambridge: Polity.
Holden, K. (1985) 'Women's Writing and the Carnivalesque', *Journal of Literary Teaching Politics* 4: 5–15.
Holquist, M. (1990) *Dialogism: Bakhtin and His World*, London: Routledge.
——(1987) 'Inner Speech as Social Rhetoric', *Dieciocho* X: 1: 41–52.
——(1986a) 'Answering as Authoring: Mikhail Bakhtin's Translinguistics', in G. S. Morson (ed.) *Bakhtin: Essays and Dialogues on his Work*, Chicago: Chicago University Press.
——(1986b) 'The Surd Heard: Bakhtin and Derrida', in G. S. Morson (ed.) *Literature and History: Theoretical Problems and Russian Case Studies*, Stanford: Stanford University Press.
——(1985a) 'The Carnival of Discourse: Bakhtin and Simultaneity', *Canadian Review of Comparative Literature* 12, 2: 220–34.
——(1985b) 'Bakhtin and the Formalists: History as Dialogue', in R. L. Jackson (ed.) *Russian Formalism: A Retrospective Glance*, New Haven, Yale University Press.
——(1983) 'Bakhtin and Rabelais: Theory as Praxis', *Boundary 2* 11, 1–2: 5–19.
——(1981) 'The Politics of Representation', in S. Greenblatt (ed.) *Allegory and Representation: Selected Papers from the English Institute 1979–80*, Baltimore: Johns Hopkins University Press.
Holub, R. (1984) *Reception Theory: A Critical Introduction*, London: Methuen.

Horkheimer, M. (1976) 'Traditional and Critical Theory', in P. Connerton (ed.) *Critical Sociology*, Harmondsworth: Penguin.

Hoy, D.C. (ed.) (1986) *Foucault: A Critical Reader*, Oxford: Basil Blackwell.

Hughes, S. (1959) *Consciousness and Society*, New York: Vintage.

Huizinga, J. (1965) *The Waning of the Middle Ages*, Harmondsworth: Penguin.

Hunter, I. (1989) 'After Representation: Recent Discussions of the Relation Between Language and Literature', in M. Gane (ed.) *Ideological Representations and Power in Social Relations: Literary and Social Theory*, London: Routledge.

Ivanov, V. (1974) 'The Significance of M. M. Bakhtin's Ideas on Sign, Utterance, and Dialogue for Modern Semiotics', in H. Baran (ed.) *Semiotics and Structuralism: Readings from the Soviet Union*, White Plains: International Arts and Sciences Press, Inc.

Jacoby, R. (1981) *Dialectic of Defeat: Contours of Western Marxism*, Cambridge: Cambridge University Press.

Jakobson, R. (1978a) 'The Dominant', in L. Matejka and K. Pomorska, (eds) *Readings in Russian Poetics: Formalist and Structuralist Approaches*, Ann Arbor: Michigan Slavic Publications.

——(1978b) 'On Realism in Art', in L. Matejka and K. Pomorska (eds) *Readings in Russian Poetics: Formalist and Structuralist Approaches*, Ann Arbor: Michigan Slavic Publications.

Jameson, F. (1981) *The Political Unconscious: Narrative as a Socially Symbolic Act*, Ithaca: Cornell University Press.

——(1979) 'Reification and Utopia in Mass Culture', *Social Text* 1: 130–48.

——(1976) 'Introduction/Prospectus: To Reconsider the Relationship of Marxism to Utopian Thought', *Minnesota Review* 6: 53–8.

——(1974) 'Review of *Marxism and the Philosophy of Language*', *Style* 8, 3: 535–43.

Jay, M. (1984a) *Marxism and Totality: The Adventure of a Concept from Lukács to Habermas*, Berkeley: University of California Press.

——(1984b) *Adorno*, London: Fontana.

——(1982) 'Should Intellectual History Take a Linguistic Turn? Reflections on the Habermas–Gadamer Debate', in D. LaCapra and S. Kaplan (eds) *Modern European Intellectual History*, Ithaca: Cornell University Press.

——(1973) *The Dialectical Imagination: A History of the Frankfurt School and the Institute of Social Research 1923–1950*, Boston: Little Brown.

Jefferson, A. (1989) 'Body Matters: Self and Other in Bakhtin, Sartre and Barthes', in K. Hirschkop and D. Shepherd (eds) *Bakhtin and Cultural Theory*, Manchester: Manchester University Press.

Jha, P. (1985) 'Lukács, Bakhtin and the Sociology of the Novel', *Diogenes* 129: 63–90.

Jones, M. (1990) *Dostoyevsky After Bakhtin: Readings in Dostoevsky's Fantastic Realism*, Cambridge: Cambridge University Press.

Kagarlitsky, B (1988) *The Thinking Reed: Intellectuals and the Soviet State from 1917 to Present*, trans. B. Pearce, London: Verso.

Kellner, D. (1978) 'Ideology, Marxism and Advanced Capitalism', *Socialist Review* 8, 6: 37–65.

Kelly, C. (1989) 'Petrushka and the Pioneers: The Russian Carnival Theatre After the Revolution', in C. Kelly, M. Makin and D. Shepherd (eds) *Discontinuous Discourses in Modern Russian Literature*, London: Macmillan.

Kinser, S. (1990) *Rabelais's Carnival: Text, Context, Metatext*, Berkeley: University of California Press.

Korsch, K. (1970) *Marxism and Philosophy*, trans. F. Halliday, London: New Left Books.

Kramer, L. (1989) 'Literature, Criticism, and Historical Imagination: The Literary Challenge of Hayden White and Dominick LaCapra', in L. Hunt (ed.) *The New Cultural History*, Berkeley: University of California Press.

Kristeva, J. (1986) 'Word, Dialogue and Novel', in *The Kristeva Reader*, T. Moi (ed.), Oxford: Basil Blackwell.

LaCapra, D. (1983) 'Bakhtin, Marxism and the Carnivalesque', in *Rethinking Cultural History*, Ithaca: Cornell University Press.

Laclau, E. (1977) *Politics and Ideology in Marxist Theory*, London: Verso.

——and Mouffe, C. (1985) *Hegemony and Socialist Strategy*, London: Verso.

Ladurie, Le Roy (1979) *Carnival in Romans: A People's Uprising at Romans 1579–1580*, trans. M. Feeney, Harmondsworth: Penguin.

Lampert, E. (1976) 'Modernism in Russia 1893–1917', in M. Bradbury and J. McFarlane (eds) *Modernism: A Guide to European Literature 1890–1930*, Harmondsworth: Penguin.

Larrain, J. (1989) 'Ideology and its Revisions in Contemporary Marxism', in N. O'Sullivan (ed.) *The Structure of Modern Ideology: Critical Perspectives on Social and Cultural Theory*, London: Edward Elgar.

——(1986) *A Reconstruction of Historical Materialism*, London: Allen & Unwin.

——(1983) *Marxism and Ideology*, London: Macmillan.

——(1982) 'On the Character of Ideology: Marx and the Present Debate in Britain', *Theory, Culture and Society* 1, 1: 5–22.

——(1979) *The Concept of Ideology*, London: Hutchinson.

Lévi-Strauss, C. (1968) *Structural Anthropology*, trans. C. Jacobsen and Brooke Schoepf, London: Allen Lane.

Levitas, R. (1990) *The Concept of Utopia*, London: Phillip Allen.

Lewis, H. (1990) *Dada Turns Red: The Politics of Surrealism*, Edinburgh: Edinburgh University Press.

Linge, D. (1976) 'Introduction', in H.-G. Gadamer, *Philosophical Hermeneutics*, ed. and trans. D. Linge, Berkeley: University of California Press.

Lodge, D. (1990) *After Bakhtin: Essays on Fiction and Criticism*, London: Routledge.

Lodziak, C. (1988) 'Dull Compulsion of the Economic: The Dominant Ideology and Social Reproduction', *Radical Philosophy* 44: 10–17.

Lombardi–Satriani, L. (1974) 'Folklore as a Culture of Contestation', *Journal of the Folklore Institute* 11: 1–2.

Lowe, D. (1982) *History of Bourgeois Perception*, Chicago: Chicago University Press.

Löwy, M. (1987) 'The Romantic and the Marxist Critique of Modern Civilization', *Theory and Society* 16: 891–904.

Lukács, G. (1971) *History and Class Consciousness: Studies in Marxist Dialectics*, trans. R. Livingstone, London: The Merlin Press.

Lukes, S. (1984) 'Marxism and Utopianism', in P. Alexander and R. Gill (eds) *Utopias*, London: Duckworth.

Lunacharsky, A. (1973) *On Literature and Art*, K. M. Cook (ed.), trans. A. Pyman and F. Glagoleva, Moscow: Progress Publishers.

Lunn, E. (1982) *Marxism and Modernism: An Historical Study of Lukács, Brecht, Benjamin and Adorno*, Berkeley: University of California Press.

Lyotard, J. F. (1984) *The Post-Modern Condition: A Report on Knowledge*, trans. G. Bennington and Brian Mussum, Manchester: Manchester University Press.

MacCabe, C. (1979) 'On Discourse', *Economy and Society* 8, 4: 279–307.

McCarney, J. (1990) *Social Theory and the Crisis of Marxism*, London: Verso.

——(1980) *The Real World of Ideology*, Brighton: Harvester.

McCarthy, T. (1978) *The Critical Theory of Jürgen Habermas*, Cambridge (Mass.) and London: The MIT Press.

Macdonell, D. (1986) *Theories of Discourse: An Introduction*, Oxford: Basil Blackwell.

Macey, D. (1988) *Lacan in Contexts*, London: Verso.

McFarlane, J. (1976) 'The Mind of Modernism', in M. Bradbury and J. McFarlane (eds) *Modernism: A Guide to European Literature 1890–1930*, Harmondsworth: Penguin.

McKinley, M. (1987) 'Bakhtin and the World of Rabelais Criticism', *Degré Second: Studies in French Literature* 2: 83–8.

McLellan, D. (1971) *The Thought of Karl Marx*, London: Macmillan.

Mann, M. (1973) *Consciousness and Action Among the Western Working Class*, London: Macmillan.

——(1970) 'On the Social Cohesion of Liberal Democracy', *American Sociological Review* 35.

Mannheim, K. (1960) *Ideology and Utopia*, London: Routledge & Kegan Paul.

Mansfield, S. (1984) 'Introduction to Gramsci's "Notes on Language"', *Telos* 59: 119–26.

Marcus, G. (1989) *Lipstick Traces: A Secret History of the Twentieth Century*, London: Secker and Warburg.

Markiewicz, H. (1984) 'Polyphony, Dialogism and Dialectics', in J. Strelka (ed.) *Literary Theory and Criticism*, New York: Peter Lang.

Markov, V. (1969) *Russian Futurism: A History*, London: MacGibbon and Kee.

Márkus, G. (1984) 'The Paradigm of Language: Wittgenstein, Lévi-Strauss, Gadamer', in J. Fekete (ed.) *The Structural Allegory: Reconstructive Encounters with the New French Thought*, Manchester: Manchester University Press.

——(1983) 'Concepts of Ideology in Marx', *Canadian Journal of Social and Political Theory* 7, 1–2: 84–103.

Marx, K. (1973) *Grundrisse: Foundations of the Critique of Political Economy*, trans. M. Nicolaus, Harmondsworth: Penguin.

——and Engels, F. (1978) *The Marx–Engels Reader*, 2nd edition, R. Tucker (ed.), New York: W. W. Norton & Company.

——(1970) *The German Ideology*, C. J. Arthur (ed.), London: Lawrence & Wishart.

Mepham, J. (1979) 'The Theory of Ideology in *Capital*', in J. Mepham and D-H. Ruben (eds) *Issues in Marxist Philosophy Vol. III: Epistemology, Science, Ideology*, Atlantic Highlands: Humanities Press Inc.

Mercer, C. (1984) 'Paris Match: Marxism, Structuralism and the Problem of Literature', in J. Hawthorn (ed.) *Criticism and Critical Theory*, London: Edward Arnold.

Merquior, J. G. (1986a) *From Prague to Paris: A Critique of Structuralist and Post–Structuralist Thought*, London: Verso.

——(1986b) *Western Marxism*, London: Granada.

——(1985) *Foucault*, London: Fontana.

Mészáros, I. (1989) *The Power of Ideology*, London: Harvester Wheatsheaf.

Minogue, K. (1989) 'Nietzsche and the Ideological Project', in N. O'Sullivan (ed.) *The Structure of Modern Ideology: Critical Perspectives on Social and Political Theory*, London: Edward Elgar.

Molina, V. (1977) 'Notes on Marx and the Problem of Individuality', in CCCS (ed.) *On Ideology*, London: Hutchinson.

Moore, H. (1990) 'Paul Ricoeur: Action, Meaning and Text', in C. Tilley (ed.) *Reading Material Culture: Structuralism, Hermeneutics, and Post-Structuralism*, Oxford: Basil Blackwell.

Morley, D. (1980) 'Texts, Readers, Subjects', in S. Hall, D. Hobson, A. Lowe and P. Willis (eds) *Culture, Media, Language*, London: Hutchinson.

Morson, G. S. (1986) 'The Baxtin Industry', *Slavic and East European Journal* 30, 1: 81–90.

——(1978) 'The Heresiarch of META', *PTL: A Journal for the Descriptive Poetics and Theory of Literature* 3: 407–27.

——and Emerson, C. (eds) (1989) *Rethinking Bakhtin: Extensions and Challenges*, Evanston: Northwestern University Press.

Mouffe, C. (1979) 'Hegemony and Ideology in Gramsci', in C. Mouffe (ed.) *Gramsci and Marxist Theory*, London: Routledge & Kegan Paul.

Mulkay, M. (1979) *Science and the Sociology of Knowledge*, London: George Allen & Unwin.

Musselwhite, D. (1977) 'Towards a Political Aesthetics', in F. Barker, J. Coombs, P. Hulme, C. Mercer and D. Musselwhite (eds) *Literature, Society and the Sociology of Literature*, Colchester: University of Essex.

Nielsen, K. (1989) 'The Concept of Ideology: Some Marxist and Non-Marxist Conceptualizations', *Rethinking Marxism* 2, 4: 146–73.

Nietzsche, F. (1966) *Beyond Good and Evil: Prelude to a Philosophy of the Future*, trans. W. Kaufman, Harmondsworth: Penguin.

Nonnekes, P. (1987) 'The Nihilism of Resistance and Freedom', *Canadian Journal of Political and Social Theory* 11, 3: 130–9.

Outhwaite, W. (1987) *New Philosophies of Social Science: Realism, Hermeneutics and Critical Theory*, London: Macmillan.

——(1975) *Understanding Social Life: The Method Called Verstehen*, London: George Allen & Unwin.

Parekh, B. (1982) *Marx's Theory of Ideology*, London: Croom Helm.

Parrott, R. (1984) '(Re)Capitulation, Parody, or Polemic', in B. Stolz, L. Dolezel and I. R. Titunik (eds) *Language and Literary Theory*, Ann Arbor: Michigan Slavic Publications.

Pateman, T. (1982) 'Discourse in Life: V. N. Voloshinov's *Marxism and the Philosophy of Language*', *University of East Anglia Papers in Linguistics*, 16–17: 26–48.

Pêcheux, M. (1982) *Language, Semantics and Ideology: Stating the Obvious*, trans. H. Nagpal, London: Macmillan.

——(1978) 'Are the Masses an Inanimate Object?', in D. Sankoff (ed.) *Linguistic Variation: Models and Methods*, New York: Academic Press.

Pechey, G. (1990) 'Boundaries vs. Binaries: Bakhtin in/and the History of Ideas', *Radical Philosophy* 54: 23–30.

——(1989) 'On the Borders of Bakhtin: Dialogisation, Decolonization', in K. Hirschkop and D. Shepherd (eds) *Bakhtin and Cultural Theory*, Manchester: Manchester University Press.

——(1986) 'Bakhtin, Marxism and Post-Structuralism', in F. Barker, P. Hulme, I. Margaret and D. Loxley (eds) *Literature, Politics and Theory: Papers from the Essex Conference 1976–84*, London: Methuen.

Perlina, N. (1984) 'Bakhtin and Buber: Problems of Dialogic Imagination', *Studies in Twentieth Century Literature* 9, 2: 13–28.

——(1983) 'Bakhtin–Medvedev–Voloshinov: An Apple of Discourse', *The University of Ottawa Quarterly* 53, 1: 35–47.

Phillips, K. H. (1986) *Language Theories of the Early Soviet Period*, Exeter Linguistic Studies Vol. 10, University of Exeter.

Pirog, G. (1987) 'The Bakhtin's Circle's Freud: From Positivism to Hermeneutics', *Poetics Today* 8, 3–4: 591–610.

Plant, S. (1990) 'The Situationist International: A Case of Spectacular Neglect', *Radical Philosophy* 55: 3–10.

Polan, D. (1989) 'Bakhtin, Benjamin, Sartre: Toward a Typology of the Intellectual Critic', in C. Kelly, M. Makin and D. Shepherd (eds) *Discontinuous Discourses in Modern Russian Literature*, London: Macmillan.

——(1983) 'The Text Between Dialogue and Monologue', *Poetics Today* 4, 1: 145–83.

Ponzio, A. (1984) 'Semiotics Between Peirce and Bakhtin', *Semiotic Inquiry* 4, 3–4: 273–92.

Poster, M. (1984) *Foucault, Marxism and History: Mode of Production vs. Mode of Information*, Cambridge: Polity.

Poulantzas, N. (1978) *State, Power, Socialism*, trans. P. Camiller, London: Verso.

Quine, W. V. O. (1960) *Word and Object*, Cambridge (Mass.): Harvard University Press.

Rabelais, F. (1955) *Gargantua and Pantagruel*, trans. J. M. Cohen, Harmondsworth: Penguin.

Radhakrishnan, R. (1990) 'Toward an Effective Intellectual: Foucault or

Gramsci?', in B. Robbins (ed.) *Intellectuals: Aesthetics, Politics, Academics*, Minneapolis: Minnesota University Press.

Richter, H. (1965) *Dada: Art and Anti-Art*, London: Thames & Hudson.

Ricoeur, P. (1986) *Lectures on Ideology and Utopia*, G. Taylor (ed.), New York: Columbia University Press.

——(1985) 'The Text as Dynamic Entity', in M. Valdes and O. Miller (eds) *Identity of the Literary Text*, Toronto: University of Toronto Press.

——(1983) 'On Interpretation', in A. Montefiore (ed.) *Philosophy in France Today*, Cambridge: Cambridge University Press.

——(1981) *Hermeneutics and the Human Sciences*, ed. and trans. J. B. Thompson, Cambridge: Cambridge University Press.

——(1978) *The Rule of Metaphor: Multidisciplinary Studies in the Creation of Meaning*, trans. R. Czerny, London: Routledge & Kegan Paul.

——(1976a) 'Ideology and Utopia as Cultural Imagination', *Philosophic Exchange* 2, 2: 17–28.

——(1976b) 'Ideology, Utopia and Faith', *The Center for Hermeneutical Studies* 17: 21–28.

——(1976c) *Interpretation Theory: Discourse and the Surplus of Meaning*, Fort Worth: The Texas Christian University Press.

——(1973) 'Ethics and Culture: Habermas and Gadamer in Dialogue', *Philosophy Today* 17: 153–67.

Roberts, J. (1990) *Postmodernism, Politics and Art*, Manchester: Manchester University Press.

Roberts, J. (1983) *Walter Benjamin*, Atlantic Highlands: Humanities Press Inc.

Rootes, C. A. (1981) 'The Dominant Ideology Thesis and its Critics', *Sociology* 15, 3: 436–44.

Rorty, R. (1979) *Philosophy and the Mirror of Nature*, Princeton: Princeton University Press.

Rose, G. (1978) *The Melancholy Science: An Introduction to the Thought of Theodor W. Adorno*, London: Macmillan.

Said, E. (1984) *The World, the Text and the Critic*, London: Faber.

Salamani, L. (1981) 'Gramsci and Marxist Sociology of Language', *International Journal of Social Languages* 32: 27–44.

Sartre, J.-P. (1976) *Critique of Dialectical Reason*, London: New Left Books.

Saussure, F. (1966) *Course in General Linguistics*, trans. W. Baskin, New York: McGraw-Hill.

Schaff, A. (1962) *Introduction to Semantics*, Oxford: Pergamon Press.

Sebeok, T. (ed.) (1984) *Carnival!*, Amsterdam: Mouton Publishers.

Selden, R. (1984) *Criticism and Objectivity*, London: George Allen & Unwin.

——(1977) 'Russian Formalism and Marxism: An Unconcluded Dialogue', in F. Barker, J. Coombs, P. Hulme, C. Mercer and D. Musselwhite (eds) *Literature, Society and the Sociology of Literature*, Colchester: University of Essex.

Shapiro, M. (1988) *The Politics of Representation: Writing Practices in Biography, Photography, and Policy Analysis*, Madison: The University of Wisconsin Press.

Shepherd, D. (1989) 'Bakhtin and the Reader', in K. Hirschkop and D. Shepherd (eds) *Bakhtin and Cultural Theory*, Manchester: Manchester University Press.

——(1986) 'The Authority of Meanings and the Meanings of Authority: Some Problems in the Theory of Reading', *Poetics Today* 7, 1: 129–45.

Sheppard, R. (1983) 'Tricksters, Carnival and the Magic Figures of Dada Poetry', *Forum for Modern Language Studies* 19, 2: 116–23.

Shklovsky, V. (1965a) 'Art as Technique', in T. Lemon and M. Reis (eds) *Russian Formalist Criticism: Four Essays*, Lincoln and London: University of Nebraska Press.

——(1965b) 'Sterne's *Tristram Shandy*: Stylistic Commentary', in T. Lemon and M. Reis (eds) *Russian Formalist Criticism: Four Essays*, Lincoln and London: University of Nebraska Press.

Shukman, A. (1984) 'M. M. Bakhtin: Notes on his Philosophy of Man', in W. Harrison and A. Pyman (eds) *Poetry, Prose and Public Opinion*, Letchworth: Avebury Publishing Co.

——(ed.) (1983) *Bakhtin School Papers, Russian Poetics in Translation* 10.

——(1980) 'Between Marxism and Formalism: The Stylistics of Mikhail Bakhtin', *Comparative Criticism* 2: 221–34.

Silverman, D. and Torode, B. (1980) *The Material Word: Some Theories of Language and Their Limits*, London: Routledge & Kegan Paul.

Simon, W. W. (1963) *European Positivism in the Nineteenth Century*, New York: Cornell University Press.

Slater, P. (1977) *Origin and Significance of the Frankfurt School: A Marxist Perspective*, London: Routledge & Kegan Paul.

Smart, B. (1986) 'The Politics of Truth and the Problem of Hegemony', in D. C. Hoy (ed.) *Foucault: A Critical Reader*, Oxford: Basil Blackwell.

——(1985) Michel Foucault, London: Tavistock.

——(1983) *Foucault, Marxism and Critique*, London: Routledge & Kegan Paul.

Soper, K. (1990) *Troubled Pleasures: Writings on Politics, Gender and Hedonism*, London: Verso.

——(1986) *Humanism and Anti-Humanism*, London: Hutchinson.

Sprinker, M. (1986) 'Boundless Context: Problems in Bakhtin's Linguistics', *Poetics Today* 7, 1: 117–28.

Stalin, J. V. (1976) *Marxism and Problems of Linguistics*, Peking: Foreign Languages Press.

Stallybrass, P. and White, A. (1986) *The Politics and Poetics of Transgression*, London: Methuen.

Stam, R. (1989) *Subversive Pleasures: Bakhtin, Cultural Criticism and Film*, Baltimore: Johns Hopkins University Press.

——(1988) 'Mikhail Bakhtin and Left Cultural Critique', in A. Kaplan (ed.) *Postmodernism and its Discontents*, London: Verso.

Stedman-Jones, G. (1977) 'The Marxism of the Early Lukács', in New Left Review (ed.) *Western Marxism: A Critical Reader*, London: Verso.

Stewart, S. (1986) 'Shouts on the Street: Bakhtin's Anti-Linguistics', in G. S. Morson (ed.) *Bakhtin: Essays and Dialogues on his Work*, Chicago: Chicago University Press.

Stites, R. (1990) 'Russian Revolutionary Culture: Its Place in the History of Cultural Revolutions', in P. Dukes and J. Dunkley (eds) *Culture and Revolution*, London: Pinter Publishers.

——(1989) *Revolutionary Dreams: Utopian Vision and Experimental Life in the Russian Revolution*, Oxford: Oxford University Press.

Sumner, C. (1979) *Reading Ideologies: An Investigation into the Marxist Theory of Ideology and Law*, London: Academic Press.

Swingewood, A. (1986) *Sociological Poetics and Aesthetic Theory*, London: Macmillan.

——(1984) *A Short History of Sociological Thought*, London: Macmillan.

——(1977) *The Myth of Mass Culture*, London: Macmillan.

Tait, A. L. (1986) 'Lunacharsky: A Nietzschean Marxist?', in B. G. Rosenthal (ed.) *Nietzsche in Russia*, Princeton: Princeton University Press.

Taylor, C. (1986) 'Foucault on Freedom and Truth', in D. C. Hoy (ed.) *Foucault: A Critical Reader*, Oxford: Basil Blackwell.

——(1985) 'Interpretation and the Sciences of Man', in *Philosophy and the Human Sciences: Philosophical Papers Vol. II*, Cambridge, Cambridge University Press.

Taylor, G. H. (1986) 'Editor's Introduction', in P. Ricoeur *Lectures on Ideology and Utopia*, Chicago: University of Chicago Press.

Thaden, B. Z. (1987) 'Bakhtin, Dostoevsky and the Status of the "I"', *Dostoevsky Studies* 8: 199–207.

Therborn, G. (1984) 'The New Questions of Subjectivity', *New Left Review* 143: 97–107.

——(1980) *The Power of Ideology and the Ideology of Power*, London: Verso.

——(1970) 'The Frankfurt School', *New Left Review* 63.

Thompson, J. B. (1988) 'Mass Communications and Modern Culture', *Sociology* 22, 3: 359–83.

——(1987) 'Language and Ideology: A Framework for Analysis', *The Sociological Review* 35, 3: 516–36.

——(1984) *Studies in the Theory of Ideology*, Cambridge: Polity.

——(1981) *Critical Hermeneutics: A Study in the Thought of Paul Ricoeur and Jürgen Habermas*, Cambridge: Cambridge University Press.

Thomson, C. (1984a) 'Bakhtinian Methodologies', *Semiotic Inquiry* 4, 3–4: 372–89.

——(1984b) 'Bakhtin's "Theory" of Genre', *Studies in Twentieth Century Literature* 9, 1: 29–40.

——(1983) 'The Semiotics of Mikhail Bakhtin', *The University of Ottawa Quarterly* 53, 1: 11–21.

Threadgold, T. (1986) 'Semiotics–Ideology–Language', in T. Threadgold, R.E.A. Grosz, G. Cress and M. A. K. Halliday (eds) *Semiotics–Ideology–Language*, Sydney: Sydney Association for Studies in Society and Culture.

Timpanaro, S. (1975) *On Materialism*, London: New Left Books.

Titunik, I. R. (1986) 'The Baxtin Problem: Concerning Katerina Clarke's and Michael Holquist's *Mikhail Bakhtin*', *Slavic and East European Journal* 30, 1: 91–5.

——(1984) 'Bakhtin &/or Voloshinov &/or Medvedev: Dialogue &/or

Doubletalk?', in B. Stolz, L. Dolezel and I. R. Titunik (eds) *Language and Literary Theory*, Ann Arbor: Michigan Slavic Publications.

Todorov, T. (1987) *Literature and its Theorists: A Personal View of Twentieth-Century Criticism*, trans. C. Porter, London: Routledge & Kegan Paul.

——(1984) *Mikhail Bakhtin: The Dialogical Principle*, trans. W. Godzich, Manchester: Manchester University Press.

Tolstoy, V., Bibikova, I. and Cooke, C. (eds) (1990) *Street Art of the Revolution: Festival and Celebrations in Russia 1918–33*, London: Thames and Hudson.

Toulmin, S. (1982) 'The Construal of Inquiry: Criticism in Modern and Post–Modern Science', *Critical Inquiry* 9: 93–111.

Tribe, K. (1980) 'Literary Methodology', *Economy and Society* 9, 2: 241–9.

Trotsky, L. (1970) *Literature and Revolution*, Ann Arbor: Michigan University Press.

Turner, V. (1974) *The Ritual Process: Structure and Anti-Structure*, Harmondsworth: Penguin.

Ulin, R. C. (1984) *Understanding Cultures: Perspectives in Anthropology and Social Theory*, Austin: Texas University Press.

Vernon, E. (1971) 'Ideology and the Social Sciences', *Semiotica* 3, 2.

Voloshinov, V. N. (1983) 'Literary Stylistics', in A. Shukman (ed.) *Bakhtin School Papers, Russian Poetics in Translation* 10: 93–152.

——(1976) *Freudianism: A Marxist Critique*, I. R. Titunik and N. Bruss (ed.), trans. I. R. Titunik, New York and London: The Academic Press.

——(1973) *Marxism and the Philosophy of Language*, trans. L. Matejka and I. R. Titunik, Cambridge (Mass.) and London: Harvard University Press.

Vygotsky, L. S. (1978) *Mind in Society*, M. Cole, V. John-Steiner, S. Scribner and E. Souberman (eds), Cambridge (Mass.): Harvard University Press.

Walicki, A. (1979) *A History of Russian Thought: From the Enlightenment to Marxism*, trans. H. Andrews–Rusiecka, Stanford: Stanford University Press.

Wall, A. (1984) 'Characters in Bakhtin's Theory', *Studies in Twentieth Century Literature* 9, 1: 41–56.

Walton, W. G. (1981) 'V. N. Voloshinov: A Marriage of Formalism and Marxism', in P. Zima (ed.) *Semiotics and Dialectics: Ideology and the Text*, Amsterdam: John Benjamins B. V.

Warnke, G. (1987) *Gadamer: Hermeneutics, Tradition and Reason*, Cambridge: Polity.

Warren, M. (1984) 'Nietzsche's Concept of Ideology', *Theory and Society* 13: 541–65.

Weber, S. (1985) 'The Intersection: Marxism and the Philosophy of Language', *Diacritics* 15, 4: 94–112.

Weedon, C., Tolson, L. and Mort, F. (1980) 'Theories of Language and Subjectivity', in S. Hall, D. Hobson, A. Lowe and P. Willis (eds) *Culture, Media, Society*, London: Hutchinson.

Wellek, R. (1980) 'Bakhtin's View of Dostoevsky: "Polyphony" and "Carnivalesque"', *Dostoevsky Studies* 1: 31–9.

Wellmer, A. (1971) *Critical Theory of Society*, trans. J. Cumming, New York: Herder & Herder.

White, A. (1987–8) 'The Struggle over Bakhtin: Fraternal Reply to Robert Young', *Cultural Critique* 8: 217–41.

——(1986) 'Bakhtin's Masks', *Partisan Review* 53, 4: 634–7.

——(1984) 'Bakhtin, Sociolinguistics and Deconstruction', in F. Gloversmith (ed.) *The Theory of Reading*, Brighton and Totowa: Harvester.

White, H. (1983) 'The Authoritative Lie', *Partisan Review* 100, 1: 307–12.

White, J. (1990) *Literary Futurism: Aspects of the First Avant-Garde*, Oxford: Clarendon Press.

Williams, H. (1988) *Concepts of Ideology*, Sussex: Wheatsheaf Books.

Williams, R. (1989) *The Politics of Modernism: Against the New Conformists*, London: Verso.

——(1986) 'The Uses of Cultural Theory', *New Left Review* 158: 19–31.

——(1977) *Marxism and Literature*, Oxford: Oxford University Press.

Willis, C. (1989) 'Upsetting the Public: Carnival, Hysteria and Women's Texts', in K. Hirschkop and D. Shepherd (eds) *Bakhtin and Cultural Theory*, Manchester: Manchester University Press.

Willis, P. (1981) *Learning to Labour*, New York: Columbia University Press.

——and Corrigan, P. (1981) 'Orders of Experience: The Difference of Working Class Cultural Forms', *Social Text* 4.

——(1980) 'Cultural Forms and Class Mediations', *Media, Culture and Society* 2: 297–312.

Wilson, R. (1986) 'Play, Transgression and Carnival: Bakhtin and Derrida on *Scriptor Ludens*', in *Mosaic* 19, 1: 73–89.

Wittgenstein, L. (1963) *Philosophical Investigations*, trans. G. E. M. Anscombe, Oxford: Basil Blackwell.

Woods, R. (1977) 'Discourse Analysis: The Work of Michel Pêcheux', *Ideology & Consciousness* 2: 57–79.

Wollen, P. (1989) 'The Situationist International', *New Left Review* 174: 67–96.

Yaeger, P. (1986) 'Emancipatory Discourse', *Contemporary Literature* 27, 2: 246–56.

Young, R. (1985–6) 'Back to Bakhtin', *Cultural Critique* 2: 71–92.

Zijderveld, A. (1982) *Reality in a Looking-Glass: Rationality Through an Analysis of Traditional Folly*, London: Routledge & Kegan Paul.

Zima, P. (1981a) 'Semiotics, Dialectics and Critical Theory: Introductory Remarks', in P. Zima (ed.) *Semiotics and Dialectics: Ideology and the Text*, Amsterdam: John Benjamins B. V.

——(1981b) 'Text and Context: The Socio-Linguistic Nexus', in P. Zima (ed.) *Semiotics and Dialectics: Ideology and the Text*, Amsterdam: John Benjamins B.V.

Name index

Subject index